D0626942

From Inner Sources

From Inner Sources

New Directions in Object Relations Psychotherapy

Edited by
N. Gregory Hamilton, M.D.

JASON ARONSON INC.
Northvale, New Jersey
London

Production Editors: Leslie Block and Judith D. Cohen

This book was set in English Times by Lind Graphics of Upper Saddle River, New Jersey, and printed and bound by Haddon Craftsmen of Scranton, Pennsylvania.

Library of Congress Cataloging-in-Publication Data

From inner sources: new directions in object relations psychotherapy
  / edited by N. Gregory Hamilton.
        p. cm.
    Includes bibliographical references and index.
    ISBN 0-87668-540-8
    1. Object relations (Psychoanalysis)   2. Psychotherapy.
  I. Hamilton, N. Gregory.
    [DNLM: 1. Object Attachment.   2. Psychotherapy.   WM 460.5.02
  F931]
  RC489.025F76 1992
  616.89′14 — dc20
  DNLM/DLC
  for Library of Congress   92–6967

Manufactured in the United States of America. Jason Aronson Inc. offers books and cassettes. For information and catalog write to Jason Aronson Inc., 230 Livingston Street, Northvale, New Jersey 07647.

Contents

Introduction   xi

1 **A Critical Review of Object Relations Theory**   1
   N. Gregory Hamilton

   Historical Overview   1
   Diagnosis   11
   Etiology   12
   Treatment   14
   Implications for the Future   19

I **DIFFERENT PATIENTS, DIFFERENT THERAPISTS,
   DIFFERENT THEORIES**

2 **An Ego Psychology-Object Relations Theory
   Approach to the Transference**   29
   Otto F. Kernberg

   An Overview of My Approach   30
   Channels of Communication of the Transference   35

Transference, Unconscious Present, and
    Unconscious Past   41
Countertransference, Empathy, Memory, and Desire   44

3 **The Interpretive Moment**   **53**
    Fred Pine

The Interpretive Setting   54
The Interpretive Moment   56
Four Clinical Interventions and Their Rationales   58
A Note on Insight and Supportive Therapies   68

4 **Formulation of States of Mind in Psychotherapy**   **75**
    Mardi J. Horowitz

Observing States of Mind   76
Naming States of Mind   77
Motivational Organization of States of Mind   79
The Structure of States   82

5 **Splitting and Projective Identification among
    Healthier Individuals**   **85**
    N. Gregory Hamilton

Splitting and Projective Identification   86
Clinical Examples of Projective Identification and
    Splitting in Healthier Patients   87
The Therapeutic Utility of Interpreting These
    Mental Processes   93

6 **Projective Identification and Couple Therapy**   **99**
    David E. and Jill S. Scharff

A Background of Object Relations Theory   100
Sources of Confusion about Projective Identification   104
Klein's Concept of Projective Identification   105
Other Contributions: Malin and Grotstein,
    Meissner, Kernberg, Ogden, Sandler   106
Contributions from Family Therapy:
    Zinner and Shapiro   110
Contributions from Sex Therapy   113

Contributing Concepts: Valency, Concordant
and Complementary Identification, and
Extractive Introjection   113
The Steps of Projective Identification   115
The Management of Impasse   118
The Treatment   120
A Session with Shifted Defensive Structure   127
Handling the Couple's Assault on the
Therapist's Capacity   132
The Countertransference of Impasse   134

II   THE THERAPIST AND THE RELATIONSHIP

7   The Selfobject Function of Projective Identification   139
Gerald Adler and Mark W. Rhine

Containing the Patient's Projections and
Provocations   141
Projective Identification   152
Selfobjects   153
Projective Identification as a Selfobject Function   154
Implications for Therapy   155
Implications for Curative Factors   157

8   The Containing Function and the Analyst's Projective Identification   163
N. Gregory Hamilton

The Container and the Contained   164
Projective Identification   164
The Containing Function as Projective
Identification   166
Clinical Example: The Therapist Containing
His Own Anxiety   167

9   Intersubjectivity in Psychoanalytic Treatment   181
*Robert D. Stolorow, Bernard Brandchaft,
and George E. Atwood*

Transference and Countertransference   183

Negative Therapeutic Reactions   184
The Psychoanalytic Understanding of
    Psychopathology   186
Clinical Example: Transference Psychosis   187
The Therapeutic Action of Psychoanalysis   189

10 Psychotherapy of the Narcissistic Personality Disorder
    Patient: Two Contrasting Approaches   195
    Gerald Adler

Description of the Narcissistic Personality Disorder
    Patient   197
Theoretical Understanding: Kernberg and Kohut   198
Psychoanalysis or Psychotherapy?   202
Theoretical Differences between Kernberg and
    Kohut and Their Relevance to Psychotherapy   204
Theories and the Psychotherapist   206
Countertransference   209

III BACK TO THE SOURCE

11 On "Doing Nothing" in the Psychoanalytic
    Treatment of the Refractory Borderline Patient   215
    Glen O. Gabbard

Theoretical and Technical Considerations   217
Clinical Example: Disengaging from the
    Patient's Projective Identification   220

12 Misrecognitions and the Fear of Not Knowing   229
    Thomas H. Ogden

A Theoretical Background   231
A Developmental Perspective   234
The Structuralization of Misrecognition   236
Clinical Example: Misrecognition of Affect   241
Misrecognition as a Dimension of Eating
    Disorders   243

Psychological Change in the Area of
Recognition and Misrecognition 245

13 The "Dis-affected" Patient: Reflections on Affect
Pathology 251
Joyce McDougall

Lifelessness of Emotional Experience 253
The Problem of Affect Pathology 254
Clinical Examples: Handling the Affectless State 258
Countertransference Pitfalls 270

14 Identification and Its Vicissitudes as Observed in
Psychosis 275
Otto F. Kernberg

Concepts Underlying the Approach 276
Clinical Example: The Identification Process in
Psychosis 281
Dual Nature of the Self 291

Afterword 299

Acknowledgments 301

Index 305

Introduction

Object relations theory evolved as a record of explorations in the internal world. Early psychoanalysts ventured into the unconscious, as if it were a strange land — foreign, distant, and primitive. Like Burton searching for the source of the Nile, they journeyed always further into the interior. Discoveries moved toward the deepest, the earliest, and the most primitive. Perhaps it was necessary to conceptualize what was closest as far away in order to discover it.

The arcane object relations literature, which chronicled these explorations, slowly gained appeal for other psychotherapists. What were these object relations therapists learning in the back wards of hospitals, talking hour after hour with solitary, seemingly incomprehensible people? What was happening between these clinicians and the borderline or narcissistic patients they saw in their private offices two and three and four times a week, year after year? What of value was being dredged up from the depths of despair or from emptiness and confusion?

As general interest in this recondite field widened, the literature became clearer and the theory consolidated. The current appeal of object relations studies has now reached a point where the theory is not only influencing psychotherapy in general, but the broader field of psychotherapy is influencing object relations theory. There has been a return from the inner source, with some new insights and some old ones. As what was discovered has been communicated, it has been altered by the context of that communication. Object relations theory is changing. This collection of papers is an indication of some of those changes.

Object relations theory developed parallel to ego psychology in the British Psychoanalytic Institute (Hamilton 1988). Since it concerns itself with how people internalize and externalize relationships, reciprocity and mutual interactions are central, unlike drive theory, which is a linear construction of cause and effect (Hamilton 1989). The infant is considered to be in relationship from birth (Isaacs 1943, Klein 1975), and its impulses are directed toward object seeking rather than tension or anxiety reduction (Fairbairn 1952). In addition to an overarching emphasis on relationship rather than drive discharge, certain object relations concepts have been most influential in psychotherapy — splitting, projective identification, containing, the holding environment, and transitional object formation.

Infants, being in relationship from the beginning, attempt to maintain themselves and their primary objects, whom they first experience as a part of themselves, by projecting destructive and painful experiences and introjecting good and nurturing qualities. Reciprocally, they can introject the "bad" and project the "good" aspects of themselves into the good object, thereby experiencing themselves removed from discomfort or danger. This process of projection and introjection is splitting and results in the split object relations unit. At its most rudimentary, the split unit consists of an all-good self, all-good object, and pleasurable affects in contrast to an all-bad self, all-bad object, and unpleasurable or overwhelming affects. Splitting does not take place as a result of drive discharge, but as an active attempt to protect the good self-object relationship.

Since the person is in relationship from the very beginning of life, self-images are always associated with object-images and with affects. They come as a package. The internal world develops and changes as new experiences of the self in relation to others are internalized. One way this happens is through projective identification (Klein 1946) and containment (Bion 1962).

Projective identification is a process whereby a person attributes an aspect of the self to the object and simultaneously identifies with the projected element in the other, attempting to control or somehow manage it. For example, Janice, a 36-year-old woman with panic disorder and agoraphobia, described her plight in such a way that her therapist, who was a male psychiatry resident, could not help but feel anxious. If she noticed signs of his discomfort, she would admonish him, "If you are so worried you don't know what to do, it only makes me more scared." With such statements, she seemed to be trying to control her own anxiety by controlling her therapist's affect.

While projective identification creates the split internal object world, it also eventually modifies it. This happens through what Bion (1962) called containment. When children have strong affects that threaten to overwhelm them, they externalize their distress. The parent takes in the projected feeling and self-object state, contains it, modulates it, gives it meaning, and returns the transformed affect in the form of holding, a meaningful comment, or some other communication. The child can now accept the metabolized affect and self-object state as his own. He eventually takes in the containing process itself along with the transformed projections, identifies with it, and learns to contain his own affects to a large degree.

Since what the child internalizes is a combination of what is projected onto the parent and what the parent gives back, there can be considerable distortion of interactions. Consequently, memories of early life are a composite of what took place and of what was projected onto the environment. From the beginning, the individual has a significant role in creating his or her interpersonal world.

If enough overwhelming or "bad" experience has been projected into the good-enough parent and been returned through containment and reintrojection, the child can now tolerate previously unwanted experience. He can do so without fear that the "bad" will swallow up the "good" internal experience. This process, the exact ordering of which remains to be determined, depends both on environmental factors and neurophysiologic development of integrative functions. It allows for development of whole object relations as opposed to split object relations. The child now knows that the mother or father whom he hated and wished to destroy for depriving him is the same parent he loves. As the child makes reparative efforts and works through feelings of remorse and guilt over wishes to destroy the beloved parent, he or she learns that the parents are primarily loving and also a bit frustrating. The self is also loving and a bit destructive. Self and object are separate, yet related. This is whole object relatedness (Mahler et al. 1975).

To achieve a secure sense of distinctness as a valuable person in relation to others, one must be provided with an adequate holding environment. This is Winnicott's (1960) term describing the good-enough parent's (Winnicott 1953) provision of optimal closeness while allowing adequate room for the child to develop autonomy. This concept is similar to Bion's idea of containment, with less emphasis on projection and introjection and more emphasis on the need for interpersonal closeness and yet separateness. A transitional object (Winnicott 1953) often provides an intermediary in the separation process. It may be represented by the child's blanket or teddy bear, which is neither self nor parent, yet is treated as if it were both the parent and the self.

In therapy influenced by object relations theory, the therapist helps the patient develop firmer boundaries and a clearer sense of self by recognizing splitting and projective identifications. More important, she or he does so while providing containment and a holding environment that the patient eventually internalizes.

Some object relations-influenced aspects of Janice's treatment follow:

Early in the therapy, she described her anxiety and panic in convincing fashion. "I get to the point where I can't do anything," she said. "I get so nervous. My daughter is beginning to stay home from school with stomachaches. Sometimes I think she is doing it to take care of me. Then I get worried about her, too. I know you can do something to help me."

When she described the damage her anxiety may be doing to an innocent child and placed responsibility for help with the therapist, he felt exceedingly anxious himself. Although this psychiatry resident at first wanted to maintain neutrality and try an expressive therapy influenced by drive theory, he kept shifting, almost unwillingly, into giving advice and encouragement. Soon he prescribed medication, too, but nothing worked.

When he recommended various antidepressants shown to have beneficial effects on panic, Janice always had high hopes until she actually took them. Once she had taken a dose or two, she developed increasing fears about minor side effects, such as dry mouth, to the point where she could no longer take the medicine.

The resident told his supervisor one day, "The harder I try, the worse she gets."

"Perhaps you shouldn't try so hard. I don't mean give up on her, but try backing off on yourself a bit," the supervisor said.

"I feel like giving up."

"Then you know what she must feel like."

"I suppose," he said. "But what good does it do for me to understand if I can't do anything to help?"

"You have very clearly let me know how difficult this case is. It must be hard to struggle through it without much help and not sure where you are going, but I guess that's where we are for now. You're doing fine. I'll see you next week."

When his patient explained her plight again the next session, she said, "I just don't know what to do," appealing to him for help.

His anxiety rose. He felt alone and wished his supervisor could have told him what to do. Without knowing exactly why, he said in a tone of voice similar to his supervisor's, "It must be very hard for you, because you don't know if anyone can ever understand how terrified and alone you feel."

"No one has ever understood," she said and sat back in her chair. She began talking in a fairly relaxed manner about how misunderstood she had felt most of her life.

According to object relations theory, the patient behaved and communicated in such a way as to elicit her unwanted feelings of anxiety, helplessness, and aloneness in the therapist. This was projective identification. Through the parallel process (Hamilton 1988) of his own projective identification, the therapist communicated his anxiety to his supervisor, who understood it and helped him contain it. When the therapist could finally tolerate these feelings, give them meaning, and return them to the patient in the form of empathic understanding, she experienced her anxiety as contained and could relax a bit. She was no longer so alone with her overwhelming feelings and could tolerate them the way the therapist could tolerate them.

Over the next several weeks, as the anxiety became contained and transformed into shared understanding, the doctor could begin to think more clearly about why the medication was not working.

One session, his patient again said, "You must know of some medicine, or something that doesn't have any side effects." This seemed to him to be the reciprocal of her projecting her anxiety. She was attributing an omnipotent self-image or caretaker-image onto him so that he felt knowledgeable and powerful. She did so by eliciting his readily available omnipotent healer fantasies.

Instead of offering a new medication, he said, "I am a bit hesitant to give you something just now, because I'm afraid it might make you feel bad about yourself. If I am the powerful doctor with the wonderful medicine, and you are the helpless patient with the disordered brain chemistry, you may feel bad about yourself, and it will only make things worse. And I don't think that."

"You don't think what?"

"That you are a helpless person with disordered brain chemistry."

"But there is something wrong with me or I wouldn't be coming to you."

"You are being pretty effective in convincing me now. That is your own power, not mine. Yes, there is something not going well, but not everything."

"I still might benefit from medication."

"Yes, you might. Let's keep talking about it."

In this example, the therapist used the concept of splitting to notice how, when the patient felt overwhelmed by anxiety, she would see herself as increasingly helpless and the doctor and his medication as increasingly perfect and omnipotent. She attributed hope and goodness to him and things associated with him in order to feel safe in his presence. This is splitting. Its mechanism is projective identification. She attributed her own coping abilities and omnipotent fantasies to the therapist and then tried to join them by being dependent on him. When he accepted her projections and acted like an omnipotent healer with magic medication, the physician colluded in splitting, only to find his medicine turned worthless once she took it into herself, where it was swallowed up by her all-bad self-experience filled with the anxiety and confusion of her hypochondriasis.

Over the next few sessions, they thoroughly discussed the benefits, side effects, and limitations of medication, as well as the meaning it had in their work together. This time, she was able to tolerate the side effects and she benefitted greatly.

Over months, Janice became convinced that the medicine her psychiatrist gave her could modulate anxiety to a manageable level, and she gradually decreased the dose in collaboration with him. One day she said, "I'm not sure I really need the pills anymore. It just makes me feel better to know I have them available to me. When I get a little nervous, I sometimes reach in my purse and make sure the bottle is there."

"It must be reassuring to know there is something outside yourself that can help you manage your feelings."

"It's odd, but I not only think of how the medicine affects me. I remember your calm voice telling me how to take it and how it works. I'm not so nervous here, especially when you talk."

"You feel secure when you're here," he said.

"Yes, secure," she said. This was the first feeling she had been able to name other than "nervousness" or anxiety.

Through his remaining emotionally attuned to the patient and also helping her regulate herself physiologically via the medication, the therapist provided a good-enough holding environment. This object relations viewpoint does not nullify the classical conditioning explanation of her feeling calmed by carrying the medication bottle, but adds a relationship component to it. Now, the patient was able to carry the medicine as a kind of security blanket, a transitional object. Eventually, she just carried an unfilled prescription written by her doctor. Months later, when she was transferring her belongings to a new purse, she found it forgotten and tattered at the bottom of her purse. She chuckled fondly at her childishness and threw it away.

Object relations approaches are radically different from drive theory and ego psychology. Although Kernberg (Chapter 2) and Pine (Chapter 3) have integrated ego psychology and object relations theory, many therapists, influenced by Fairbairn, do not do so. The main advantage of object relations ideas for the therapist in this example is that they provide a way of understanding the emotional context of therapy, a way of understanding the therapist's countertransference feelings in relation to the patient, and a method of handling splitting and projective identification.

According to this model, the patient's expectable feelings of security with the doctor are not repressed at the beginning of therapy because of unconscious erotic or aggressive transference or unconscious association with a previous unfortunate medical event. A secure feeling is absent because, on the one hand, the patient had never been provided a good-enough holding environment to feel secure and, on the other hand, whenever she begins to feel safe, she splits off and projects that affect to protect it from being swallowed up by her overwhelming anxiety. The patient develops a feeling of safety in relation to the therapist when he provides a holding environment and contains and eventually returns to her, in the form of understanding, aspects of her own self that she has split off and projected. This takes place before any uncovering of unconscious impulses can be done and before anything can be derepressed.

The main drawback of this approach for the therapist is that it requires so much self-scrutiny and seems so hazy at first. Some therapists are tempted to see affects and self-images shuttling back and forth between therapist and patient in a quasimystical fashion. There is also a temptation to overemphasize the containing and nurturing function of the therapist, as if caring and tolerance are all that is required, resulting in an underemphasis of the hard work and effort psychotherapy requires of both therapist and patient.

This theory, like any set of ideas, can be overly reductionistic. Just as drive theory can reduce relationships to erotic and aggressive drives, object relations theory can reduce erotic and aggressive feelings to issues exclusively dealing with closeness, distance, and self–other boundaries. For example, the therapist and patient in the example could have easily avoided the sexual aspects, that is, how the patient may have felt seduced by the therapist into taking medication, which reminded her of an actual seduction by a neighbor when she was a little girl. Such an avoidance is not required by object relations theory, but it can be facilitated by it.

Each contribution in this book indicates a new direction in psychotherapy arising out of object relations approaches. Self psychology and ego psychology are included in that they pertain to and overlap with object relations understandings, but the central emphasis remains on object relations psychotherapy, where it has been and where it is going. Object relations theory is influencing hospital administration, group therapy, psychiatric case management, and studies of the arts, history, and the roles of men, women, and children in the family and society. To include these areas, however, would be too vast an undertaking. This book is about psychotherapy.

One movement within object relations literature is toward an emphasis on psychotherapy in general, including work with healthier individuals in addition to intensive treatment of patients who have narcissistic, borderline, or psychotic disorders. A second is toward a greater appreciation of alternative viewpoints and how they relate to one another. A third movement is in the direction of regarding the source of insight as equally within the therapist and the patient, using the concepts of empathy, projective identification, countertransference, containing, and selfobject function. These three themes are expected to determine the way object relations approaches affect psychotherapy over the next several years.

After an introduction providing a brief overview of object relations in general, the chapters are arranged in three sections. Each one addresses, to a slightly different degree, all three themes — wider psychotherapy applications, appreciation of theoretical diversity, and awareness of the therapist's experience as central.

The first section, "Different Patients, Different Therapists, Different Theories," focuses on how object relations theory is beginning to be adapted to various psychotherapy styles with divergent clinical groups. Object relations theory was once the basis for treating borderline disorders and little else. Now it is being used more widely.

The second section, "The Therapist and the Relationship," is composed of chapters, each from a slightly different perspective, and each dealing with what is created or exists or takes place between therapist and patient. Emphasis is no longer solely on technical neutrality and what takes place within the patient, but also upon what takes place within the therapist and between the therapist and the patient. While these contributions are theoretical in tone, they are clinical in relevance and contain extensive examples. They draw heavily upon ideas from both self psychology and object relations theory.

The final section, "Back to the Source," consists of four chapters that illustrate advances in understanding and treating difficult patients. This section returns to the source of object relations theory, since it deals with the intensive individual treatment of severe disorders. Yet, each contribution suggests new directions in that it employs a way of comprehending the self in the other, which will undoubtedly yield further insights in the future.

The writings are recent, many of them by the most influential object relations theorists, such as Kernberg, Adler, McDougall, and Ogden. Gabbard and Hamilton are newer on the scene. Horowitz and Stolorow are included to represent an overlap with ego psychology and self psychology, respectively. All the contributions, even the few theoretical ones, were chosen for their direct clinical relevance and case examples, which therapist-readers can compare to their own work. Another criterion for selection was that each chapter must be clearly written and understandable to psychotherapists, regardless of their level of experience, yet without sacrificing depth of meaning.

This collection is brought together for the reader's convenience in studying the influence object relations theory is beginning to have on psychotherapy in general. It is an anthology and, as such, is not intended to be comprehensive. Neither is it intended merely as a sampler. Each chapter is sufficiently thorough to present a useful viewpoint in its own right. Additionally, the arrangement and comments introduce a new element, a theme.

The collection arises out of the recent past and looks forward to the future. It predicts a continued movement within object relations theory toward greater application to psychotherapy in general, increasing theoretical diversity, and clearer acknowledgment of the source of insight within the therapist, as well as within the patient. Its success in prediction, of course, is a question that remains for the future.

N. Gregory Hamilton, M.D.
Portland, Oregon

REFERENCES

Bion, W. R. (1962). *Learning from Experience*. London: Heinemann.

Hamilton, N. G. (1988). *Self and Others: Object Relations Theory in Practice*. Northvale, NJ: Jason Aronson.

_____ (1989). A critical review of object relations theory. *American Journal of Psychiatry* 146:1552–1560.

Isaacs, S. (1943). The nature and function of phantasy. In *Developments in Psychoanalysis*, ed. M. Klein, P. Heimann, S. Isaacs, and J. Riviere, pp. 67–121. London: Hogarth, 1952.

Klein, M. (1946). Notes on some schizoid mechanisms. *International Journal of Psycho-Analysis* 27:99–110.

_____ (1975). *Envy and Gratitude and Other Works 1946–1963*. New York: The Free Press.

Mahler, M. S., Pine, F., and Bergman, A. (1975). *The Psychological Birth of the Human Infant*. New York: Basic Books.

Winnicott, D. W. (1953). Transitional objects and transitional phenomena. *International Journal of Psycho-Analysis* 34:89–97.

_____ (1960). The theory of the parent–infant relationship. In *The Maturational Process and the Facilitating Environment*, pp. 37–55. New York: International Universities Press.

A Critical Review of Object Relations Theory

N. Gregory Hamilton

The place of drive theory and ego psychology in general psychiatry was well discussed in the 1950s. Since that time, object relations theory has made a tremendous impact on American psychiatry. Like any advance, it has brought its own problems, and an overview and critical reassessment are in order.

This chapter provides a historical account of the development of object relations theory and discusses the theory's contributions to diagnosis, etiologic concepts, and treatment. Particular attention is paid to those strengths and weaknesses which run through all its applications.

HISTORICAL OVERVIEW

Object relations theory concerns itself with how individuals develop in relation to the people around them. Internalizing and externalizing relationships (Hamilton 1988, Kernberg 1976), attachment and separation (Bowlby 1969, 1973, 1980), introjection and projection (Klein 1946), and transmuting internalization (Kohut 1971) are the key issues in development. This emphasis on relationships is in contradistinction to classic psychoanalytic drive theory with its focus on how the individual organism discharges its impulses.

Freud (1905) conceptualized the infant as having drives that have an aim and are directed toward an object. The direction of causation is linear, from subject to object. According to this model, psychological growth takes place as impulses are frustrated and the organism seeks increasingly efficient avenues for discharge of energy. The needs of the object are accommodated only as a compromise.

In the first months of life, the child's drives are primarily oral. The person who allows the infant to suck becomes an object of attachment because that person provides for the discharge of oral impulses. Through physiological development, the most invest-ment of emotional energy shifts from the oral mucosa to the anal mucosa when the child is about 18 months to 2 years of age. Thus, the relationship with parents now begins to center on bowel function and training, including issues of control and power. At 3 to 4 years, the genitals become (again, physiologically) the most important organs of instinctual discharge. The stage is now set for oedipal conflicts concerning impulses to engage in sexual activi-ties.

In this model, pathology arises when the drives are excessively frustrated or gratified, leading to symptomatic inhibitions, re-newed attempts to gratify impulses through convoluted channels, or impulse control problems. Psychological energy, like steam in a boiler, can only be diverted or discharged (Freud 1887–1902). This schema is consistent with the linear causality model so influential in medicine at the beginning of the twentieth century. It is both deterministic and reductionistic. Drives, which are unidi-rectional, from inward to outward, are frustrated, leading to the peculiarities of civilized behavior as well as to pathology.

Anna Freud (1936) eventually helped create a shift in analytic theory by focusing on one aspect of her father's work. She devoted increasing attention to the ego and its attempts to handle conflict. While not supplanting drive theory, she and other ego psycholo-gists did not dwell on the damming up of energy as pathogenic but concentrated on the ego's attempts to protect its integrity through an increasingly elaborate series of defense mechanisms, which contribute both to growth, when managed well, and to pathology, when managed poorly. Still, however, these theorists saw relationships among people as being maintained primarily to gratify drives or to defend against their unwanted expression.

Sigmund Freud developed an object relations theory, which received less attention than did his drive and structural theories. He described how, following a loss, people seek to continue receiving gratification from the lost person by internalizing the person's image and relating to this now internal object as if it were the actual person (Freud 1917). People not only internalize lost objects but identify with them; they make the object-image a part of themselves and thereby develop their identity.

Following Freud, Melanie Klein (Klein 1975, Segal 1964) increasingly emphasized internal relationships. She and her colleagues (Isaacs 1952, Klein 1975) took the crucial step of asserting that infants are object related from birth — possibly earlier. They do not merely become attached to the parent because the parent satisfies their oral drives. Since infants are in a relationship from the beginning, they attempt to protect their integrity as an organism and that of the primary object of attachment (which they experience as a part of themselves) by projecting their innate destructiveness onto the environment and introjecting its good aspects or, reciprocally, by projecting the good aspects of themselves onto the good object and experiencing themselves removed from discomfort or danger. Thus, they split their self-and-object world into all-good and all-bad camps.

An illustration of splitting may prove useful.

Case 1.

Ms. A., a 28-year-old woman, sought treatment with a psychiatrist because she had chaotic, unstable emotions and did not feel that she knew who she was or what she wanted to do with her life. After she had been in therapy for two months, she described a scene with her husband the previous night. She had been reading a book about how to have a more gratifying relationship with a man and decided to follow its directions. When her husband returned from work, she served him a fine meal, with flowers on the table. He was appreciative and attentive. They drank a bottle of wine and afterward enjoyed an hour of sexual activity in which she felt totally gratified and at one with her husband. She had thought it was perfect, she said, but she should have known better.

After he had talked with her for 15 or 20 minutes more, her husband dozed off. She began to feel lonely and afraid and awoke him to seek reassurance. When he rather groggily replied that she would be all right, she felt slighted. He was inconsiderate and inattentive, she thought. She became furious and woke him up, shouting at him that he did not really love her, that his lovemaking had been ungenuine and selfish, that she had had to seduce him, and that he did not really care for her at all. In fury she smashed a glass against the wall above his head.

With further exploration, it could be seen that the patient kept her blissful, gratified, united experience with her husband entirely separate from her enraged, abandoned, neglected feeling. When she felt abandoned and full of rage, she revised history so that she could not remember how good she had felt just a little while previously. The whole world seemed to change for her. The psychiatrist pointed out how this also happened in her feelings about him and her therapy. Because of her extreme splitting she could not develop continuity of experience and a clear sense of identity.

Splitting as a primary developmental and psychological mechanism remains central to modern object relations theory (Adler 1985, Burnham 1966, Gabbard 1989, Grotstein 1981, Hamilton 1988, Kernberg 1969, 1976, Mahler et al. 1975, Masterson and Rinsley 1975). Pruyser (1975) wrote a major paper questioning the usefulness of this concept; his main objection was the lack of clarity in terminology which suggests that what is divided—the ego—is also the agent which does the dividing. More recent work has attempted to address this issue by distinguishing the self from the ego (Hamilton 1988).

Klein strove to maintain a drive theory by using Freud's idea of life and death instincts (Freud 1920), which most American analysts now consider an aberration in his thought. Despite this effort, in her concept the primary motivation of development shifted from instinctual discharge to the need to maintain continuity of the relationship: good self and good object.

As splitting resolves, whole object relations become central to mature functioning in normal development. The maturing child learns that his loving wishes are directed toward the same object as his destructiveness (Klein 1975). The mother whom he hates and wishes to destroy for depriving him is the same mother he loves for nurturing him. The child then develops remorse and guilt and wishes to restore or repair the object he had previously wanted to diminish. As he works through his guilt, he comes to recognize his loving and destructive impulses as his own and his mother's nurturing and depriving qualities as her own. The self is loving and also somewhat destructive. The object is loving and also a bit destructive. The self and object are separate, yet related. This is whole object relatedness (Mahler et al. 1975).

> In the example of Ms. A., the psychiatrist treated the patient with lithium carbonate and psychotherapy. The lithium seemed to help her modulate her affects to some degree, but she continued to show prominent splitting and concomitant affective shifts, now somewhat attenuated, until she worked on recognizing her contradictory feelings about the therapist, about people in her current life, and about her parents during her early years. It was a long time before she could say to her therapist, "When I look back, I realize I made such unreasonable demands on you. I feel kind of ashamed. You must have had some concern for me then, just as you do now, but I'd punish you so, because I couldn't see it."
>
> At this point, the patient was beginning to experience the therapist who cared about her and whom she valued as the same person who was sometimes frustrating and whom she had hated. Similarly, she began to integrate her feelings toward her husband. She could now experience her loving and punishing aspects as part of herself and could experience the remorse, as well as the meaningful relatedness, that accompanies whole object relationships.

In this view of development, the primary problem of the individual is how to maintain continuity of relationships in the presence of contradictory loving and hating feelings — love being associated with gratification-attachment and hate being associated with deprivation-abandonment. This is quite different from the problem in drive theory of how to gratify internal genital impulses in spite of outside prohibition and overwhelming force. Maturity is no longer conceptualized as relatively unconflicted, if compromised, drive discharge.

In addition to emphasizing object relatedness, splitting, and reparation, Klein (1946) introduced the concept of projective identification, whereby a person attributes an aspect of the self to the object and reidentifies with the projected element in the other, attempting to control it. The following case is an example.

Case 2.

> Ms. B., a 35-year-old woman with unusual intelligence and education, said at her first appointment, "I can't have a relationship with a man for more than a few months because I see the man as so wonderful that I begin to feel empty. Then it's like I have to become him, get into him some how to be valuable and feel good about myself." Here she was describing a process of seeing her own value as a person in another person and then needing to join that aspect of herself in the other.

Similarly, projective identification can take place with negative feelings, as in the patient who elicits helpless or angry feelings in the doctor so that the patient does not feel so alone with overwhelming affect. This concept has been elaborated and applied to understanding countertransference (Kernberg 1965), splitting in hospital treatment teams (Adler 1985, Gabbard 1989), and parallel processes in clinical administration and supervision (Hamilton 1988). The use of two logically mutually exclusive processes, projection and identification, as a single entity powerfully describes a kind of blurring of the boundary between self and object that takes place during projective identification, but it has led to considerable theoretical controversy (Gabbard 1989, Grotstein 1981, Hamilton 1986, 1988, Kernberg 1965, Klein 1946, Ogden 1982, Sandler 1987, Spillius 1983) and has resulted in confusion of patient and clinician attributes as well as individual and group variables.

Klein's ideas about splitting as a mechanism for maintaining intactness and object relatedness, her emphasis on projection and introjection, and her concept of developing whole object relatedness have been important contributions. However, her odd terminology, her insistence on concrete, anatomical metaphors, her concept of an inborn death instinct, her recommendation of deep interpretation early in therapy, her ideas about innate knowledge of sexual intercourse, her overemphasis on constitutional as opposed to environmentally determined development, and her idea that psychic development is condensed into the first months of postnatal life have interfered with both the understanding and the acceptance of her ideas (Kernberg 1969).

Fairbairn (1954) went further than Klein. He and his student Guntrip (1969) entirely relinquished drive theory and focused on the need to seek objects and attach meaningfully to other people as the central elements in personality development. Like Klein, Fairbairn considered infants to be object related from birth, but whereas Klein highlighted the inherent destructiveness in human beings, Fairbairn saw human beings as originally innocent of aggression, which only arises from frustration within a depriving environment. He further elaborated the idea of a divided self or ego — libidinal ego, antilibidinal ego, and central ego (Fairbairn 1954).

Relying on Klein's concept of projective identification (Klein 1946), Bion (1962) used the metaphor of the container and the contained to show how infants overcome the isolation and fragmentation of their split internal world. Children have strong affects that threaten to overwhelm them. They externalize their distress and project it onto the parent, who takes in the projected feeling, contains it, modulates and alters it, and gives the transformed affect back to the child in the form of holding behavior or a meaningful comment. The child can now accept the metabolized affect and self-image as his own. He eventually identifies with the containing process itself and learns to contain his own affects. Bion's ideas have been widely used in both the psychotherapy and the hospital treatment of borderline and psychotic patients (Adler 1985, Gabbard 1989, Hamilton 1988, Haugsgjerd 1987, Singer 1987). However, because he did not consistently distinguish between the internal and the external worlds and between the self and the internal object, and did not discuss mechanisms by which affects cross personal boundaries, his theory has taken on the aura of mysticism.

Unlike Fairbairn and Bion, Winnicott did not have a penchant for theory; nevertheless, he introduced the widely accepted concepts of the holding environment (Winnicott 1960) and the transitional object (Winnicott 1953). The holding environment describes the good enough mother's (Winnicott 1953) function of providing the child with optimal closeness while allowing adequate room for development of autonomy. This idea is similar to Bion's concept of container, with less emphasis on the projection of destructiveness and more emphasis on the need for closeness yet separateness. Eventually, the child can internalize the holding functions so that he can self-soothe (Tolpin 1971) and separate from the parent. An important step in this process is development of a transitional object (Winnicott 1953) — often represented by the child's blanket or teddy bear — which is neither self nor object and yet may be treated as if it were the beloved parent and simultaneously the self. Again, the issue is relationship, not mechanism of drive discharge. These concepts are circular, with unclear boundaries between environment and infant, so they cannot describe linear causation, but they are powerful and useful descriptions of personal systems interactions.

It was not until the work of Kernberg (1976) that object relations theory achieved a firm place in American psychoanalysis and a growing influence on general psychiatry. Kernberg, influenced by Klein and Jacobson (1964), concluded from his analytic studies of adult patients that infants develop through phases of a split internal world and gradually shift toward whole object relatedness. Kernberg (1982) later attempted to bring his object relations theory into line with drive theory and ego psychology by conceptualizing the infant as being born with an undifferentiated energy and responsiveness. This energy becomes organized into the traditional two drives of sex and aggression by polar affects experienced in the split all-good, all-bad world of the infant. Making drives secondary came late in Kernberg's theory. Earlier, he emphasized the innateness of aggressive and libidinal drives (Kernberg 1975). Kernberg has not yet reconciled this aspect of his later theory with his earlier thinking.

Kernberg's ideas have been found to be compatible with Mahler's observations of infants and their mothers (Mahler et al. 1975). Mahler described the phases of autism, symbiosis, separation-individuation, and whole object relations. Children begin in a relative but not complete psychological insulation at birth (autism). By the age of 2 months, they move toward an experience in which they are one pole of a dual unity with the symbiotic mother (symbiosis). At 6 months or so, the child begins physically and psychologically separating himself from the primary parent (separation-individuation). During the practicing subphase of separation-individuation (10–16 months), the child becomes exhilarated by his new mobility and moves off to explore his world. By 16–24 months, he acquires an increased cognitive awareness of his vulnerability and separateness, which leads to an uneasy return to the mother (rapprochement subphase of separation-individuation). His attempts to divide the world into all good and all bad, nurturing and depriving, are redoubled; splitting becomes the prominent defense mechanism. This uneasy solution eventually gives way to developing whole object relations (24–36 months) in which infant and parent are separate yet related, the relationship being primarily good but also having some less than optimal qualities.

Mahler's studies have been found to be largely consistent with those of Spitz (1965) and Piaget (Cobliner 1965, Fraiberg 1969, Lester 1983, Mahler et al. 1975, Piaget 1954) as well as with the work of Kernberg (1980), and Masterson and Rinsley (1975).

Rinsley (1982) brought the American and British schools of object relations theory closer by showing how Fairbairn's concept of the divided self, or ego, was the intellectual forerunner of the American understanding of split object relations units. These units consist of all-good or all-bad affects that are associated with a set of self- and object-images.

Unlike Kernberg, Kohut (1971) developed an object relations theory that denies inherent human aggression. Infants are born with needs, not drives. They need self-cohesion and self-regulation, functions that the parent originally performs for the child. Through empathic attunement the parent integrates and modulates for the baby. Kohut considered splitting not as a congenitally determined developmental step but as a fragmentation product resulting from inadequate empathic attunement. Since the parent performs a self-modulation function for the infant and is still an object, the parent serves as a "selfobject." Through what Kohut called transmuting internalization, that is, introjecting and identifying with the sustaining selfobject, the child learns to self-soothe and develop self-esteem and a cohesive sense of self (Kohut 1971, Tolpin 1971), although even adults continue to need sustaining objects to some degree. Kohut entirely did away with the concept of an organizing ego.

Kohut's self psychology is an object relations theory because it focuses on the development of personality through the internalization of relationships. The fact that he dropped the concept of ego and deemphasized the role of aggression in development causes serious problems in his theory. Focusing only on the self allows for no autonomous, organizing ego (Hartmann 1964) that matures with neurologic consolidation and helps some infants cope with less carefully attuned parents. His deemphasis of aggression invites neglect of this important clinical factor or facile reinterpretation of it as the patient's innocent frustration at being "misunderstood." His descriptions of selfobject function, empathy, and transmuting internalization, however, are important contributions with considerable intuitive and clinical power.

Stern (1985) has drawn together numerous observational studies and delineated phases in developing a sense of self (emergent self, core self, subjective self, verbal self) and concomitant phases in developing relatedness (emergent relatedness, core relatedness, intersubjective relatedness, and verbal relatedness). He argues against Mahler's idea of an autistic phase. His phrasing and emphasis are compatible with Kohut's work (1971) and deemphasize drives, particularly aggression.

At present, the main difference between Stern's work and that of Piaget, Spitz, and Mahler is that Stern emphasizes the newborn infant's rudimentary object relatedness, whereas the others emphasize the undeveloped nature of that relatedness by contrast to later stages of growth. The primary similarity among all of these developmental studies is that the unit of investigation has become the infant–parent relationship. They are studies of personal interaction — of a system, not an isolated entity with pent-up drives forcing outward (Beahrs 1986, Bertalanffy 1950, Menninger et al. 1963). The similarities between Stern's work and that of Mahler may outweigh the differences, but critical review and integration of Stern's work remain areas for further study.

All of the object relations theories have in common an emphasis on the importance of internalization and externalization of relationships in development and thus in all psychological change, including recovery from psychiatric illness. They are systems theories (Beahrs 1986, Bertalanfffy 1950, Menninger et al. 1963) that describe interactions across boundaries and emphasize complex patterns and relationships instead of linear causality. Thus, they are readily applicable to the complexities of clinical practice; but, while useful to the art of medicine, they are difficult to reconcile with the traditional, positivistic, scientific tradition of medicine, which attempts to isolate variables and demonstrate specific cause and effect. Thus, many psychiatric clinicians and researchers remain skeptical of these theories.

The theories also share, in varying degree, a lack of preciseness in terminology. Ego, self, object, selfobject, transitional object, internal and external world, and intersubjective experience (Stolorow et al. 1983) are not clearly distinguishable concepts. Processes of projection, introjection, identification, projective identification, merger, fusion, blurring of boundaries, transmuting internalization, and empathic understanding (Buie 1981, Hamilton 1981, Kohut 1971) are not specific actions in which one thing acts on another. This terminology serves the purpose of eliciting in the reader a feeling for the blurriness under consideration but leads to misunderstanding within the field of object relations theory and, to no less a degree, in general psychiatry.

These theories do not agree on the importance of drives versus needs (Greenberg and Mitchell 1983), the role of aggression in development (Kernberg 1980, Kohut 1971), and the existence of an autistic phase of interpersonal unrelatedness in the newborn (Mahler et al. 1975, Stern 1985).

DIAGNOSIS

Object relations theorists have used clinical and developmental studies to delineate a system of classifying mental illness (Adler 1985, Hamilton 1988, Horner 1984, Kernberg 1976) that is irreconcilable with the phenomenologic approach of general psychiatry (Hamilton and Allsbrook 1986).In the psychoanalytic tradition of placing disorders on developmental continua, these authors have created their own continuum. Classical psychoanalysis described fixations at the level of psychosexual development (oral, anal, phallic, genital) (Freud 1905). Object relations theorists classify mental disorders according to the degree of separation-individuation and development of whole object relations achieved by the patient. This schema does not imply a fixation per se, but notes similarities between certain disorders and developmental issues at various phases of growth. The psychoses display a severe degree of self-object confusion and fragmentation; they are placed at the presymbiotic or symbiotic level of development described by Mahler (Hamilton 1988, Mahler 1952, Rinsley 1972). Borderline disorders, in which splitting all-good and all-bad experience is predominant, are placed at the rapprochement level (Adler 1985, Kernberg 1975, Masterson and Rinsley 1975). Narcissistic idealizing and devaluing are seen as associated with the late rapprochement subphase or the early phase in developing whole object relations (Hamilton 1988, Rinsley 1972, 1980). Neurotic disorders with greater tolerance of ambivalence are considered whole object relations issues (Horner 1984). This linear system is based on the similarity between the object relations of patients and those of children at various developmental levels. Kohut's schema (1971) is based on the degree of self-cohesion as manifested in merger, mirroring, and idealizing transferences.

Developmental diagnosis has contributed greatly to the systematic investigation of borderline and, to a lesser degree, narcissistic disorders. A continuum, however, is fundamentally incompatible with the either–or, algorithmic, phenomenologic classification of general psychiatry. Most medical specialties rely on such algorithmic systems. While continua are systematic and comprehensive, they are unlikely to evolve into a classification according to etiology (Hamilton and Allsbrook 1986). Object-relations-oriented developmental diagnosis (Blanck and Blanck 1979) is most useful in planning psychotherapies and less useful for choosing somatic interventions.

ETIOLOGY

This set of object relations theories constitutes a developmental psychology that focuses on the earliest years. The fact that there are parallels between the object relations of persons with certain disorders and the infantile developmental phases has led to an often implied and sometimes explicit assumption that later difficulties are caused by earlier ones. For example, Kohut (1971) attributed narcissistic disorders to inadequate parental empathic attunement. This failure leads to defective self-soothing and an ongoing desperate search for external sources of self-esteem. Masterson and Rinsley (1975) suggested that borderline splitting results from maternal behavior that alternately rewards clinging symbiosis and punishes appropriate individuation by emotional abandonment. Kernberg (1975) considered borderline splitting to be derived from an attempt to keep overwhelming aggression from annihilating feeble good internal objects. While he emphasized a constitutional excess of aggression as central, he acknowledged that extreme environmental frustration in early life could lead to increased internal aggression. The role of adult psychological trauma in the emergence of splitting and projective identification as predominant defense mechanisms has been discussed by only a few authors (Brende 1983, Hamilton 1988). Horowitz (1976) described the dynamics of adult stress response syndromes in systems terms, which include shifting internal self and object representations, but he emphasized cognitive information processing instead of projection, introjection, splitting, and identification.

Because object relations theory is an intrapsychic and interpersonal construct focusing on emotional interactions, cognitive and perceptual-motor factors have been relatively ignored. There has been little consideration of the observation that splitting can result from an autonomous ego deficit (Hartmann 1964) in cognition so that the patient is unable to hold opposites in mind at the same time (Hamilton 1988). There has been even less emphasis on how such factors as adult brain trauma, temporal lobe epilepsy, and chemical intoxication can lead to reemergence of poorly integrated and differentiated patterns of object relatedness (Andrulonis et al. 1981, Hamilton and Allsbrook 1986). This shortcoming of object relations theory has serious drawbacks for the general psychiatrist, whereas the theory's explanatory power in interpersonal treatment of certain psychotic, borderline, and narcissistic disorders can be useful.

TREATMENT

Individual Psychotherapy

Object relations theory has been derived from and has made its most profound contribution to the individual psychotherapy of severe disorders. The literature is so extensive that only its highlights can be summarized here (Adler 1985, Blanck and Blanck 1979, Giovacchini 1979, Hamilton 1988, Horner 1984, Kernberg 1975, Masterson 1976, Rinsley 1982). The concepts of splitting and projective identification have proven indispensable for understanding and treating borderline disorders (Kernberg 1975).

There is need for further investigation into how modern object relations techniques, such as interpretation of splitting, can also be useful in the treatment of less severe disorders. The following case is an example.

Case 3.

Ms. C., a 42-year-old woman, complained of a recurrent nightmare. She was a well-functioning, somewhat overcontrolled woman who had maintained a difficult marriage for twenty years, had been steadily employed, and successfully raised two children. In her nightmare, her ex-husband appeared, walking down a hall toward her. She was glad to see him, as if he were coming home from work. Suddenly, a fog appeared and the scene changed. A different man was lurching down the hall toward her. She was frightened but not terrified. He disappeared and she was left weeping bitterly. She would awaken because of her sobbing. "I don't know why I would keep dreaming about my husband and keep crying over him," she said. "I was so glad to be rid of him." They had been divorced for three years.

Using a drive theory and ego defense model, Ms. C. and the therapist explored her repression and isolation of her anger at her husband, who had become alcoholic and had beaten her severely late in their marriage. They discussed how she had been spanked occasionally by her admired father when she was a young girl. She became aware of some masochistic, sexual excitement when being spanked. A few sessions later, they discussed her repetition compulsion, an attempt to master an old trauma by repeating it again and again in the dream. This discussion of her drives and defenses over several sessions relieved some tension, but the nightmare continued about twice a month until they explored the splitting revealed in the dream.

There were two figures in the dream. The first one represented her good, loved, sober husband, and the second one represented her split-off drunken, dangerous, abandoning husband. The two experiences of her mate had been so incompatible to her that she had separated the loved figure and kept him as a secret, isolated object-image inside her. The more she was traumatized, the more it aroused her dependent needs for reassurance and the more she clung to her secret good object, the sober husband of the past and the hoped-for future when he would stop drinking. The secret, dependent, loving self-image was inextricably intertwined with the good object-image and associated affects. Because these images of her husband and her relationship were split, she had only been able to focus on the relief of her divorce and could not mourn the loss of her good husband. With this understanding, the nightmares disappeared, and Ms. C. developed a more integrated understanding of her ex-husband and her life experience. She was now able to mourn the loss of the good aspects of her relationship.

It is likely that this patient benefited from insight into drive and defense as well as into splitting of object-images in an attempt to maintain a relationship. Clinically, drives, defenses, and object relations all need attention.

In addition to the concept of splitting, object relations insights into envy as a prominent dynamic in negative therapeutic reactions have been equally valuable (Kernberg 1969). The psychiatrist's awareness of the need to confront negative transference and acting out and to work through abandonment depression has helped many patients (Masterson 1976, Masterson and Rinsley 1975). Juxtaposing positive and negative self- and object-images and clarifying self-other boundaries are more recent additions (Hamilton 1988). Recognition and interpretation of mirroring and idealizing transferences have helped in treating narcissistic disorders (Kohut 1971).

The object relations emphasis on external as well as internal relationships has contributed to an understanding of the importance of providing a holding environment (Modell 1976, Winnicott 1960), containment (Bion 1962), empathic attunement (Kohut

1971), and sustaining relatedness (Adler 1985) in therapy. These relationship aspects of psychotherapy have been reintegrated with the technical aspects of treatment (Hamilton 1988), largely overcoming the previous polarization between corrective emotional experience (Alexander 1950) and interpretation (Eissler 1953, Waelder 1964) as the legitimate agents of change (Lipton 1977, Schafer 1983, Stone 1961).

The interpersonal and systems nature of object relations theory has played a prominent part in the legitimization of countertransference as an important source of information and a powerful tool in the treatment of patients (Kernberg 1965). Elucidation of how projective identification stimulates powerful and primitive countertransference reactions has made it possible for therapists to work with many patients previously considered untreatable (Giovacchini 1979, Kernberg 1980, Masterson 1976). The recognition that empathic sources of information are equal in validity to cognitive sources (Fromm-Reichmann 1950, Kohut 1971, Lichtenberg et al. 1984) has proven valuable, and understanding the effects on the patient of the therapist's empathic failure has helped in therapy with these patients (Kohut 1971).

Inherent in the hopefulness that new insights and treatments bring is a tendency to overapply these recent advances. Some patients may have congenital or acquired cognitive and neuroregulatory deficits that make it impossible for them to internalize any therapeutic experience as benign. The therapist may have no more ability than the parents had to help a particular impaired individual differentiate and integrate emotional experience. Since the object relations diagnostic continuum is a systems theory that categorizes according to patterns of relatedness and not according to cause of dysfunction, symptom pattern, course of illness, and prognosis, it is difficult to differentiate patients who may benefit from interpretation and those who cannot. Through object relations theory itself, unlike cognitive and ego psychologies, one cannot determine which patients might benefit from the time-honored psychiatric interventions of education, advice, encouragement, and prohibition. It is perhaps a necessary risk in a treatment which pays close attention to the therapist's affects that some psychiatrists might consider their treatment failures to be personal failures.

Family Therapy

Family therapy and object relations theory have both loosely allied themselves with general systems theory (Bowen 1978, Hamilton 1988, Kernberg 1976, Minuchin 1974). Each deals with internal and external boundaries, movement of energies, supplies, and information across those boundaries, and patterns of dynamic relationship over and above linear causation. With this common theoretical basis, one would expect an interchange between object relations theorists and family therapists. This cross-enrichment, however, has just begun (Scharff 1989).

While Minuchin's (1974) and Bowen's (1978) systems theories seem compatible with object relations theory, there have been few systematic efforts to integrate their work. Some authors Scharff 1989, Slipp 1984) have attempted to create a theoretical bridge, but these approaches have been more satisfactory to individual psychotherapists than to family therapists, because they emphasize the effect of early family dynamics on later personality development more than the present effect of family dynamics on the current internal world of a particular patient. Shapiro and colleagues (1977) found that "families demonstrate a tendency towards splitting which parallels that of their borderline adolescent" (p. 79). Their therapy approach suggests that changing current family splitting may help the borderline family member overcome his or her tendency toward internal splitting. Solomon (1985) has discussed marital therapy and Brown (1987) has discussed family interviews in object relations terms.

Group Therapy and Psychiatric Administration

Discussions of group therapy for patients with borderline and narcissistic disorders (Horowitz 1977, Roth 1980, Solomon 1987, Wong 1979) and posttraumatic stress disorder (Frick and Bogart 1982) and for incest victims (Ganzarain and Buchele 1988) have used object relations concepts. This literature is still nascent.

The object relations school of group therapy based on whole-group interpretation (Bion 1961, Rice 1965, Sutherland 1952), as opposed to making comments concerning the individual in the group, has not gained prominence among American psychiatrists. Object relations concepts, particularly Bion's ideas (1961), however, have had an impact on milieu therapy and psychiatric administration (Kernberg 1976, Rice 1965). Bion's insights into the importance of focusing on clear, meaningful, and accomplishable tasks in work groups to keep them from regressing into basic-assumption groups preoccupied with dependency, fight-flight, or pairing have helped inpatient and outpatient psychiatrists focus their administration of potentially disorganizing milieus.

Object relations theorists have discussed the influence of the group on the leader and the leader on the group (Kernberg 1976). They have provided insights into group splitting, which takes place on wards when certain borderline patients are hospitalized. Discussion of how a patient can re-create his split internal object world outside himself through projective identification (Adler 1985, Gabbard 1989) has made the orderly hospital treatment of borderline patients much more common in recent years. The concepts of providing a holding environment (Winnicott 1960) and containing functions (Bion 1962) have been applied to both long-term (Gabbard 1989, Haugsgjerd 1987) and short-term (Adler 1985, Singer 1987) hospital treatment (Friedman 1969, Hartcollis 1980, Sadavoy et al. 1979). Day hospital treatment has been discussed by Crawford (1977), among others.

Kohut's ideas have been less useful on inpatient units because his theory, derived from the psychoanalysis of fairly well functioning outpatients with narcissistic concerns, emphasizes therapist empathy as a major agent of change and has no clear framework for understanding how and when patients may benefit from structure, limits, and even physical restraint.

Insights into group functioning and milieu therapy derived from object relations theory have provided a framework for fruitful discussion of the observation that affects and viewpoints seem to pass from individual to group and from group to individual. This systems theory, however, being nonlinear, sheds little light on the direction of causation in any particular instance — for example, does splitting in the patient result in increased staff divisiveness (Main 1957) or does covert staff disagreement (Stanton and Schwartz 1954) exacerbate fragmentation in the patient? Most often, both factors are cited as contributory

(Adler 1985, Burnham 1966, Colson et al. 1985, Gabbard 1989, Hamilton 1988).

IMPLICATIONS FOR THE FUTURE

Object relations theory is an important psychoanalytic viewpoint that has broadly influenced general psychiatry but is far from an overall psychology. It is best considered an addition to drive theory and ego psychology within psychoanalysis rather than an entirely different theory. One way to reconcile drive theory and object relations theory is to consider attachment as primary and as forming a backdrop on which impulses are played out. Such a schema would change both drive theory and ego psychology. The ego functions of cognition, memory, modulation of affect, and integration of experience would be seen as designed to preserve relationships, which has survival implications for the species. They would be seen primarily as creating channels for relatedness and only secondarily as managing and diverting drives. Impulses would always be seen in the context of relationships; the self–other connection would no longer be considered an unsought byproduct of instinctual gratification. However, the power of both conscious and unconscious impulses would not be denied. Another possibility is to consider object relations theory as a new psychoanalytic viewpoint that would complement the present topographic, genetic, economic, and structural points of view. However, integration and differentiation of drive theory and object relations theory in classical usage and metapsychology has barely begun. It remains for the future.

Object relations theory has provided general psychiatrists with a deeper emotional understanding of many severe disorders. It has developed a therapeutically useful conceptualization of patients whose object relations difficulties can be traced back to the earliest period of their lives. The power and compellingness of its early developmental and interpersonal focus, however, may lead to the relative neglect by some clinicians of cognitive, organic, and later developmental contributions to psychopathology. There also needs to be an expansion of object relations studies—which have thus far focused on infantile psychological life and severe pathology—into the arena of the neuroses and normal adult everyday life (Hamilton 1988).

As drive theory provided theoretical links between psychology and the linear causation biology of the late nineteenth century, object relations theory provides important links between individual psychology and social systems, as well as between more modern systems theories of biology and social relationships (Beahrs 1986, Bertalanffy 1950). Those links, so important to biopsychosocial psychiatry (Beahrs 1986, Fink 1988), have yet to be thoroughly explored and delineated.

Many psychiatrists have developed an interest in this new turn of psychoanalytic thought, because it fills a niche in the biopsychosocial model and has still-unrealized potential for integration. Further work is needed in defining terminology, describing the theory more clearly and concisely, comparing and contrasting approaches, and finding the place of object relations theory in general psychiatry, rather than attempting to establish its preeminence or eliminate its influence.

REFERENCES

Adler, G. (1985). *Borderline Psychopathology and Its Treatment*. Northvale, NJ: Jason Aronson.

Alexander, F. (1950). Analysis of the therapeutic factors in psychoanalytic treatment. *Psychoanalytic Quarterly* 19:482–500.

Andrulonis, P. A., Glueck, B. C., Stroebel, C. F., et al. (1981). Organic brain dysfunction and the borderline syndrome. *Psychiatric Clinic of North America* 4:47–66.

Beahrs, J. O. (1986). *Limits of Scientific Psychiatry*. New York: Brunner/Mazel.

Bertalanffy, L. (1950). An outline of general systems theory. *British Journal for the Philosophy of Science* 1:134–163.

Bion, W. R. (1961). *Experiences in Groups*. London: Tavistock.

———— (1962). *Learning From Experience*. London: Heinemann.

Blanck, G., and Blanck, R. (1979). *Ego Psychology*. Vol. 2. *Psychoanalytic Developmental Psychology*. New York: Columbia University Press.

Bowen, M. (1978). *Family Therapy in Clinical Practice*. New York: Jason Aronson.

Bowlby, J. (1969). *Attachment and Loss.* Vol. 1. New York: Basic Books.
———— (1973). *Attachment and Loss.* Vol. 2. New York: Basic Books.
———— (1980). *Attachment and Loss.* Vol. 3. New York: Basic Books.
Brende, J. O. (1983). A psychodynamic view of character pathology in Vietnam combat veterans. *Bulletin of the Menninger Clinic* 47:193–216.
Brown, S. L. (1987). Family therapy and the borderline patient. In *The Borderline Patient,* vol. 2, ed. J. S. Grotstein, M. F. Solomon, and J. A. Lang, pp. 201–209. Hillsdale, NJ: Analytic Press.
Buie, D. (1981). Empathy: its nature and limitations. *Journal of the American Psychoanalytic Association* 29:281–307.
Burnham, D. L. (1966). The special-problem patient: victim or agent of splitting? *Psychiatry* 29:105–122.
Cobliner, W. G. (1965). The Geneva School of genetic psychology: parallels and counterparts. In *The First Year of Life,* ed. R. A. Spitz, pp. 301–356. New York: International Universities Press.
Colson, D. B., Allen, J. G., Coyne, L., et al. (1985). Patterns of staff perception of difficult patients in a long-term psychiatric hospital. *Hospital and Community Psychiatry* 36:168–172.
Crafoord, C. (1977). Day hospital treatment for borderline patients. In *Borderline Personality Disorders,* ed. P. Hartocollis, pp. 385–397. New York: International Universities Press.
Eissler, K. R. (1953). The effect of the structure of the ego on psychoanalytic technique. *Journal of the American Psychoanalytic Association* 1:104–143.
Fairbairn, W. R. D. (1954). *An Object Relations Theory of Personality.* New York: Basic Books.
Fink, P. J. (1988). Response to the presidential address: is "biopsychosocial" the psychiatric shibboleth? *American Journal of Psychiatry* 145:1061–1067.
Fraiberg, S. R. (1969). Libidinal object constancy and mental representation. *Psychoanalytic Study of the Child* 24:9–47. New York: International Universities Press.
Freud, A. (1936). *The Ego and the Mechanisms of Defense.* New York: International Universities Press.
Freud, S. (1887–1902). Project for a scientific psychology. *Standard Edition* 1:283–397, 1966.
———— (1905). Three essays on the theory of sexuality. *Standard Edition* 7:121–245, 1953.
———— (1917). Mourning and melancholia. *Standard Edition* 14:243–258, 1957.

_____ (1920). Beyond the pleasure principle. *Standard Edition* 18:3–64, 1955.

Frick, R., and Bogart, L. (1982). Transference and countertransference in group therapy with Vietnam veterans. *Bulletin of the Menninger Clinic* 49:151–160.

Friedman, H. J. (1969). Some problems of inpatient management with borderline patients. *American Journal of Psychiatry* 126:299–304.

Fromm-Reichmann, F. (1950). *Principles of Intensive Psychotherapy.* Chicago: University of Chicago Press.

Gabbard, G. O. (1989). Splitting in hospital treatment. *American Journal of Psychiatry* 146:444–451.

Ganzarain, R. C., and Buchele, B. J. (1988). *Fugitives of Incest.* Madison, CT: International Universities Press.

Giovacchini, P. L. (1979). *Treatment of Primitive Mental States.* New York: Jason Aronson.

Greenberg, J. R., and Mitchell, S. A. (1983). *Object Relations in Psychoanalytic Theory.* Cambridge, MA: Harvard University Press.

Grotstein, J. S. (1981). *Splitting and Projective Identification.* New York: Jason Aronson.

Guntrip, H. J. S. (1969). *Schizoid Phenomena, Object-Relations and the Self.* New York: International Universities Press.

Hamilton, N. G. (1981). Empathic understanding. *Psychoanalytic Inquiry* 1:417–422.

_____ (1986). Positive projective identification. *International Journal of Psycho-Analysis* 67:489–496.

_____ (1988). *Self and Others: Object Relations Theory in Practice.* Northvale, NJ: Jason Aronson.

Hamilton, N. G., and Allsbrook, L. (1986). Thirty cases of "schizophrenia" reexamined. *Bulletin of the Menninger Clinic* 50:323–340.

Hartocollis, P. (1980). Long-term hospital treatment for adult patients with borderline and narcissistic disorders. *Bulletin of the Menninger Clinic* 44:212–226.

Hartmann, H. (1964). *Ego Psychology and the Problem of Adaptation.* New York: International Universities Press.

Haugsgjerd, S. (1987). Toward a theory for milieu treatment of hospitalized borderline patients. In *The Borderline Patient,* vol. 2, ed. J. S. Grotstein, M. F. Solomon, and J. A. Lang, pp. 211–226. Hillsdale, NJ: Analytic Press.

Horner, A. J. (1984). *Object Relations and the Developing Ego in Therapy.* New York: Jason Aronson.

Horowitz, L. (1977). Group psychotherapy of the borderline patient. In *Borderline Personality Disorders,* ed. P. Hartocollis, pp. 399–422. New York: International Universities Press.

Horowitz, M. J. (1976). *Stress Response Syndromes*. New York: Jason Aronson.

Isaacs, S. (1943). The nature and function of phantasy. In *Developments in Psychoanalysis,* ed. M. Klein, P. Heimann, and S. Isaacs, and J. Riviere, pp. 67–121. London: Hogarth, 1952.

Jacobson, E. (1964). *The Self and the Object World*. New York: International Universities Press.

Kernberg, O. F. (1965). Notes on countertransference. *Journal of the American Psychoanalytic Association* 13:38–56.

———— (1969). A contribution to the ego-psychological critique of the Kleinian school. *International Journal of Psycho-Analysis* 50:317–333.

———— (1975). *Borderline Conditions and Pathological Narcissism*. New York: Jason Aronson.

———— (1976). *Object Relations Theory and Clinical Psychoanalysis*. New York: Jason Aronson.

———— (1980). *Internal World and External Reality*. New York: Basic Books.

———— (1982). Self, ego, affect, and drives. *Journal of the American Psychoanalytic Association* 30:893–917.

Klein, M. (1946). Notes on some schizoid mechanisms. *International Journal of Psycho-Analysis* 27:99–110.

———— (1975). *Envy and Gratitude and Other Works, 1946–1963*. New York: Free Press.

Kohut, H. (1971). *The Analysis of the Self*. New York: International Universities Press.

Lester, E. P. (1983). Separation-individuation and cognition. *Journal of the American Psychoanalytic Association* 31:127–156.

Lichtenberg, J., Bornstein, M., and Silver, D., eds. (1984). *Empathy*. Vols. 1, 2. Hillsdale, NJ: Analytic Press.

Lipton, S. B. (1977). The advantages of Freud's technique as shown in his analysis of the Rat Man. *International Journal of Psycho-Analysis* 58:255–273.

Mahler, M. S. (1952). On child psychosis and schizophrenia. *Psychoanalytic Study of the Child* 7:286–305. New York: International Universities Press.

Mahler, M. S., Pine, F., and Bergman, A. (1975). *The Psychological Birth of the Human Infant*. New York: Basic Books.

Main, T. F. (1957). The ailment. *British Journal of Medical Psychology* 30:129–145.

Masterson, J. F. (1976). *Psychotherapy of the Borderline Adult*. New York: Brunner/Mazel.

Masterson, J. F., and Rinsley, D. B. (1975). The borderline syndrome:

the role of the mother in the genesis and psychic structure of the borderline personality. *International Journal of Psycho-Analysis* 56:163–177.

Menninger, K. A., Mayman, M., and Pruyser, P. (1963). *The Vital Balance.* New York: Viking.

Minuchin, S. (1974). *Families and Family Therapy.* Cambridge, MA: Harvard University Press.

Modell, A. H. (1976). "The holding environment" and the therapeutic action of psychoanalysis. *Journal of the American Psychoanalytic Association* 24:285–307.

Ogden, T. H. (1982). *Projective Identification and Psychotherapeutic Technique.* New York: Jason Aronson.

Piaget, J. (1954). *The Construction of Reality in the Child.* New York: International Universities Press.

Pruyser, P. W. (1975). What splits in splitting? *Bulletin of the Menninger Clinic* 39:1–46.

Rice, A. K. (1965). *Learning for Leadership.* London: Tavistock.

Rinsley, D. B. (1972). A contribution to the nosology and dynamics of adolescent schizophrenia. *Psychiatry* 46:159–186.

———— (1980). The developmental etiology of borderline and narcissistic disorders. *Bulletin of the Menninger Clinic* 44:127–134.

———— (1982). *Borderline and Other Self Disorders.* New York: Jason Aronson.

Roth, B. E. (1980). Understanding the development of a homogeneous, identity-impaired group through countertransference phenomena. *International Journal of Group Psychotherapy* 30:405–426.

Sadovoy, J., Silver, D., and Book, H. E. (1979). Negative responses of the borderline to inpatient treatment. *American Journal of Psychotherapy* 33:404–417.

Sandler, J., ed. (1987). *Projection, Identification, Projective Identification.* Madison, CT: International Universities Press.

Schafer, R. (1983). *The Analytic Attitude.* New York: Basic Books.

Scharff, J. S. (1989). *Foundations of Object Relations Family Therapy.* Northvale, NJ: Jason Aronson.

Segal, H. (1964). *Introduction to the Work of Melanie Klein.* New York: Basic Books.

Shapiro, E. R., Shapiro, R. L., Zinner, J., et al. (1977). The borderline ego and the working alliance: indications for family and individual treatment in adolescence. *International Journal of Psycho-Analysis* 58:77–87.

Singer, M. (1987). Inpatient hospitalization for borderline patients. In *The Borderline Patient,* vol. 2, ed. J. S. Grotstein, M. F. Solomon, and J. A. Lang, pp. 227–242. Hillsdale, NJ: Analytic Press.

Slipp, S. (1984). *Object Relations: A Dynamic Bridge Between Individual and Family Therapy.* New York: Jason Aronson.

Solomon, M. F. (1985). Treatment of narcissistic and borderline disorders in marital therapy. *Clinical Social Work Journal* 13:141–156.

——— (1987). Therapeutic treatment of borderline patients by nonanalytic practitioners. In *The Borderline Patient,* vol. 2, ed. J. S. Grotstein, M. F. Solomon, and J. A. Lang, pp. 243–259. Hillsdale, NJ: Analytic Press.

Spillius, E. B. (1983). Some developments from the work of Melanie Klein. *International Journal of Psycho-Analysis* 64:321–332.

Spitz, R. A. (1965). *The First Year of Life.* New York: International Universities Press.

Stanton, A., and Schwartz, M. (1954). *The Mental Hospital.* New York: Basic Books.

Stern, D. N. (1985). *The Interpersonal World of the Infant: A View from Psychoanalysis and Developmental Psychology.* New York: Basic Books.

Stolorow, R., Brandchaft, B., and Atwood, G. (1983). Intersubjectivity in psychoanalytic treatment. *Bulletin of the Menninger Clinic* 47:117–128.

Stone, L. (1961). *The Psychoanalytic Situation.* New York: International Universities Press.

Sutherland, D. J. (1952). Notes on psychoanalytic group therapy, I: therapy in training. *Psychiatry* 15:111–117.

Tolpin, M. (1971). On the beginnings of a cohesive self. *Psychoanalytic Study of the Child* 26:316–352. New Haven, CT: Yale University Press.

Waelder, R. (1964). *Basic Theory of Psychoanalysis.* New York: International Universities Press.

Winnicott, D. W. (1953). Transitional objects and transitional phenomena. *International Journal of Psycho-Analysis* 34:89–97.

——— (1960). The theory of parent–infant relationship. In *The Maturational Process and the Facilitating Environment,* pp. 39–55. New York: International Universities Press.

Wong, N. (1979). Clinical considerations in group treatment of narcissistic disorders. *International Journal of Group Psychotherapy* 29:325–345.

I

DIFFERENT PATIENTS, DIFFERENT THERAPISTS, DIFFERENT THEORIES

Object relations approaches arose from the source of psychoanalytic explorations in the internal world. Although these concepts were once most widely used in North America to understand individuals with borderline pathology, there has been a shift toward wider application. The chapters in this section demonstrate that shift, which is taking place as object relations approaches are being infused into general psychotherapy.

The movement here is from intensive treatment of borderline disorders to supportive-expressive therapy in general and even to work with normal couples. As will be seen in subsequent sections, when these ideas are applied to different patients by different therapists, both the tone and tenor of the theory shift. It is characteristic of the newer therapies influenced by object relations theory, and self psychology, for that matter, that theory must take into account the person of the therapist as well as the patient.

The clinical literature in this area lags far behind the reality of practice. Object relations approaches have become much more widely disseminated in psychotherapy than formal discussion suggests. Consequently, these papers are merely an indication of what is beginning and what is hopefully to come.

27

An Ego Psychology–Object Relations Theory Approach to the Transference

Otto F. Kernberg

Otto Kernberg has played a major role in introducing concepts from British and South American object relations theory into North American ego psychology. This section begins with a comprehensive and understandable summary of his clinical approach.

In both his clinical theory and case examples, Kernberg acknowledges intertwining contributions from ego psychology and object relations traditions, while taking care to distinguish those lines of thought. This utilization of varying traditions within psychoanalysis represents one new direction in psychotherapy influenced by object relations. Even his discussion of disagreement with certain aspects of self psychology shows respect for the contributions from that school of thought.

Because Kernberg differentiates among clinical approaches more than most contributors in this collection, there is an exciting tension in his writing that requires the reader's attention. The reader is always rewarded with greater insight into the subtleties of clinical work.

As an example of Kernberg's tendency to differentiate, he more clearly distinguishes neurotic from borderline patients and the preferred clinical approaches to their difficulties than might many, if not most, psychotherapists in daily practice. Nevertheless, his clarity and careful dissection of issues can help therapists better understand their patients and their own work.

A more thorough account of Kernberg's clinical approach can be found in Object Relations Theory and Clinical Practice (Kernberg 1976) and Severe Personality Disorders: Psychotherapeutic Strategies (Kernberg 1984).

AN OVERVIEW OF MY APPROACH

Having spelled out my general theoretical and technical approach in earlier work (1975, 1976, 1980, 1984), and having illustrated it with extended clinical material more recently (1986a, 1986b, 1987), I will limit myself here to providing the briefest outline of that approach, to be followed by a description of its clinical aspects as applied to the management of the transference.

My ego psychology-object relations theory is anchored in the theoretical and clinical contributions of Jacobson (1964, 1967, 1971) and Mahler (1971, 1972, Mahler and Furer, 1968, Mahler et al. 1975). I have also been influenced by Erikson (1951, 1956, 1959), Melanie Klein (1945, 1946, 1952a, 1957), Fairbairn (1954), Winnicott (1958, 1965), and Sandler (Sandler and Rosenblatt 1962, Sandler and Sandler, 1978).

My theory of motivation adheres closely to Freud's dual drive theory, but considers drives indissolubly linked to object relations; I also consider the separation of source, pressure, aim, and object of drives, as in traditional metapsychology, artificial. I think that libidinal and aggressive drive derivatives are invested in object relations from the very onset of the symbiotic phase, that the ideational and affective representations of drives are originally undifferentiated from each other, and that affect states representing the most primitive manifestations of drives are essential links of self- and object representations from their origins on.

My theoretical formulation proposes that affects are the primary motivational system and, internalized or fixated as the frame of internalized object relations, are gradually organized into libidinal and aggressive drives as hierarchically supraordinate motivational systems. This concept distinguishes my position from the theories of motivation of the major contributors I have listed, but the emphasis on the central clinical position of affects is common to all of us. In my view, affects are constitutionally determined and developmentally activated primary motivators. I believe that after they have been integrated into the drives, they become the signals of drive activation.

Also in agreement with the authors I have mentioned, I believe that the internalizations of object relations are originally dyadic, and that self- and object representations established under the impact of various affect states are the building blocks of what eventually constitutes the id, the ego, and the superego.

In agreement with Jacobson and Mahler, I have proposed a developmental model for the conceptualization of the structural characteristics of psychotic, borderline, and neurotic psychopathology, and stressed differences in the structural characteristics of these three levels of emotional illness.

I have considered the ego, superego, and id the underlying structural organization of the classical psychoneuroses and neurotic characters and stressed that at this level the vicissitudes of impulse-defense configurations are predominantly expressed as conflicts involving the three psychic agencies and external reality. The Oedipus complex is the dominant conflictual constellation that reflects the culmination of the development of sexual and aggressive drives in the context of the representational world of early childhood, and is crucially involved in the consolidation of the superego.

Patients with neurotic personality organization present well-integrated superego, ego, and id structures; within the psychoanalytic situation, the analysis of resistances brings about the activation, in the transference, first, of relatively global characteristics of these structures, and later, the internalized object relations of which they are composed. The analysis of drive derivatives occurs in the context of the analysis of the relation of the patient's infantile self to significant parental objects as projected onto the analyst.

The borderline personality organization, in contrast, shows a predominance of preoedipal conflicts and psychic representations of preoedipal conflicts condensed with representations of the oedipal phase. Conflicts are not predominantly repressed and therefore unconsciously dynamic. Rather, they are expressed in mutually dissociated ego states reflecting the defense of primitive dissociation or splitting. The activation of primitive object relations that predate the consolidation of ego, superego, and id is manifest in the transference as apparently chaotic affect states, which have to be analyzed in sequential steps (Kernberg 1984). In summary, I wish only to stress that the approach to the interpretation of the primitive transferences of borderline patients suggested in my earlier work may bring about a transformation of part object relations into total object relations, of primitive transferences (largely reflecting stages of development that predate object constancy) into the advanced transferences of the oedipal phase.

Within my ego psychology-object relations theory framework, unconscious intrapsychic conflicts are always between (1) certain units of self- and object representations under the impact of a particular drive derivative (clinically, a certain affect disposition reflecting the instinctual side of the conflict) and (2) contradictory or opposing units of self- and object representations and their respective affect dispositions reflecting the defensive structure. Unconscious intrapsychic conflicts are never simply between impulse and defense; rather, the drive derivative finds expression through a certain internalized object relation, and the defense, too, is reflected by a certain internalized object relation.

At severe levels of psychopathology, splitting mechanisms stabilize such dynamic structures within an ego-id matrix and permit the contradictory aspects of these conflicts to remain — at least partially — conscious, in the form of primitive transferences. In contrast, patients with neurotic personality organization present impulse-defense configurations that contain specific unconscious wishes reflecting sexual and aggressive drive derivatives embedded in unconscious fantasies relating to the oedipal objects. Here, we find relatively less distortion both of the self-representations relating to these objects and of the representations of the oedipal objects themselves. Therefore the difference between past pathogenic experiences and their transformation into currently structured unconscious dispositions is not as great as is found in the primitive transferences in patients with borderline personality organization.

My emphasis is on the internalized object relation rather than on the impulse-defense configuration per se: the unconscious, wishful fantasy expresses such an object relation. The two ways in which, according to Freud (1915), unconscious wishes may become conscious (in the form of ideational representatives and as affects) are, in my view, evident in the relation between a self-representation and an object representation under the impact of a certain affect. Glover (1955), when he pointed to the need to identify both libidinal drive derivatives and ego- and superego-derived identifications in the transference, was, I believe, pointing in the same direction. If the transference neurosis is expressed in (1) instinctual impulses expressed as affects and (2) identifications reflecting internalized object relations, then the object relations frame of reference I propose may be considered a direct clinical application of the metapsychological concept of the dynamic unconscious and the conditions under which it appears in consciousness.

The analysis of the transference is a central concern in my general technical approach. Transference analysis consists in the analysis of the reactivation in the here-and-now of past internalized object relations. The analysis of past internalized object relations in the transference constitutes, at the same time, the analysis of the constituent structures of ego, superego, and id and their intra- and interstructural conflicts. In contrast to the culturalists or interpersonal object relations theoreticians, such as Sullivan (1953, 1962) and Guntrip (1961, 1968, 1971), and to Kohut's (1971, 1977) self psychology, I conceive of internalized object relations as not reflecting actual object relations from the past. Rather, they reflect a combination of realistic and fantasied — and often highly distorted — internalizations of such past object relations and defenses against them under the effects of activation and projection of instinctual drive derivatives. In other words, there is a dynamic tension between the here-and-now, which reflects intrapsychic structure, and the there-and-then unconscious genetic determinants derived from the "actual" past, the patient's developmental history.

I assume that in all cases the transference is dynamically

unconscious in the sense that, either because of repression or of splitting, the patient unconsciously distorts the current experience because of his fixation to pathogenic conflicts with a significant internalized object of the past. The major task is to bring the unconscious transference meanings in the here-and-now into full consciousness by means of interpretation. This is the first stage in analyzing the relation between the unconscious present and the unconscious past.

Rather than making a direct connection between currently conscious or preconscious experiences in relation to the therapist and the conscious past, or to an assumed unconscious past (as I believe self psychologists tend to do), I expect the patient's free associations to the uncovered unconscious transference meanings in the here-and-now to lead us into the unconscious past. I therefore suggest reconstructions to the patient in tentative and open-ended formulations that should permit him to proceed in any one of several directions.

My theoretical framework is expressed clinically in the way I listen to patients. My only expectation is that the patient's free associations will lead to the emergence in the transference of past internalized object relations superimposed on the actual interactions of patient and analyst.

I wish to stress again that I leave the question of assumed genetic origins in the process of uncovering the unconscious meaning in the here-and-now as open-ended as I can. Although it is true that the nature of the activated object relation itself points to its probable genetic and developmental origins, I think it premature to pin down this hypothetical origin before the patient's free associations and exploration of unconscious meanings of his behavior in the here-and-now have given access to new evidence. I am always acutely aware of the danger that any preconceived notions the analyst has may close this investigative field prematurely. A theoretical frame that locates dominant conflicts of the patient in a predetermined area or time seems to me to constitute an important limitation to the analyst's and the patient's freedom to explore the origins of the unconscious present in the unconscious past.

The Kleinian tendency to relate primitive defensive operations and object relations to the first year of life (Klein 1945, 1946,

1952b, 1957), or Kohut's assumption that an ever-present fragility of the self is the primary determinant (Reed 1987), or, for that matter, to consistently search for the oedipal determinants or for pathology of separation-individuation, etc., brings about an unwarranted narrowing of the interpretive frame and limits the analyst's capacity for discovering and investigating the unknown.

CHANNELS OF COMMUNICATION OF THE TRANSFERENCE

The unconscious object relations that superimpose themselves on the actual one—the patient and the analyst working together within the jointly agreed upon boundaries of the psychoanalytic situation—might be either a variety of unconscious object relations in conflict with each other or a defensively functioning object relation activated against an underlying, contrasting one with impulsive functions. These unconscious object relations may emerge through various "channels." With patients presenting neurotic personality organization, and in the advanced stages of treatment of patients with more severe character pathology and borderline pathology, they emerge mostly from the patient's free associations.

Let me illustrate with a clinical vignette.

Ms. A., an architect in her early thirties, consulted me because of chronic interpersonal difficulties in her work and a severe depression related to the breakup of an extramarital relationship with a senior business associate she described as being sadistic. Diagnostic evaluation revealed a hysterical personality with strong masochistic features. A happy early childhood relation with her father had turned into bitter struggles with him during her adolescence, in the context of his having severe marital difficulties. Ms. A. saw her mother as an innocent victim. A sexually intolerant, suppressive atmosphere in the home had become internalized in Ms. A.'s own rigid repression of all sexual impulses until only a few years before starting her analysis: she was frigid with her husband and was able to achieve orgasm only in extramarital affairs.

A few weeks after beginning her analysis, her mood improved, and she now conveyed the impression of a nice, "innocent," submissive little girl who seemed eager to please the analyst. She was obviously trying hard to say whatever came into her mind, and the dominant content of her early free associations related to her work, particularly to her bosses, who seemed to her narrow-minded, biased, uninformed professionals, lacking an original, creative approach to design. She was so obviously dismissive of her bosses that she herself raised the question during a session whether she might be risking losing her job. She had, indeed, lost a job with another firm in the not so distant past because of her interpersonal difficulties.

When I said I was puzzled by the cheerful way in which she expressed her concerns over the prospect of being thrown out, she acknowledged a "dare-devil" attitude in herself, adding that this might indeed be dangerous but it was gratifyingly exciting, too. Further associations revealed her fantasies of meeting her boss, who would sternly notify her that she would have to leave, and whom she would then let know by means of subtle insinuations that she was interested in him as a man. This, in her fantasy, might lead to a sexual relation with him at the very time he was dismissing her from the business. It was exciting to be sexually involved with a man who had thrown her out.

I think this vignette illustrates the early emergence of a "nice little girl" attitude in the transference as a defense against the underlying temptation of a pseudorebellious, provocatively aggressive attitude toward a male authority aimed at bringing about an underlying, desired self-punitive sexual relation (presumably, with a sadistic father image). The fact that the apparently positive early transference relationship permitted the emergence of the underlying negative transference dispositions in the content of the patient's free associations, rather than directly in the transference relationship itself, actually gave us a lead time to elaborate this unconscious conflict before its full actualization in the transference. The focus on the contents of free association, on the communication of Ms. A.'s subjective experience, was the predominant communicative channel through which the unconscious pathogenic object relation emerged in the transference.

In patients with severe character pathology and borderline personality organization, the emergence of dominant unconscious object relations in the transference typically occurs by means of another channel, namely, nonverbal communication. This does not mean that what is verbally communicated through free association in these cases is not relevant or important, but rather that the nonverbal communication acquires economic (that is, affective) predominance in conveying information to the analyst.

A postgraduate college student in his late twenties, Mr. B. came for consultation because of chronic difficulties in relationships with women, uncertainty about his professional interests and future, and deep passivity in his work and daily life. Mr. B., in his early analytic sessions, dwelt on detailed descriptions of the altercations he was having with his present woman friend. My efforts to clarify further what the issues were in what appeared to me confusing descriptions of these arguments elicited ironic comments from him that I was slow and pedestrian and did not grasp the subtlety of what he was telling me. He also expected me to approve immediately the statements he had made and the actions he had taken regarding his woman friend. I asked why he felt the need for me to immediately support his actions or agree with his evaluation of her. He now angrily accused me of not being sympathetic to him and of being the traditional, poker-faced psychoanalyst.

Soon Mr. B. also began to complain that I was not providing him with any new understanding that would permit him to deal more effectively with his woman friend. But when, after getting a better feeling for what was actually going on in their interactions, I did question his interpretations of her behavior and also wondered about the reasons for some of his behaviors, he accused me of taking her part, of being unfairly biased against him, and, in fact, of making his relations with her worse by undermining his own sense of security. He also offered me various psychoanalytic theories to account for his woman friend's sadistic behavior toward him. He pointed out to me that he himself was obviously a masochistic character and, with growing anger, that I was not doing my job—I was not relating what was happening to him now with his childhood experiences.

Although my initial diagnosis of Mr. B. had been severe character pathology with paranoid, narcissistic, and infantile features—and I was prepared for stormy transference developments—I was taken aback by the intensity of his complaints and accusations, and I became increasingly cautious in making any comments to him. He immediately perceived my cautiousness and accused me angrily of treating him like a "sickie," rather than being direct with him. I then focused on his difficulty in accepting anything I said that was different from his own thinking, pointing to the internal conflict he experienced in his relationship with me: he very much wanted me to help him and to be on his side while, at the same time, he experienced everything that came from me as either hostile and damaging or absurd and worthless. Mr. B. agreed (for the first time) with my assessment of the situation. He said that he found himself very much in need of help and faced with an incompetent and hostile analyst. I then asked whether he was indeed convinced that this was a reality because, if it was, it would naturally lead him to ask why he had selected me as his therapist, and he was not raising that question. He immediately accused me of trying to throw him out. I told him I was trying to understand how he felt and not necessarily confirming his views of me.

He then reviewed the circumstances that had led him to consult with me and to select me as an analyst after several unhappy experiences with other psychotherapists. In the course of this review, it emerged that Mr. B. had been very pleased when I accepted him as a patient, but had also felt very unhappy about what he experienced as the enormous difference in our status. He talked about how painful it was to him to have to consult professionals he considered representative of the most conservative psychiatric and psychoanalytic establishment. Because I had been highly recommended to him, he had consulted me, but now he was wondering whether a brief psychotherapy with a therapist from one of the "antipsychiatry" schools might help him much more. I suggested that it might be preferable for him to perceive me as incompetent and hostile if this permitted him to preserve his own self-esteem, although this perception of me was also frustrating his wish to be helped. In other words, I began to interpret the acting out of needs to devalue and disparage me that reflected dissociated envy of me.

I believe that this case illustrates how, from the beginning of the treatment, the principal channel of communication for unconscious object relations activated in the transference was reflected in the patient's attitude toward me rather than in the content of free associations per se. Certainly the content of his verbal communication was important in clarifying what went on in the relationship with me, but the nature of Mr. B.'s behavior was the dominant focus of communication.

On the surface, he was devaluing me as an admired yet enviously resented parental authority, with himself a grandiose and sadistic child. At a deeper level, he was enacting unconsciously the relationship of a frustrated and enraged child with a much needed parental image; but he also deeply resented that parental figure because he perceived it as controlling and devaluating. This view of the parental object triggered intense rage, expressed in the wish to devalue and destroy the object while, at a still deeper level, he unconsciously hoped that it might survive. In fact, it took many weeks to unravel these unconscious meanings in the here-and-now. Months later, we learned that this object relation reflected an unconscious relationship with Mr. B.'s mother and that his repeated failure in relationships with women followed a strikingly similar pattern to the one described in his relationship with me. All these women and I myself represented mother in this transference enactment.

There is still a third channel of communication, which might be considered an outgrowth of the second one, except that here the nonverbal communication is expressed in the apparent absence of any specific object relation in the transference. Under these circumstances, over a period of many months or even years, there is minimal transference regression and an almost total absence of manifest aggression or of libidinal investment in the transference, an indication of the patient's incapacity to depend upon the analyst.

I have stressed elsewhere (Kernberg 1984) that such patients present subtle, pervasive, and highly effective transference resistances against being dependent on the analyst and against the related regression in the transference in general, a condition that might be described as a "closure of the analytic space." To put it more concretely, an absence of emotional depth, of emotional reality, and of fantasy in the analytic encounter becomes the dominant resistance in the treatment.

I described elsewhere (Kernberg 1986b) an artist in his late twenties who consulted because of his dissatisfaction with his bisexual style of life and his growing sexual inhibition.

This man's personality had strong narcissistic features and an "as if" quality. His mother had died when he was 9 years old, and an older sister had taken over her household duties while his father took over many of the mother's functions. The description of both parents was vague and contradictory. The patient conveyed a quality of unreality about his entire history. He had an adequate surface social adaptation, but there was something artificial in his appearance. He was one of those patients whose "perfect free association" effectively mimics an authentic analytic process. There was something mechanical about him, and I found it extremely difficult to link this impression to any concrete manifestations in the transference. He showed similar lack of involvement with his woman friend, toward whom, in spite of good reasons to the contrary, he showed absolutely no signs of jealousy.

By the third year of his analysis, although I was able to maintain my interest in him, I felt that I was being seduced into a strange inactivity and tolerance of this situation, as if I were watching a theatrical display that had no depth and presented itself as from a film screen. It was as if the patient could neither acknowledge me as a person different from himself yet available to him, nor acknowledge his own presence in the room beyond that of recorder of external reality. I finally decided to focus on the nature and the symptoms of his consistent unavailability to me and my unavailability to him as he conveyed it in his attitude in the hours. I used the technique I have described elsewhere (Kernberg 1984) of imagining how a "normal" patient might behave in a particular hour in order to sharpen my focus on the concrete manifestations of the artificiality in this man's relation with me.

The effect of my focus on this "absence" in the transference was striking: the patient began to experience anxiety in the sessions. Over a period of several weeks, his anxiety increased, and his associations changed significantly. He developed an intense fear of me, with an image of me as somebody totally unreal, who presented the facade of a friendly psychoanalyst that covered an underlying frightening empty space. He was alone in the middle of a devastating experience of himself as damaged, disintegrating, incapable of being either boy or girl. It was as if only dead objects surrounded him.

In the course of a few weeks this man changed from an almost inanimate robot to what can best be described as an abandoned, terrified child. Activated in the transference was an intense primitive object relation and, as part of my countertransference reaction, a concordant identification (Racker 1957) with that self-representation. Following this episode, an intensely ambivalent relation to a powerful father emerged in the transference, with projection onto me of the image of a sadistic, controlling, savage father who would be disgusted by the patient's sexual fantasies and wishes. In short, for the first time it was as if elements that had previously been presented in a flat mosaic of past experiences now acquired depth in the transference.

This case, I believe, dramatically illustrates the predominance of the "third channel" of the constant yet latent "space" of the analytic encounter.

TRANSFERENCE, UNCONSCIOUS PRESENT, AND UNCONSCIOUS PAST

I have stressed that it is crucial to first uncover the unconscious meanings of the transference in the here-and-now and to make fully conscious the expression of this object relation in the transference before attempting reconstructions of the past. In the course of this process, the previously unacknowledged, denied, repressed, projected, or dissociated object relation may now be fully acknowledged and become ego-dystonic. This is where the analytic questions can be raised: what are the genetic determinants of the presently activated unconscious intrapsychic conflict, and how are these interpreted to the patient?

Our first case, Ms. A., provided dynamic information that would seem quite naturally to reflect a masochistic transformation of a positive oedipal relationship. As is characteristic of better functioning patients, the links between the consciously known history from the past and the unconscious activation of repressed object relations in the here-and-now were apparently direct. I nevertheless avoided any reference to her relationship with her father until the patient herself, wondering about her need to first transform a good relationship with a man into a bad one in order to then sexualize it, started to associate about her adolescent interactions with her father.

With Mr. B., the postgraduate college student, a very chaotic and complex acting out in the transference could not be linked directly with any known aspects of the patient's past: the information he had conveyed about his past was itself so contradictory and chaotic that it would have been difficult to accept any of its aspects at face value. It took a long time to clarify the unconscious meanings in the here-and-now; only when that had been accomplished could I begin to raise the question of what should be explored in terms of genetic and developmental antecedents.

The dynamics of Mr. B.'s desperate search for dependency

upon a dangerously and cruelly controlling object might lead
theoreticians of different persuasions to different conclusions: (1)
a Mahlerian might conclude that it related to the rapprochement
subphase of separation-individuation; (2) a Kleinian might relate it
to an envied good (and/or bad) breast; (3) a traditional ego
psychologist might think in terms of the guilt-determined anal
regression from a positive oedipal conflict. But because I had no
information about what developmental stage this conflict had
originated in, or regressed to, I avoided speculating about it before
the unconscious here-and-now developments had become completely conscious and ego-dystonic.

In the case of the artist, the danger of premature genetic
reconstructions is really highlighted. Here, even at the time of a
breakthrough from a long analytic stalemate, I refrained from
linking the activated primitive object relation with any aspect of
the past before further evidence emerged in the transference, in the
patient's free associations, in short, in the emergence of new and
unexpected material.

In summary then, I attempt to carry out, first, "atemporal"
constructions of the unconscious meanings in the here-and-now,
and only later, when the conditions warrant it, cautiously to
transform such constructions into reconstructions of the unconscious past. Similarly, I try to avoid the genetic fallacy of equating
the most primitive with the earliest, as well as any mechanical
linkage of certain types of psychopathology with fixed stages of
development.

My three cases also illustrate another aspect of my technique:
namely, the importance of carefully exploring the developments in
the patient's experience both outside the analytic hours and in the
analytic relationship itself. With Ms. A., I spent considerable time
exploring the relationship with her colleagues and superiors at
work before attempting to link that material to the relationship
with me: and that, in spite of my very early observation of her
"nice little girl" attitude in the analytic hours.

My first efforts with Mr. B. were genuinely focused upon the
clarification of the chaotic relationship with his woman friend.
Only when, in the course of the paralysis of all my efforts to help
him gain further understanding, it became obvious that the
transference issues had acquired highest interpretive priority, did

I focus consistently on his relationship with me. I had to wait a long time before I could link the relationship with his woman friend and the relationship with me.

In the third case, of course, a long history of failure of efforts to explore both the patient's extra-analytic and his analytic relationships led to the diagnosis of what I have referred to as the closure of the analytic space with this patient. In general terms, economic criteria (that is, the search for areas of dominant affective activation, whether conscious or unconscious) should dictate whether the focus of intervention is predominantly on an interaction with the patient in the hour, or in the patient's external reality (Kernberg 1984).

It must be apparent by now that while I strongly emphasize the analysis of the unconscious meanings of the transference in the here-and-now, I do not neglect the importance of the analysis of genetic antecedents, the there-and-then. In my emphasis on the here-and-now, I am in agreement with Gill's proposals. I do believe, however, that, by overextending the concept of the transference as "an amalgam of past and present," Gill (1982, p. 177) blurs the differentiation of what is inappropriate in the here-and-now and needs to be explained by its origin elsewhere.

I think it is an error to include the actual aspects of the analyst's behavior that trigger and/or serve to rationalize the patient's transference as part of the transference itself. For the analyst to phobically avoid acknowledging the reality of an aspect of his behavior noticed by the patient, and which triggers a certain reaction by the patient, is a technical error; even further, the analyst's failure to be aware of what in his own behavior may have unconsciously triggered aspects of the transference is also an error of technique. I think it is a distortion of the classical concept of transference to assume that the analyst's realistic contributions to the interaction with a patient should be ignored or denied; to do so is to misuse the concept of transference as a distortion of actual reality because it implies that the analyst is perfectly adjusted and one hundred percent normal. As I pointed out in earlier work (Kernberg 1984),

Patients rapidly become expert in detecting the analyst's personality characteristics, and transference reactions often first emerge in this context. But to conclude that all transference reactions are at bottom, at least in part, unconscious or conscious reactions to the reality of the analyst is to misunderstand the nature of the transference. The transference is the inappropriate aspect of the patient's reaction to the analyst. The analysis of the transference may begin by the analyst's "leaving open" the reality of the patient's observations and exploring why particular observations are important at any particular time.

If the analyst is aware of realistic features of his personality and is able to accept them without narcissistic defensiveness or denial, his emotional attitude will permit him to convey to the patient: "So, if you are responding to something in me, how do we understand the intensity of your reaction?" But the analyst's character pathology may be such that the patient's transference reaction to him results in the erosion of technical neutrality. When the analyst is incapable of discriminating between the patient's realistic and unrealistic perceptions of him, countertransference is operating. [p. 266]

In my view, what is enacted in the transference is never a simple repetition of the patient's actual past experiences. I agree with Melanie Klein's (1952b) proposal that the transference derives from a combination of real and fantasied experiences of the past, and defenses against both. This is another way of stating that the relations between psychic reality and objective reality always remain ambiguous: the more severe the patient's psychopathology and the more distorted his intrapsychic structural organization, the more indirect is the relation between present structure, genetic reconstruction, and developmental origins. But to conclude that reconstruction of the past is impossible because it is difficult, and to use the difficulty of connecting past with present to question the possibility of uncovering the past is really an evasion and is unwarranted.

COUNTERTRANSFERENCE, EMPATHY, MEMORY, AND DESIRE

My views of countertransference have been spelled out in earlier work (Kernberg 1975, 1984). Here, in summary, I want to stress the advantage of a "global" concept of countertransference, which includes, in addition to the analyst's unconscious reactions to the patient or to the transference (in other words, the analyst's transferences), (1) the analyst's realistic reaction to the reality of the patient's life, (2) the analyst's realistic reaction to his own life as it may become affected by the patient, and (3) the analyst's realistic reaction to the transference. For practical purposes, all these components — but not the analyst's realistic emotional reaction to the patient's transference — should remain rather subdued under ordinary psychoanalytic circumstances.

Obviously, if the analyst has retained severe nonanalyzed character pathology or if an unfortunate mutual "resonance" exists between the patient's and the analyst's character pathology, the analyst's transferences to the patient may be accentuated. The greater the patient's psychopathology and the more severely regressive the transference, the more intense the therapist's realistic emotional responses to the patient. It is this area of the realistic responses to the patient and their links with the analyst's deeper transference dispositions that presents both potential dangers for countertransference acting out and potential assets in the form of clinical material to be explored by the analyst and integrated in his understanding of the transference.

I assume that Racker's (1957) concepts of concordant and complementary identifications in the countertransference are well known by now. Their respective functions in increasing empathy with a patient's central subjective experience (in concordant identification) and in maintaining empathy with what the patient is dissociating or projecting (in complementary identification) are also well known. In my view, complementary identification in the countertransference is of particular importance in the analysis of patients with severe character pathology and regressive transference developments. By means of unconscious defensive operations, particularly projective identification, patients are able, through subtle behavioral communications, to induce emotional attitudes in the analyst that reflect aspects of the patient's own dissociated self-representations or object representations.

The psychoanalyst's introspective analysis of his complementary countertransference reaction thus permits him to diagnose projected aspects of the patient's activated internalized object relations, particularly those communicated nonverbally and by alteration in the "analytic space" — the habitual, silent relationship between patient and analyst. Under optimal circumstances, the analyst's understanding of his own affective pressure that derives from the patient's unconscious communications in the transference may lead to a fuller understanding of the object relation activated in the transference.

My attitude regarding the activation in the analyst of intense emotional dispositions toward the patient, particularly at times of transference regression, is to tolerate my own feelings and fantasies about the patient, with the clear understanding that I attempt to use them to better understand what is going on in the transference. I remain consistently alert to the need to protect the patient from any temptation I might have to act on these feelings or to communicate them to him or her. Absolute noncommunication of countertransference reactions to the patient is the counterpart of the analyst's freedom to work with them and use them in his interpretations.

A related issue is to determine the nature of what is projected onto the analyst and activated in the countertransference. In essence, patients may project a self-representation while they enact the object representation of a determined object relation activated in the transference, or, vice versa, they may project an object representation while enacting the corresponding self-representation. These projections tend to be relatively stable in patients with neurotic personality organization, but are unstable and rapidly alternating in patients with severe character pathology and borderline personality organization.

For example, the architect, Ms. A., unconsciously tried to ingratiate herself with me as an object representation of her father in order to protect herself against her own impulses to defy me as a father and to seduce me into an aggressive — and sexualized — counterattack. There was a relatively stable activation of several self-representations under the impact of different affective states in the patient, and a relatively stable projection onto me of object representations unconsciously representing father under different affective states. In other words, we did not "exchange personalities."

But Mr. B. showed a rapid and almost chaotic alternation of

self- and object representations in his identifications and in his projections onto me, reflecting different affective states as well. For example, at one point, he would project onto me a withholding, indifferent, and rejecting parental image, perceiving me as dominant, self-centered, unable to tolerate any view different from my own, and ready to angrily dismiss the patient (my child) who dared to think differently. Only minutes before or after such an experience, Mr. B. would identify himself with the image of such a parental figure, and dismiss me (his child), declaring that he had just decided to stop his analysis because he could not tolerate such a totally misguided and obstinate analyst. His attitude implied that such a sudden termination of his relationship with me would come most naturally, and without any risk of missing me. In other words, there was a rapid exchange between us of the roles of the sadistic, neglecting parent and the neglected, mistreated child.

I think it is of crucial importance that the analyst tolerate the rapidly alternating, at times completely contradictory, emotional experiences that signal the activation of complementary self- and object representations of a primitive internalized object relation. The analyst's capacity to tolerate such rapid changes in his emotional responses to the patient without denial or acting out includes several preconditions.

First, the analyst must maintain strict boundaries in the analytic situation of space, time, privacy outside the treatment hours, and a sense of his own physical security during the sessions.

Second, the analyst must be able to tolerate, as part of his empathic response to the patient, the activation of primitively aggressive, sexual, and dependent affect states in himself. Thus, for example, the analyst must accept his own aggression in the countertransference (Winnicott 1949), such as the gratifying experience of sadistic control; this experience may be much more of a problem for the analyst than tolerating, for example, developmentally more advanced levels of sexual arousal.

Third, it is important that the analyst maintain sufficient confidence in his creativity as part of his analytic work so that he may tolerate the patient's need to destroy his efforts without a reactive counterattack, devaluation of the patient, or withdrawal from him. Only if the analyst can feel comfortable with his own aggression will he be able to interpret aggression in the patient without fearing that this is an attack on the patient, or without submitting to the patient's accusation that he is being attacked (a manifestation of the patient's intolerance of his own aggression).

The impression I have gained from studying the clinical material presented by self psychologists is that they implicitly or explicitly accept the view that the analyst's interpretation of aggression in the patient corresponds to an attack on the patient, as if all aggression were "bad." Obviously, such a view of the analyst cannot but reinforce the patient's own conviction that aggression is bad and that he must defend himself against this "accusation" by whatever means at his disposal.

As I have stressed in earlier work (Kernberg 1975), empathy must therefore include not only concordant identification with the patient's ego-syntonic, central subjective experience, but also complementary identification with the dissociated, repressed, or projected aspects of the patient's self-concept or his object representations.

Wilfred Bion, in a paper he called "Notes on Memory and Desires" (1967), stressed the importance of facing the patient's material in each session without preconceived notions about the patient's dynamics ("memory") and without any particular wishes regarding the patient's material, functioning, and experience, as well as any wishes not related to the patient at all ("desire"). Insofar as this contribution, in my view, marks an indirect criticism of the formulations of interpretations prevalent in the Kleinian school, and a plea for complete openness to new material with a minimum of analytic preconceptions, his point is well taken. I think, however, that Bion neglected the importance of the analyst's long-range experience with the patient's material, the understanding of an analytic process that develops over a period of weeks and months, an understanding that may become a frame of reference to be used by the analyst without his becoming enslaved by it.

My point is that the analyst needs to maintain a sense of the continuity of the analytic process and, particularly, a view of the patient, his behavior, and his reality that transcends the subjective view of the patient at any particular moment, in any particular hour, as well as the patient's own "myths" or preconceived organization of his own past. Such a frame of reference ("memory") is the counterpart to the analyst's tolerating periods of nonunderstanding, in the course of which he may expect new knowledge to emerge eventually. Similarly, regarding the analyst's "desire," the tolerance of impulses, wishes, and fears about the patient that evolve throughout time may provide the analyst with important information that may enter his awareness in the sessions, again, without necessarily enslaving him.

While much of what I have said may apply to psychoanalytic psychotherapy with nonanalyzable borderline and narcissistic patients, my intention has been to spell out my basic approach to the transference in the context of standard psychoanalysis with a broad spectrum of patients. It has been my experience that when I apply this approach to patients with neurotic personality organization (Kernberg 1987), it differs little from a traditional ego psychology approach or from other object relations theories. In contrast, the differences between my approach and that of self psychology are obviously profound and global. In my work with regressed patients, however, important differences between my approach and traditional ego psychology, the British object relations schools, and the culturalists' object relations techniques in this country seem to emerge.

REFERENCES

Bion, W. R. (1967). Notes on memory and desire. *Psychoanalytic Forum* 2:272–280.

Erikson, E. H. (1951). Growth and crises of the healthy personality. In *Identity and the Life Cycle: Selected Papers,* pp. 50–100. New York: International Universities Press, 1959.

———— (1956). The problem of ego identity. *Journal of the American Psychoanalytic Association* 4:56–121.

———— (1959). *Identity and the Life Cycle: Selected Papers.* New York: International Universities Press.

Fairbairn, W. R. D. (1954). *An Object-Relations Theory of the Personality.* New York: Basic Books.

Freud, S. (1915). The unconscious. *Standard Edition* 14:159–215.

Gill, M. M. (1982). *Analysis of Transference.* Vol. 1. *Theory andTechnique. Psychological Issues,* Monograph 53. New York: International Universities Press.

Glover, E. (1955). *The Technique of Psychoanalysis*. New York: International Universities Press.

Guntrip, H. J. S. (1961). *Personality Structure and Human Interaction: The Developing Synthesis of Psychodynamic Theory*. New York: International Universities Press.

_____ (1968). *Schizoid Phenomena, Object Relations and the Self*. New York: International Universities Press.

_____ (1971). *Psychoanalytic Theory, Therapy, and the Self*. New York: Basic Books.

Jacobson, E. (1964). *The Self and the Object World*. New York: International Universities Press.

_____ (1967). *Psychotic Conflict and Reality*. New York: International Universities Press.

_____ (1971). *Depression: Comparative Studies of Normal, Neurotic, and Psychotic Conditions*. New York: International Universities Press.

Kernberg, O. F. (1975). *Borderline Conditions and Pathological Narcissism*. New York: Jason Aronson.

_____ (1976). *Object Relations Theory and Clinical Psychoanalysis*. New York: Jason Aronson.

_____ (1980). *Internal World and External Reality: Object Relations Theory Applied*. New York: Jason Aronson.

_____ (1984). *Severe Personality Disorders: Psychotherapeutic Strategies*. New Haven: Yale University Press.

_____ (1986a). Identification and its vicissitudes as observed in psychosis. *International Journal of Psycho-Analysis* 67:147–159.

_____ (1986b). "Mythological encounters" in the psychoanalytic situation. Proceedings of the First Delphi International Psychoanalytic Symposium.

_____ (1987). Projection and projective identification: developmental and clinical aspects. *Journal of the American Psychoanalytic Association* 35:795–819.

Klein, M. (1945). The oedipus complex in the light of early anxieties. In *Contributions to Psycho-Analysis, 1921–1945*, pp. 339–390. London: Hogarth.

_____ (1946). Notes on some schizoid mechanisms. In *Developments in Psycho-Analysis*, ed. J. Riviere, pp. 292–320. London: Hogarth, 1952.

_____ (1952a). Some theoretical conclusions regarding the emotional life of the infant. In *Developments in Psycho-Analysis*, ed. J. Riviere, pp. 198–236. London: Hogarth.

_____ (1952b). The origins of transference. *International Journal of Psycho-Analysis* 33:433–438.

_____ (1957). *Envy and Gratitude: A Study of Unconscious Sources.* New York: Basic Books.

Kohut, H. (1971). *The Analysis of the Self: A Systematic Approach to the Psychoanalytic Treatment of Narcissistic Personality Disorders.* New York: International Universities Press.

_____ (1977). *The Restoration of the Self.* New York: International Universities Press.

Mahler, M. S. (1971). A study of the separation-individuation process and its possible application to borderline phenomena in the psychoanalytic situation. *Psychoanalytic Study of the Child* 26:403–424. New Haven: Yale University Press.

_____ (1972). On the first three subphases of the separation-individuation process. *International Journal of Psycho-Analysis* 53:333–338.

Mahler, M. S., and Furer, M. (1968). *On Human Symbiosis and the Vicissitudes of Individuation.* Vol. 1. *Infantile Psychosis.* New York: International Universities Press.

Mahler, M. S., Pine, F., and Bergman, A. (1975). *The Psychological Birth of the Human Infant: Symbiosis and Individuation.* New York: Basic Books.

Racker, H. (1957). The meanings and uses of countertransference. *Psychoanalytic Quarterly* 26:303–357.

Reed, G. S. (1987). Rules of clinical understanding in classical psychoanalysis and self psychology: a comparison. *Journal of the American Psychoanalytic Association* 35:421–446.

Sandler, J., and Rosenblatt, B. (1962). The concept of the representational world. *Psychoanalytic Study of the Child* 17:128–145. New York: International Universities Press.

Sandler, J., and Sandler, A. (1978). On the development of object relationships and affects. *International Journal of Psycho-Analysis* 59:285–296.

Sullivan, H. S. (1953). *The Interpersonal Theory of Psychiatry.* New York: Norton.

_____ (1962). *Schizophrenia as a Human Process.* New York: Norton.

Winnicott, D. W. (1949). Hate in the countertransference. In *Collected Papers: Through Paediatrics to Psycho-Analysis,* pp. 194–203. New York: Basic Books, 1958.

_____ (1958). *Collected Papers: Through Paediatrics to Psycho-Analysis.* New York: Basic Books.

_____ (1965). *The Maturational Processes and the Facilitating Environment: Studies in the Theory of Emotional Development.* New York: International Universities Press.

The Interpretive Moment

Fred Pine

*F*red Pine combines object relations concepts with those of drive theory and ego psychology in a coherent, readable, and convincing fashion. He describes how insights concerning object relatedness, affect modulation, self-cohesion, and the holding environment can be learned and used by therapists at all levels of experience. He shows how and when to infuse the deeper insights of object relations approaches into what was once known as ego-supportive psychotherapy for "fragile" patients.

Pine points out how fragility versus resilience varies within patients from moment to moment depending upon the here-and-now therapeutic relationship, a view consistent with self psychology. Rather than proposing empathic attunement as the only intervention, however, he suggests that the approach must shift back and forth between supportive and interpretive modalities, even within a single session. He emphasizes the overlap of these two modalities more than Kernberg did in the preceding chapter.

Tolerance of variation in approach, taking into account the needs of the patient and the personality of the therapist *without sacrificing theory, is characteristic of a new direction psychotherapy is taking.*

A more detailed account of how Pine brings together elements of ego psychology, object relations theory, and self psychology, can be found in his influential book, Drive, Ego, Self, and Object (Pine 1990).

My aim in this chapter is to present a style of interpretation, along with certain supportive props, for occasional use with fragile patients who are ordinarily unable to work in an insight-oriented interpretive mode. This chapter results from my efforts over the years to bring my own psychoanalytical orientation to bear on therapeutic work with seriously disturbed patients—the kinds of patients whose treatment I frequently supervise with psychiatric residents and psychology interns at a large urban hospital outpatient clinic. In that work, I have found it ethically more comfortable not to search for the so-called "good" patient for insight therapy but instead to try to develop "good" variations on technique for less-than-optimal therapeutic situations. In this chapter, I report on a limited area of success in that attempt. To develop my theme, I shall (1) consider the interpretive setting, (2) describe aspects of the interpersonal and intrapsychic psychology of what I call "the interpretive moment" in order to provide a rationale for consciously and intentionally varying that psychology, (3) discuss four clinical variations of that moment, and (4) make some concluding remarks regarding insight and supportive therapies.

THE INTERPRETIVE SETTING

Interpretation is generally regarded as the central mutative agent in psychoanalytic work—whether it ties together past, present, and transference; examines the "here and now" of the transference (Gill 1979); or focuses especially on what analysts call "constructions" (Freud 1937). Although the mechanism of action of interpretation is arguable, each of the many arguments is based on the recurring observation of the potential power of such action. Thus, interpretation may have its effect (1) by increasing the dominion of the ego, thus subjecting unconscious content to more rational thought processes (Freud 1933); (2) by permitting old, poorly resolved fears and fantasies to achieve a new organization within the patient's current capacity for mental functioning in the implicit parent–childlike setting of the analyst–patient relationship (Loewald 1960, Pine 1976); or (3) by lessening the condemnations of conscience by the very fact that the interpreting analyst is not judgmental as he speaks of (and permits the patient to speak of) wishes and fears that are ordinarily taboo to the patient (Strachey 1934).

To be sure, interpretation does have its shortcomings. No one who has ever sat behind an analytic couch can fail to be aware of them. Over the years, numerous concepts have been advanced to account for interpretive failures — from the analyst's inexact interpretation (Glover 1931) and poor timing (Freud 1913) to the patient's unconscious guilt that makes him want to stay ill, his compulsion to repeat, and the "resistance of the unconscious" (Freud 1926, p. 160). But all these problems exist within a setting where interpretation is nonetheless conceived as the central and most efficacious therapeutic intervention.

What is that setting? Keeping in mind the contrasts that I shall later describe, I would emphasize that, for the patient, the setting includes — besides some minimum of intelligence, motivation, and suffering — at least (1) some array of reasonably reliable intrapsychic defenses, which enable the patient to protect himself against overwhelming affect and the experience of disorganization; (2) some capacity to comprehend that the therapist, who points out unpleasant inner or life history realities, does *not* do so to condemn, humiliate, provoke, or ultimately abandon the patient; and (3) some broad, inner psychological organization that can receive the offered interpretation — some soil on which the interpretation can fall and take root. The therapist cannot assume, however, that all these elements are consistently present in all patients (even though they may be present at moments).

In this paper, I describe an attempt to work with these latter, more fragile patients at times in a distinctive, interpretive manner. This work did not result from any self-conscious attempt to "apply" interpretive procedures to these patients but rather developed over the years through trial-and-error attempts which showed that these procedures "worked" in small ways. This chapter and the mode of working described in it are extensions of an earlier effort in this direction (Pine 1976).

The patients I shall discuss, whether children or adults, are generally characterized by a fragility of defense; a tendency toward panic anxiety, depression, rage, or other affects they experience as overwhelming; occasional moderate disorganization; and perhaps even flight from treatment because of these characteristics. These features do not form a specific diagnosis; rather these patients may vary diagnostically across the range of severe character disorders, impulsive personalities, depressions, and reintegrated postpsychotic states. At the time of this work, these patients are not overtly psychotic or grossly disorganized, and although they may not always be able to retain the idea of the object's goodness, they do – often in desperation – want help and can make a basic attachment of considerable force. Nevertheless, this overall setting makes it difficult to use interpretive approaches, not only because of the patient's panic-driven flight from or rejection of these approaches, but also because of the therapist's fear of upsetting the patient's shaky balance.

While the work that I am going to describe did not develop this way historically, for the sake of exposition I shall approach it in terms of the psychology of the interpretive moment: what is going on in the patient that leads the analyst to judge that the moment is right for interpretation, and what goes on in the patient after the interpretation is given. A few comments on these moments are in order.

THE INTERPRETIVE MOMENT

For the patient ordinarily considered analyzable, the "right" moment for interpretation is often characterized by a certain affectivity – a surfacing and aliveness of conflict – that heightens the likelihood that the analyst's words will have impact, triggering further affect and productive thought processes. But in the more fragile patient this very affectivity creates a psychological situation of risk and potential disorganization. For him, the moment of

potential influenceability is simultaneously a moment of vulnerability. Is there a way out of this dilemma?

As for what goes on in the patient after the interpretation is
given: the patient can respond not only, say, with confirming
associations or total rejection, but also, say, with suspicion, as
though it were a seduction or a condemnation. Waelder (1936)
points out that every psychic act has multiple functions related to
drive gratification, the demands of conscience, adaptation to
reality, and repetition. I want to highlight the fact that a patient's
reception of an interpretation *is itself a psychic act having
multiple functions.* Today, we might modify Waelder's work by
noting that the functions of a psychic act include not only drive
gratification, the demands of conscience, and adaptation to
reality (as he saw them), but also repetition of old internalized
object relationships (Kernberg 1976, Sandler and Rosenblatt
1962) and the maintenance of self-cohesion and self-esteem
(Kohut 1971, 1977). Thus, in schematic outline, a patient may
"hear" an interpretation in any or all of these ways: as a
gratification or deprivation (from the standpoint of drive); as a
condemnation or permission (from the standpoint of conscience);
as an access to a new view of reality or as a stimulus to cling to
one's old defenses (from the standpoint of adaptation); as a
repeated or a reparative object-relation experience (from the
standpoint of internalized object relationships); and as a
humiliation or a sign of special attention (from the standpoint of
self-esteem).

In work with fragile patients, I have found it of considerable
clinical value to present the interpretation in such a way as to
increase the probability that it will be received with functions
relevant to good object relationships, benign aspects of the
superego, and support for flexible defenses. As for the dilemma
that the moment of influenceability in the fragile patient is
simultaneously a moment of vulnerability, I have found that
interpretations formulated to support these positive functions
provide an escape from the dilemma. By actively supporting the
patient's best possible level of functioning, the therapist minimizes
the patient's vulnerability; such support therefore makes interpretive intervention possible.

In the following section, I shall present four overlapping ways of speaking to fragile patients that not only carry interpretive content but also make it more possible for the patient to receive and work with that content. I refer to "interpretive content" rather than interpretation because the whole speech act that carries the content differs radically from the classical mode. But there is no question that the therapist introduces difficult content for the patient to work with.

FOUR CLINICAL INTERVENTIONS AND THEIR RATIONALES

A fragile patient reveals just as much, and often more, comprehensible content as a better organized patient. The question is whether and how this content can or should be interpreted to the fragile patient. The interventions I suggest are all based on two assumptions: (1) that the therapist understands something and (2) that clinical considerations indicate that the time is right for imparting that knowledge to the patient. The question I wish to address is *how* the therapist does so. In each of the four modes of intervention, I first attempt to clarify aspects of the interpersonal and intrapsychic psychology of the interpretive moment and then to vary that moment in ways that seem suitable for the fragile patient. The variations are based on efforts to minimize the shock of the interventions and/or to emphasize the therapist's benevolent presence. As a vehicle for discussion, I contrast the specifics and the rationales of these variations with classical technique. But because suggestions in this area are so readily overextended or misunderstood, I add two important cautions: (1) these interpretive variations are only *moments* in a treatment that, like any other, is based primarily on quiet listening; and (2) they are not accompanied at all by any advice or active "doing for" the patient. The *style* of intervention is gentle and supportive, but its *aim* is to make difficult interpretive work possible. It has been my distinct experience that by making the interpretive work possible, the therapeutic process can be moved ahead in small ways.

1. Close Off the Implicit Expectation of Patient Responsibility for Associative Response to the Interpretation.

In classical psychoanalysis, an interpretation is ordinarily open-ended. Through vocal tone or sentence structure, the therapist leaves a demand floating in the air that allows the patient to react to what has been said; indeed, the whole prior analysis sets up the expectation of such a response. A prime indicator confirming an interpretation is the new material — memories or other spontaneous thoughts — that the interpretation elicits. I believe that the therapist's open-ended expectation of response, at least as much as the interpretive content itself, can trigger panic and flight (or rage or depression and flight) in the fragile patient. The patient may react in any of these ways because his experience of interpretation is that he has been given new and frightening information and then left alone with it; he faces a void, not being sure what the interpretation "means" (e.g., in terms of his own badness, dangerousness, or babyishness), where it will lead, what he is to do with it, whether he should act on it, and what attitude the therapist has toward it.

I shall illustrate this situation with the case of a woman who was raised by her mother and maternal grandmother and who has always idealized them and her whole childhood. Her various defenses against awareness of her anger were interpreted, and memories suggestive of quite painful early caretaking events emerged (though almost as "asides"). In a session when she did not feel that the therapist had taken good care of her, her anger mounted, but she seemed unaware that it was linked to her feeling of being neglected. In this case, the therapist might say: "I wonder if the anger you feel has anything to do with your idea that I can't really understand you, and whether those feelings also came when you felt uncared for by your mother and grandmother as a child." The next move would then be the patient's, for the therapist would have implicitly said, "Take what I said and do something with it."

In this particular case, it was known what the patient would do with such an interpretation: she would panic, feel guilt-ridden, and stay away from subsequent sessions. If the therapist were to take into account that the patient had experienced moments of real eruptive violence in the past, as well as some confusion of reality in relation to anger, he might well have hesitated to make such an interpretation. Yet the patient was in the office. The material was active. It *was* the material of the session. And it was linked to the patient's decision to seek help in the first place.

In such a case, does the therapist "support" the patient? If so, how? Should he look the other way, ignoring the material? Perhaps. But I have found that the interpretation can sometimes be conveyed more successfully if the therapist clearly indicates that the patient does not have to make an immediate "next move." The patient is not left alone with the interpretation—alone to face the thoughts it stimulates or to wonder what the therapist thinks about her anger or whether she is "supposed" to act on it or feel guilty about it. Thus, *in an explanatory and sympathetic tone,* the therapist might say to this patient:

> Do you see what's happening, Ms. X.? You're getting angry again and I don't think you really know why. But I believe it's because you felt I wasn't taking proper care of you. That's probably coming up now because of those memories you told me about your mother and grandmother not taking care of you as well as you like to believe. You know, children get angry when that happens, and you must have, too. But you want so much to believe they were perfect that every time you get anywhere near your angry feelings, you get frightened and stay away from therapy. But that's just what our work is about. Look, you *were* angry. That *does* frighten you. We are going to discover that together again and again. And we will work on it together as time goes on, and you will be able to see how it affects you even now.

In some ways, this intervention is like that of a traditional family doctor: "here are the diagnosis and the treatment plan; cooperate with me and we will get you back on your feet again."

There is more in this interpretation than just not leaving the patient alone with the responsibility of thinking about the content. Any interpretation is likely to be multiply functional; my aim is not to extract a pure type. The therapist promises to be with the patient, not in outside life but in therapeutic *work.* The therapist makes clear his acceptance of the aggressive content; not only is he nonjudgmental but, in fact, he views the anger as inevitable and entirely expected. Furthermore—and I consider this point central—the patient is not implicitly asked to associate immediately to the content. The importance of this delay is confirmed by two observations I have made again and again: (1) after a while, when the material is more familiar and the patient is not surprised by it, he *can* allow spontaneous thoughts about it at the moment the interpretation is made; and (2) the therapist's suggestion that the material can be worked through "later on" takes some pressure off and, surprisingly, often enables the patient to work on the material *now*.

The female patient I have just described was given a statement similar to the suggested one and was able to move along one small step. There is no magic here. Interpretive interventions of this sort are not the whole of any treatment; but neither are they one-shot affairs. Like any other intervention, they are repeated again and again when the session content and the patient's state seem to demand it.

2. Strike While the Iron is Cold.

Issues of timing are significant in relation to any interpretation. Among other considerations, timing involves interpretation at the moment the conflictual issues are active and "bubbling over" in some way. In such cases, the issues are usually active in the here and now of the transference, and the patient is suffering some degree of affective discomfort that, whether he knows it or not, is linked to these conflictual issues. But this factor, affective discomfort related to active conflict, is precisely the problem in the fragile and panic-prone patient. His anxiety (or rage or depression) tends to mushroom, to swamp him; and any interpretive input threatens to tip the balance *toward* that full and painful affective reaction rather than to help the patient understand what is going on inside him so that he can come to terms with it.

Sometimes the therapist may decide that the patient simply cannot deal with interpretation at the "hot" moment. On such occasions, I have found it useful to delay the interpretive work until a later session, when the conflict is not active or "hot"—in short, when "the iron is cold." Then the form of the interpretation would be: "Do you remember last week when you were so upset about . . . [and a reminder is given]. I think perhaps you were feeling . . . [and an interpretation is given]." Or: "I've been trying to understand what happened a few days ago when we were talking about . . . [again, a reminder] and you began to feel really troubled. Maybe what happened was . . . [and again, an interpretation]."

The therapeutic aim is to make the interpretation *usable* by the patient, who must have an adequate control structure to receive it. Adaptive capacities in any individual vary over time, and although some intact individuals may be at their adaptive best under pressure, such is not the case, *by definition,* with fragile patients. It is certainly true that neurotic patients, perhaps especially obsessional ones, will not receive interpretations with full emotional force if they are given when "the iron is cold." The analytic posture, the ambiguities created by the patient's lack of knowledge of the behind-the-couch analyst, and the interpretation at the time of active conflict all increase the likelihood that an interpretation will be received with emotional force and not, for example, simply contribute to further intellectualization. But at times some fragile patients require precisely the opposite; they need an increase in control capacity and a decrease in emotional force to be able to hold, and perhaps use, the difficult interpretive material. For such patients, disorganization, not intellectualization, is the danger; flight is the outcome to avoid. I have found that after these patients become familiar with the content through repeated interventions such as I have described, they become able to hear related interpretations even if the therapist later does "strike while the iron is hot." The familiarity itself permits patients to gain some capacity for coping in that specific area.

3. Increase the Patient's Relative Degree of Activity vis-à-vis the Interpretive Content.

In classical psychoanalysis, the patient's supine position on the couch, the analyst's position outside the patient's visual field, and the basic rule of free association lead to a regressive tendency—a passivity in the patient's relation to his own thought processes which facilitates the exploratory work. At the same time, the patient is required to exercise judgment, to think in an orderly fashion, and to be capable of shifting to psychological activity, i.e., he must be able to call upon the observing ego. These shifts between passivity and activity in relation to the emerging associations are not contradictory but central to the mode of the analytic work.

However, for a patient who is generally passive in the face of his inner experience and who cannot reliably regulate either the control or the expression (Rapaport 1953) of what goes on within him, a still greater passivity toward freely flowing mental content is too great a threat to his control structures. Unless he is already slipping into psychosis and experiencing a relatively gross collapse of controls, the patient who is in such a passive-helpless state vis-à-vis both control and discharge of inner impulse/ fantasy/affect processes will not ordinarily be able to assume a passive, free associative relation to his own inner life. Any clinician certainly knows this fact, and the patient himself will regulate this situation by massive blocking or by flight if necessary.

But the patient in the therapeutic situation also may experience another kind of passivity — passivity toward interpretive content introduced by the *therapist*. That is the kind of passivity I want to focus on here. The emergence of this new content and its penetration into the patient's consciousness is *entirely* out of his hands — i.e., it is beyond any available "activity" of his control processes. The therapist decides when and what to say; the patient can only react — perhaps with understanding and relief, but all too often in these fragile, near-panic situations with rigid and reflexive rejection of the content and/or flight and/or disorganization. It is the capacity for ego activity (e.g., bringing the observer function into play) that allows the better functioning analytic patient to successfully use these "intrusions" by the therapist. In work with more fragile individuals, can the therapist increase the *patient's* activity with respect to the content the *therapist* introduces? I believe so, according to how the therapist presents the material. Greater activity in the patient can be induced in either of two quite different ways: (1) by arousing the patient's readiness, an anticipatory or orienting response that allows available defensive processes to be called into play, and (2) by explicitly giving the patient more control over the fate of the interpretive content offered.

Trauma is defined in terms of a flood of stimulation too great for mastery at a given moment. The arousal of anticipation—the activation of small degrees of preparatory anxiety—increases one's readiness to cope with the stimulus influx, probably by calling into play one's defensive repertoire. For example, in recent years, young children have been introduced to surgery with advance information about it. This information does not eliminate anxiety; quite the reverse, it produces anxiety at low levels over considerable time. The effect appears to be a lessening of the traumatic, all-at-once, shock effect of unprepared-for surgery. The same preparation can be done prior to the shock effect of the stimulus influx that we call an "interpretation." Although the therapist would not ordinarily want to activate the control/defense repertoire with neurotic and well-controlled patients before interpretation for fear of diluting its effect, the activation of readiness/control and the resulting dilution of the force of the interpretation may be precisely what makes it possible for poorly controlled patients to receive the interpretation.

Thus, with children who hold their ears or screech or run out of the office or break into panicky rage when something difficult is verbalized to them, I have found it useful to increase their readiness (their degree of activity vis-à-vis what I have to say) by warning them that I am about to say something difficult for them to hear and by giving them some control over its timing. I might say: "Johnny, I want to tell you something that you're not going to like hearing. I'll wait until after you finish that drawing and then I'll tell you." Or: "Johnny, I have something important to say. Tell me when you're ready to hear it." Then after a while, since the child almost never tells when he is "ready": "I'll wait five more minutes and then I'll tell you." I might add, drawing on my discussion about not requiring a response, that "you won't have to say anything, Johnny. I just want you to listen." Or: "Johnny, I have something a little scary to say but it will just take a minute. After the checkers game, I'm going to tell you." Then, after the game, perhaps even giving the child my watch as a crutch to time the minute if he needs to do so, I will say what I have to say. To increase the child's control over the material, I may also tell him that he can stop me for a little while if it is too hard for him to listen and that we can continue after a few minutes. My experience with this procedure has been excellent. The child more often than not *can* listen and take in some of what I have to say; it gets easier each time, and after some months formerly untouchable content becomes a regular part of our work.

These modes of alerting patients to activity or readiness have felt right to me in working with young children. With adults, I have given control to the patient in other ways. For example: "I'm not sure about this idea; I'd like you to tell me what you think. It occurred to me that . . . [and the interpretation is given]. Does that sound possible to you?" Or: "Look, I have a thought about what may be going on. I'm not sure of it, but I'd like to tell you so you can see what you think. Perhaps you can think it over and tell me your reaction next time we meet . . . [and then the interpretation is given]." Clearly, I am attempting to alert the patient that an interpretation is coming, thus allowing him to prepare himself. But this manner of speaking especially aims to decrease the therapist's omniscience and the certainty-of-truth quality of his words; it also *explicitly aims to increase the patient's right to accept or reject* the content. Whether the patient accepts or rejects the content, it *can* more likely be heard when given in this way, gradually becoming more familiar so that later on it enters the work less frighteningly in more usual ways.

4. Increase the "Holding" (Winnicott 1963) Aspects of the Therapeutic Environment.

The classical analysis of more or less intact patients is conducted under conditions of abstinence. The therapist avoids direct gratification of the patient's wishes by not participating in word or deed as an actor in the patient's life. This condition of deprivation increases the likelihood that derivatives of unconscious content will make their way into the patient's associations and fantasies, where they can be analyzed both because they are present and because they are not being acted upon.

But abstinence or deprivation is a relative matter. Patients experience some analysts as distant, others as concerned, some as warm and kindly, others as cold and awesome. A substantial portion of this variation lies in a patient's perceptions, but another portion lies in actualities of the analyst's person (cf. Stone 1961). Furthermore, even identifying abstinence or deprivation as a technical "ideal" misses the point regarding the very real gratifications inherent in the analytic setting, which provide the "stage" on which the analytic action takes place (Pine 1976). These gratifications are inherent in the very presence of the analyst — his reliable presence at sessions, his full attention focused on the patient for the entirety of the sessions, and his consistent and nonjudgmental work to understand what the patient brings to the sessions. As I (1976) wrote previously,

> the analytic setting, like the average expectable environment (Hartmann 1939) that includes good-enough mothering [Winnicott 1960], provides a context of safety in which . . . the child's growth on the one hand, or the analysand's communication, developing insight, and trying out of change on the other can take place. . . . The analysis, like the child's growth, is acted upon the solid stage of safety in a relationship. Without the stage, which we too easily take for granted (when it is there), the action would not take place. [p. 546]

With the patients whose treatments I am discussing, one can assume neither the analytic stage of safety and reliability of relationship nor a patient's capacity to successfully regulate his internal psychological homeostasis. The work can proceed more successfully when the therapist allows the patient to "borrow" the therapist's control/defense capacity and when he highlights his consistent presence for the patient by vocal tone, phrasing of sentences, sheer extent of speech, and some explicit remarks. It is this activity I refer to when I speak of explicitly increasing the "holding" aspects of the therapeutic environment.

Thus, the therapist might say: "I know this thought is going to be painful to you, and we can work on it together over time, but it seems clear to me that . . . [and the interpretation is given]." Or: "Look, you've gone through this experience before and have been just as frightened. Let's see if we can make some headway with it.

I think you're feeling . . . [and again the interpretation is given] and every time that happens you feel you're falling apart. Perhaps we can catch it this time and help you get it under control." The critical factor to the patient is not the wording alone but also a reassuring tone. But the words, although supportive, and the tone, although reassuring, are carriers of difficult-to-hear interpretive content. I believe that this latter point is critical for the entire set of approaches I am advocating.

Let me review and add a closing note on the place of interpretation within the approaches I have offered. I have described several overlapping ways of imparting interpretive material to patients. To highlight their rationale, I have counterpointed each of them to intervention in classical psychoanalysis, for that is the way they evolved for me, as marked shifts against a backdrop of my own training and continuing way of working. Each approach draws, to varying degrees, upon two basic techniques: (1) working with the patient's defenses at their optimal level (by interpreting away from the heat of conflict, by setting up an anticipatory readiness response in the patient, and by giving the patient a sense of greater control and activity toward the content), and (2) actively conveying a sense of the therapist's understanding and participatory presence (by tone, by duration of speech, or by explicit wording). These approaches are reserved for certain fragile patients and, at that, only for certain (albeit significant) moments in their treatment.

In relation to this style of intervention, the fact that these variations are always around *interpretation* is what, in my experience, prevents the work from ever becoming simply caretaking, in which patient pseudosafety and passivity are the outcomes. For the patient's hand is being held (figuratively, by the style of interpretive intervention) *only* and *always* so that he can take a difficult and threatening next step in the therapy. My impression is distinctly that patients who are worked with in this way feel themselves *supported in hard work* and not just "taken care of by a kindly doctor." I cannot stress this point too strongly. The intent (and, in my experience, the effect) of this interpretive work is to make it possible for the fragile patient to work with the interpretation of active and frightening content. He is given a lot of "support," but in the end he feels quite challenged — stressed by the content. Yet this stress is at some optimal, workable level — a level achieved through one or another of the variants of intervention I have described.

A NOTE ON INSIGHT AND SUPPORTIVE THERAPIES

The clinical procedures I have described blur the distinction between insight and supportive therapies in at least two ways. The first way is that *support* (a style of intervention that attempts to keep the patient's defenses functioning at their best and that provides a "holding," object-related context in the patient–therapist relationship) helps to advance interpretations, i.e., to work toward *insight*. The second way stems from the underlying belief that insight is one of the best forms of *support*. This belief is true not only in the sense that self-understanding gives the patient an increased capacity for self-control and a decreased experience of vague fear regarding things within, but also in the sense that such therapeutic work helps the patient understand what is going on within him and is thus one of the principal experiences facilitating his ultimate use of the therapist as a supportive (structure-maintaining and growth-producing) object.

In an earlier paper (Pine 1976), I examined the problem of therapeutic change from the standpoint of the parent–child relationship (cf. Loewald 1960). I also argued that too great a separation between insight and supportive therapies has been detrimental to theory-building regarding supportive work.

It seems to me that a therapist who is "psychoanalytically oriented" is psychoanalytically oriented in whatever he or she does, though just *what* he does (especially beyond the range of the "average expectable analyzable patient") should vary with the patient's psychic structure. Technical variations, too, even major ones, can be "psychoanalytically oriented." Although the terms "psychoanalytically oriented psychotherapy" and "insight therapy" are often used synonymously, such an equation is actually a usurpation of the former term, implying that insight therapy has drawn on the vast contributions of psychoanalysis whereas supportive therapy has not. It is as though the latter is a mindless wasteland, not guided by a theory of human functioning. Psychoanalysis has status, and naming has power; and one result of contrasting psychoanalytically oriented (insight) therapy with supportive therapy has been that psychoanalytic theoretical considerations have only very slowly been applied to the work of supportive therapy.

I would propose instead two parallel terms: psychoanalytically oriented *insight* therapy and (equally) psychoanalytically oriented *supportive* therapy. . . . For if we genuinely operate with a theory of human development, structure, and change, such as psychoanalysis (among others) provides, then all of our thinking, no matter what the problem, no matter who the patient, is influenced by — i.e., "oriented" by — that theory (cf. Blanck and Blanck 1974, 1979). It is true in considerable degree that insight therapy, far more than supportive therapy, draws upon — is oriented by — psychoanalytic *technique,* but both can be equally oriented by psychoanalytic *theory* more generally — in particular its conceptions of development and change on the one hand, and of psychic structure and human thought, affect, and drive processes on the other. [Pine 1976, pp. 553-554]

In this chapter, I have drawn especially upon the psychoanalytic theory of technique to develop procedures for working with unanalyzable patients; but I have drawn upon it in two distinctly different ways: first, by relying heavily on interpretation, as does classical psychoanalysis; and, second, by examining the psychology of the interpretive act to understand how that psychology can be significantly *reversed,* thus making it possible for these fragile patients to work with interpretations.

The Role of Interpretation

In my 1976 paper, I questioned what supportive therapy supports, suggesting that "at the least, the presence of an interested therapist 'supports' the brittle or severely ill patient's *ties to human objects* and capacities for the *maintenance of defense*" (p. 549). But to the question of how such support can become more permanent I could only say that the answer was not readily at hand. In this chapter,

I approach these issues quite differently. Rather than seeing the support of the patient's object ties and defenses as somehow effecting therapeutic change, *I propose using such support in the here and now of the patient–therapist interaction so that the patient may receive and work with interpretation* and, through doing so, slowly achieve some limited self-understanding.

But why use interpretation? It is hardly sacred. As I said at the outset, this work grew through trial and error, not as an effort to "apply" interpretation, but rather through many frustrating therapy supervisions and experiences that often ended with stalemate or flight, until I discovered that these clinical interventions often eventually facilitated the work's progress. In retrospect, the value of interpretive work with fragile patients is apparent in at least three ways.

1. Interpretation is efficacious in itself (provided it is well timed and tactfully offered). The naming (Katan 1961)—the clarification—of inner experience helps bring the patient's experiences out of the shadows, gives them shape, and permits the patient to draw upon his cognitive powers for aid in adaptation. In the setting of the supportive and nonjudgmental relationship to the therapist, these possibilities certainly exist for the more fragile patient just as they do for the more intact patient.

2. Interpretation is one of the unique tools the therapist has to offer. The nonspecific, supportive aspects of the patient–therapist relationship are inherent in the therapist's presence, benevolent concern, and consistent empathic listening. He need do nothing special to bring these elements about. But when the patient is in acute distress and the content is clear, the therapist is in a unique position to offer what no one else ordinarily can offer the patient—a new level of self-understanding. If interpretive work is done in the ways I have described here, I find that fragile patients can use it.

3. Whatever the developmental and therapeutic processes are that enable a person to "take in" another person in order to use that internal object to foster better functioning or growth, they seem to be expedited between a patient and his therapist when the therapist has been able to help quiet some of the patient's anxieties by promoting self-understanding, thus becoming a "good object" in actuality. This theory is more hunch than certainty, and I offer

it as bearing on the question of how the supportive aspects of the relationship are internalized.

Reversals of the Psychology of the Interpretive Moment

In each of the clinical procedures I have described, I offered interpretive content while stimulating the patient's defenses to their highest possible level and while actively giving the patient a sense of the therapist's supportive presence. In contrast to the interpretive moment with a more analyzable patient, where the therapist might want to heighten the affective impact of interpretation, here the effort is to soften that impact.

Analytic work requires the patient to work at some optimal level of tension. If a conflict is not active or if the patient is too well defended, or, on the other hand, if a patient is too flooded with affect or his reality situation is too chaotic, analytic work does not proceed as well as it might otherwise. Either too little or too much anxiety interferes with the ordinary process of analysis. Clearly, however, "optimal tension" is a relative term; what is optimal varies from person to person. Individuals vary in the degree to which they can sustain adequate functioning in the face of anxiety without it reaching disruptive or incapacitating levels.

In the treatment of the patients I have discussed, the possibilities for change that result from interpretation inevitably are accompanied by reactions of anxiety, guilt, rage, or depression at a level far beyond what is optimal for these patients. The question of how to work with these possibilities for change while keeping the level of anxiety tolerable is one that underlies the variations in interpretive style. *The intent of these variations is to increase the defense and object-relational support structure while increasing the anxiety level (through the interpretation), thus supporting patients' tolerance for strain at a higher level of demand.* This supportive approach in the here and now of the therapy relationship makes it possible to introduce interpretive work and its potential benefits into treatments that otherwise might not be amenable to interpretation.

In analytic therapy, the optimal moment for interpretation is often characterized by a receptive affectivity in the patient so that active conflicts can be touched by the interpretive intervention. But in certain fragile patients who are subject to emotional flooding, this very affectivity is experienced as a danger that may lead to disorganization or flight if an interpretation is offered. In this chapter, I have described several modes of offering interpretations that provide pathways out of this dilemma; they aim to activate the patient's defenses to their maximal level while simultaneously giving the patient a sense of the therapist's supportive presence. My focus has been on the rationale of these technical variations, the role of interpretive work with such patients, and the blurring of distinctions between insight and supportive therapies.

Overall, I suggest that the distinction between interpretive (insight) therapy on the one hand and supportive therapy on the other is not the most useful one. A better distinction would be between *interpretation given in the context of abstinence* (i.e., classical psychoanalysis) and *interpretation given in the context of support* (the work described herein).

REFERENCES

Blanck, G., and Blanck, R. (1974). *Ego Psychology: Theory and Practice*. New York: Columbia University Press.
_____ (1979). *Ego Psychology II: Psychoanalytic Developmental Psychology*. New York: Columbia University Press.
Freud, S. (1913). On beginning the treatment. (Further recommendations on the technique of psycho-analysis I). *Standard Edition* 12:123–144.
_____ (1926). Addenda to inhibitions symptoms, and anxiety. *Standard Edition* 20:157–172.
_____ (1933). New introductory lectures on psychoanalysis. *Standard Edition* 22:7–182.
_____ (1937). Constructions in analysis. *Standard Edition* 23:257–269.
Gill, M. M. (1979). The analysis of the transference. *Journal of the American Psychoanalytic Association* 27:263–288, Supplement.
Glover, E. (1931). The therapeutic effect of inexact interpretation: a contribution to the theory of suggestion. *International Journal of Psycho-Analysis* 12:397–411.
Hartmann, H. (1939). *Ego Psychology and the Problem of Adaptation*. Trans. D. Rapaport. New York: International Universities Press, 1958.

4

Formulation of States of Mind in Psychotherapy

Mardi J. Horowitz

*M*ardi *Horowitz is best known for his innovative study of individuals with dissociative states, especially those arising from previous psychological trauma.*

In this chapter, he describes psychotherapeutic approaches to patients with shifting states of mind. Although Horowitz has not been as heavily influenced by the British school of object relations, as have other authors in this collection, his description of states of mind is entirely compatible with Kernberg's and Rinsley's concepts of object relations units derived from Fairbairn's work. Because Horowitz includes self-image, affect, intended action, and perception of others in his components of mind states, his can be considered an object relations theory applied to the dissociation of post-traumatic stress disorders rather than to the splitting of borderline disorders.

In this selection, Horowitz does not emphasize transference, countertransference, projective identification, and experience-near empathy as central treatment elements. Instead, he advises a somewhat educative approach, teaching the patient to recognize various mind states. If successful, this process will foster fuller self-awareness and better inte-

gration of self- and object experiences. This emphasis on the patient understanding him- or herself rather than on the patient–therapist interaction (transference, countertransference, projective identification, and empathy) distinguishes it from object relations or self psychology work with borderline and narcissistic disorders. Perhaps the patients Horowitz is describing do not find it helpful for the therapist to enter too fully into their overwhelmed states of mind. Once again, theory is adapted to the patient and the therapist without disregarding theory altogether.

A useful account of Horowitz's work can be found in States of Mind (Horowitz 1987).

One should not oversimplify symptoms as always present. Symptoms in some people come and go. The state of mind in which symptoms tend to occur thus becomes a matter of attention.

We have found analysis of states of mind to be a useful tool for organizing systematic review of videorecorded psychotherapies (Horowitz 1985, 1987, Horowitz et al. 1985). As a consequence of these efforts, we have also found that active formulation of states of mind with the patient may be an effective early step in psychotherapeutic technique. This chapter reviews the latter utility of analyses of states of mind.

OBSERVING STATES OF MIND

A state of mind is a relatively coherent pattern, a composite of diverse forms of experience and expression that appear almost simultaneously. An observer could describe a person's state of mind in terms of expressive speech patterns, noticing vocal inflection, pace, tone, or other verbal qualities that occur more noticeably in one state of mind than in another. Do the expressed contents dwell on particular ideas, feelings, and subjective experiences? What kinds of gazes, facial expressions, postures, gestures, actions, or other qualities separate this state of mind from a contrasting one?

An important aspect of describing a state of mind involves noting the congruence or disparity between different expressive signal systems. In some states of mind verbal and nonverbal messages are comparable, compatible, and complementary. In other states of mind there is a discrepancy between what the person is saying, his tone of voice, his bodily movements, and the expression on his face.

Important issues to be observed in both the verbal and nonverbal expressive systems are prevailing mood or emotion as well as the degree of modulation exerted over the communicated expression. The "degree of modulation" is a description of the quality of control over behavioral impulse. Are there leakages beyond what is intended? Does some other state seem to shimmer, co-exist, or try to come into existence along with this one? An expression of fear can, for example, be quite frank and direct. In contrast to such *well-modulated* expression, the expression of fear can be *overmodulated,* and take the form of feigned nervousness. *Undermodulated* states of pure terror complete the spectrum of this example.

Well-modulated states are those in which a person appears to be in self-command, appropriately spontaneous, openly expressive, and adequately controlled in terms of releasing and containing impulses. *Overmodulated* states are those in which the person seems to be excessively self-controlled, veiled, shielded, contrived, or pretending to emotions that are signaled but not really felt. *Undermodulated* states are those in which the expressions seem lacking in self-command, excessively impulsive, undercontrolled, or to be just "leaking out."

NAMING STATES OF MIND

Giving states more descriptive and customized names is desirable as a method to facilitate the recognition and explanation of those states. For example, if the person has a throbbing pulse, weak knees, feelings of faintness, intense sweatiness, and thoughts of impending harm, with confusion about what to do next, a label of *distraught fear* or *flooded panic* might be used as a shorthand attempt to name the state. The patient is thus provided with more clarity and more empathy than if the clinician used the word "anxiety." At other times, a personal symbol may serve as a name and say a lot, as in a patient who called a particularly florid panic state a mood of "purple terror."

The name for an important state of mind can then be used in the dialogue of psychotherapy, and can be used by the patient in independent self-observation as well. It helps to clarify what is happening in experiences that otherwise may threaten the patient with flooding in a jumbled series of ideas and intense emotional surges. The naming process gives the patient an increased sense of shared understanding that helps to develop a therapeutic alliance. In addition, enhanced reflective self-observation helps the patient feel increased control over symptoms.

Naming states leads to understanding in terms of multiple states. Particular symptoms are related to the states that contain them. Transition into and out of these states becomes a theme of self-observation, with an aim to find ways to avoid or escape from problematic states. An example of such a list of multiple states follows.

Case Example

The patient was a quite intelligent 40-year-old business executive. He was referred by his internist at the end of a three-month period of treatment for an anxiety disorder and for social phobia. The benzo-diazepine that had been prescribed had only partially relieved his anxiety symptoms and the supportive advice had not counteracted his phobic withdrawal. Upon exploration it was determined that his symptoms were closely related to the fear of being fired from his position, and his withdrawal had been enough to make this eventuality an impending possibility.

In situations where he worked on his own within the corporation he had been quite successful in forming a creative approach to marketing the company's products. After being promoted he took on supervisory responsibilities, and there were important occasions in which he had to present the work of his unit to a management committee. When people he supervised did not meet his expectations, or when he was criticized by superiors, he flew into a rage. He withdrew, in order to avoid these explosions, but both patterns severely threatened his career. He had been warned but could not change; he was tense and jittery over the anticipation of being fired.

He experienced his rage attacks as quite out of control, and yet was at first vague about them. When he spoke of anger it was clear that his angry states of mind must range from a blind and violent rage to a more acceptable annoyance. Yet he spoke ambiguously of being angry, without further qualification. It was easy to apply the same label and just say during psychotherapy, "When you get angry. . . ." But such dialogue seemed confusing, since he was angry in different ways, and with quite different views of himself and the relationship in question.

As part of a gradual clarification, a list of states of mind concerning anger emerged (See Table 4–1). In this list it was useful to group the most important states not only by their emotional coloration but in terms of degree of apparent self-control over the experiences and behaviors.

The task of clarifying different states of mind around the theme of anger provided a useful exploration for this patient who had a poor acquaintance with any language for emotion. State analysis emphasized the importance of the anger theme and the interpersonal patterns involved. Through this type of work the patient became more aware that anger was not an all-or-nothing proposition, that he did not have to act upon his hostile impulses expressively and fully, nor did he need to totally stifle them.

In the next phase the patient revealed a fantasy of what he expected from therapy. He desired to have no further experiences at all of rage, to have me remove this theme and emotion from contaminating his life. I should, thereby, also completely relieve him of his chronic anxiety about the problems his rage might cause. Once this expectation was clearly communicated to me, it became obvious to him that it was not within the range of human possibilities for him to be expunged of all rage and fear. Nonetheless he was angry with me and expected me to feel ashamed that I could not produce this type of psychotherapeutic triumph. This led to work on the dreaded state of shame, and to work on the self-concepts, role-relationship models, and impulsive aims that tended to generate expectations of humiliation.

MOTIVATIONAL ORGANIZATION OF STATES OF MIND

Formulation of states of mind is a useful procedure early in insight-oriented psychotherapy; such formulation can introduce concepts about the dynamic triad of intersecting wishes, threats, and defenses. The state of mind that contains symptoms is often itself a *defensive* compromise. There may be other compromise

Table 4-1. Example of Six Anger-Related States in a Patient

Label	Description
	UNDERMODULATED STATES
Blind rage	Not thinking, all feeling. He wants to demolish and destroy persons who frustrate him. He is not aware of ever loving or even faintly liking the object. He has no awareness that his rage is a passion that will decline. He believes he will hate the object forever.
Blurting out	He feels bursts of hostility but knows it will not last forever. His aim is to defuse the feeling and reduce his passion, to express himself but not to destroy the other person. Nonetheless he blurts out irritation about any theme that comes up during this state, not just the particular source of frustration or insult.
	WELL-MODULATED STATES
Annoyance	His rage doesn't take over his intentions and actions. He is aware of his anger. His expressions are of irritation, controlled yet appropriately sharp. He views others as equal to him although he is angry with them. His annoyance is not generalized to other themes. He is consciously self-reflective about his anger.
Bantering sarcasm	He delivers teasing, good-tempered, but hostile barbs while remaining aware that he likes the current object of his hostility and that he is converting anger to humor. He tolerates being the butt of similar barbs or rejoinders from others.
	OVERMODULATED STATES
"Pro forma"	He feels numb, although he is aware of his current potential for anger, and his inhibition of it at an intellectualized level. He exhibits a conspicuously insulated interpersonal behavioral pattern in which his actions are too formal.
Sullen and grudging	He tends toward a surly, sullen, irritable, but suppressed display of irritation. He is not aware of loving or liking anyone and is aloof or prickly interpersonally. This state is relatively stable in that it has a slow onset and long continuance.

states that do not contain symptoms but simply omit desired experiences to avoid threats associated with wishes. *Wishes* can be understood at the level of what states of mind the person would like to enter and continue to be in. *Threats* can be understood as risk of entry into dreaded states of mind, especially those colored by strong and undermodulated negative emotions such as fear, shame, guilt, despair, or hate.

To continue the example of the man with several angry states of mind, consider a *desired* state of mind, that of *exhibitionistic excitement*. By showing off his work to others, he hoped to exhibit his prowess. This action could lead into either the desired state of *exhibitionistic excitement* or the *dreaded* state of *shameful mortification*. If he did not show his work, he avoided entry into the dreaded state of *shameful mortification,* but also reduced his chances of entering a gratifying state. Instead of either the desired or dreaded states he entered a defensive compromise state of *ruminative rehearsal* colored by some anxious anticipation but without fantasies of humiliation. This *ruminative rehearsal* state was a compromise in that he could not get the joyous excitement he desired, because he rehearsed without ever concluding that he was ready to perform.

This patient tended to externalize the threat of humiliation by blaming others, placing them in the shamed role he feared he might occupy. He feared his subordinates would fail and make him look bad. When he saw such behavior, he became angry with them (Horowitz 1981, Lewis 1971, Wurmser 1981). The resultant state of *blind rage* was also a defensive compromise; it helped him avoid his own state of *shameful mortification.* Yet the *blind rage* presented its own problems since it threatened relations with his subordinates. Thus it is called a problem state in the motivational layout of his states in Table 4-2.

Table 4-2. A Conflict Analysis at the Level of States of Mind

Desired State	exhibitionistic excitement
Dreaded State	shameful mortification
Attempted Compromise State	ruminative rehearsal
Actually Emergent Problem State	blind rage

THE STRUCTURE OF STATES

States of mind are determined by a combination of external observations, as perceived and appraised, and internal factors such as schemas, motivations, and excitation levels. Views of self and others as entering into interpersonal relationships are especially important. These may be called person schemas. (I use the modern form for schemata.) Each state of mind tends to be organized by activation of particular schemas from the person's repertoire of such forms. These views of self and others are not conscious, yet they determine repetitive patterns by the way they affect the organization of thought and emotion.

State analysis may be the first step to inference of repetitively misused inner views about self and others. Role-relationship models for each state of mind can be developed, as shown in Table 4–3, for the patient already described. Self-concepts as the great star, foolish jerk, capable loner, and righteous avenger were

Table 4–3. Each State Is Associated with a Role-Relationship Model

State label	Self	Expected Action	Others
DESIRED: Exhibitionistic Excitement	Great Star	Show Admire	Group
DREADED: Shameful Mortification	Foolish Jerk	Show Scorn	Group
COMPROMISE: Ruminative Rehearsal	Capable Loner	Work Judge	Perfectionist Appraisers
PROBLEM: Blind rage	Righteous Avenger	Harm Harm	Malicious Marauders

neither totally unconscious nor clearly conscious. Such ideas and such role labels played upon the periphery of this patient's awareness, occurring as fantasy images poorly related to lexical representations such as the kind of words used in Table 4–3.

The patient's fleeting and ambiguous fantasies about himself in relation to others were both private and privately discounted. Adding names to states and views of self-facilitated communication in therapy reduced avoidance and increased self-reflective observation. In this way conscious clarification of preconscious views occurred and permitted this patient to contemplate his wishes, fears, and defensive compromises.

When different verbal and nonverbal characteristics occur in a pattern, this is termed a "state of mind." Once these characteristics are defined, the state of mind may be labeled. This name gives therapist and patient quick access to a memory of the overall pattern of features. Naming a state of mind serves as a handle in psychotherapy, improving both the therapist's capacity to observe the patient and the patient's capacity to observe himself. Analysis of states of mind explores an important therapeutic question: Which views of self and other are significant in organizing the pattern of features within a state of mind? Analyzing the characteristics in a state of mind can heighten understanding of otherwise obscure working models of situations, thereby helping the patient to alter the irrational aspects of his views of self and other.

REFERENCES

Horowitz, M. J. (1981). Self-righteous rage and the attribution of blame. *Archives of General Psychiatry* 38:1233–1238.

_____ (1985). Psychoanalytic activities and research. In *New Ideas in Psychoanalysis,* ed. C. Settlage and R. Brockbank, pp. 141–154. Hillsdale, NJ: Analytic Press.

_____ (1987). *States of Mind.* New York: Plenum.

Horowitz, M. J., Marmar, C., Krupnick, J., et al. (1984). *Personality Styles and Brief Psychotherapy.* New York: Basic Books.

Lewis, H. B. (1971). *Shame and Guilt in Neurosis.* New York: International Universities Press.

Wurmser, L. (1981). *The Mask of Shame.* Baltimore, MD: Johns Hopkins Press.

5

Splitting and Projective Identification among Healthier Individuals

N. Gregory Hamilton

Object relations theory derived from intensive psychoanalytic work with narcissistic, borderline, and psychotic patients. This was the source. Since healthier individuals have object relations, too, I have suggested in earlier works that looking at better integrated and differentiated patients using object relations concepts might be useful.

This chapter represents one attempt to employ the concepts of splitting and projective identification in once-weekly psychotherapy with healthier patients. Here, Pine's idea of moment-to-moment shifts in fragility and resilience is extended by suggesting that many, if not all, fairly mature individuals can become fragile in their sense of self and others under certain circumstances. This examination of what is common to both neurotic and borderline patients runs somewhat counter to Kernberg's differentiation of the two groups. Since Kernberg recognizes that any individual may use splitting and projective identification occasionally, and since among patients there are varying degrees of integration and differentiation that persist over time and are of diagnostic significance, this difference is one of emphasis, tone, and clinical application more than one of theoretical substance.

Splitting and projective identification are useful concepts in once-weekly psychotherapy with patients who have normal and neurotic character structure, just as they are in the intensive therapy of individuals with borderline personality. This use of object relations theory is part of a recent widening application of these ideas (Hamilton 1988, 1989a).

Although some authors (Kernberg 1970, Masterson and Rinsley 1975) have indicated that splitting and projective identification are hallmarks of primitive character disorders, others have emphasized their ubiquity (Grotstein 1981, Hamilton 1988, 1990, Langs and Searles 1980, Ogden 1986). Even these latter authors, however, have not systematically explored how the concepts of splitting and projective identification can be used with higher functioning patients. To examine this issue, case examples will demonstrate the existence of splitting and projective identification in patients with more mature character structure. The therapeutic utility of interpreting and otherwise commenting on these ways of experiencing and thinking will be illustrated. The presence of these patterns in borderline and more neurotic personalities will be compared and contrasted. Finally, discussion of possible historical and theoretical reasons for the delay in application of these ideas to healthier individuals will be provided.

SPLITTING AND PROJECTIVE IDENTIFICATION

Before proceeding to the clinical evidence, we must attend to definitions.

Splitting is defined in this chapter as the keeping apart of contradictory mental contents or experiences (Kernberg 1980). The two divided poles often remain conscious, but are separated in time or space, and do not influence one another (Hamilton 1988). In extreme forms, both self- and object-images connected by associated drives and affects are split as units (Rinsley 1978). Splitting also sometimes refers to division of incompatible self- or object images alone.

The relationship between splitting and repression is a complex one, which I have described elsewhere (Hamilton 1988). Suffice it to say that repression divides along conscious–unconscious lines, not along self–other and good–bad lines, as in splitting.

Projective identification, according to Klein's (1946) original usage, is the attribution of an aspect of the self to the object, while simultaneously reidentifying with the projected aspect. There is usually an attempt to control, manipulate, or change the projected quality in the other person. Both good and bad aspects of the self can be involved in projective identification (Hamilton 1986).

There is an interpersonal concomitant to projective identification. Here, the subject behaves in such a way as to elicit from another person affects and self-images that are projected. Thus, both parties can feel that the subject has actually put something into the object. Some authors (Gabbard 1989, Ogden 1982) have defined projective identification so that both interpersonal and intrapsychic processes must take place for it to be present. Others (Hamilton 1988, 1989b, Sandler 1987) have pointed out the utility of describing intrapsychic and interpersonal projective identification as separate, but often parallel phenomena.

With these definitions, we can now look at the case material.

CLINICAL EXAMPLES OF PROJECTIVE IDENTIFICATION AND SPLITTING IN HEALTHIER PATIENTS

Case 1. Projective Identification

Ms. A. was a 32-year-old comptroller for a large hotel. She had become increasingly anxious over the past few months. She had a pattern of working at her relationship with her fiancé, until it was "all fixed up." She would then become anxious and feel neglected during a stable period. Finally, she would engage in an angry exchange, leading to temporary distancing. She would feel terribly guilty for hurting the feelings of her fiancé, whom she loved deeply. She said, "I lose my temper with my mother, too, on occasion, and I shouldn't do that."

She had had a stable first few years in an upper middle-class family. She had friends and did well in elementary school. When she was 8 or 9, however, her father began to drink excessively. When she was 10, her mother suffered a cerebral vascular accident resulting in paraplegia. Her father left the care of the mother to his two daughters. The patient also became his confidante, while he drank and complained about the burden of caring for the mother. When the patient was 16, her father died in an automobile accident. She took over the family finances and worked evenings so she could continue to attend private school without using family capital, which she saved for her younger sister, and to provide for her mother's care. After successfully completing college, during which she had an active social life, she worked as an accountant and advanced rapidly because of her charm and helpfulness, as well as professional competence. She had lived on her own for two years before meeting her fiancé, but now stayed with him on weekends. She maintained her own apartment, where she installed her mother, because she felt guilty that professionals were not providing enough personal care.

On weekends, Ms. A. cleaned, prepared meals for herself and her fiancé, helped him with his business and worked with him in the garden. He was a competent and successful man in his own right and hired a housekeeper, but the patient liked to take on these chores, despite her busy life-style. When her fiancé was content, she would feel increasingly anxious and look for new ways to take care of him, until he began to feel intruded upon and controlled. He would then withdraw and she would anxiously pursue him until they had an argument and would agree to not see one another except for lunch, for a period to time.

Early in the therapy, she became a "good patient," providing material and having insights regularly. Within a few months, she began to refer several of her friends and employees to the therapist. In the countertransference, he at first felt he "needed to" take one of these referrals, though his caseload was a bit full at the time. He did take one of these patients and wondered to himself why he felt grateful for this particular referral.

In the fourth month of therapy, in the middle of a session, the therapist and patient had the following conversation:

Patient: But I won't talk any more about that because it has to do with Carla.

Therapist: So you will sacrifice the freedom to say what comes to mind rather than interfere with the therapy of your friend whom you referred.

Patient: But it must be such a burden for you. It must be hard to keep it all straight.

Therapist: You want to help me with the effort of my work, as you want to help Carla, and as you help your mother and your fiancé. But who is looking out for you? Who is taking care of your dependency needs?

Patient: Don't you think dependency is a bit too strong a word? I think you may be onto something, but I'm not sure.

Therapist: When you were 8, 9, and 10, you were very resourceful, though you were still a little girl and needed someone to take care of you, too. But your father began drinking, and you had to take care of him. Then your mother was paralyzed. There was no one to help you. What I think you did with your needs was to see them in the people around you. You try to manage whatever weakness or sadness or dependency you feel in them. You do it with your lover, your mother, your boss, your friends, and with me.

Patient: You mean, I get my needs met vicariously? I need people to need me?

Therapist: Exactly.

Patient: I'm having so many thoughts at once, I don't quite know which to talk about first. Well, at any rate, I was going to refer one of my employees who is having trouble with her marriage, but maybe you could give me the name of someone else. You probably don't need the referrals anyway, and I don't have to give my therapy away to anyone.

Two months later, she was able to help her mother move into a care home and to ask her younger sister to help with her mother, also. Eventually, she was able to let her fiancé look out for her a little bit. He was gratified to be able to give to her, too.

This patient did not have a borderline personality organization. She was able to tolerate ambivalence, empathize, delay gratification, and self-observe. She was not impulsive, but a bit overcontrolled. She did not have a fragmented identity, but a firm sense of self as a caretaker. Yet, she displayed projective identification.

She experienced the dependent aspect of herself in others and then needed to fix that aspect in the other. She was gratified by doing so because she simultaneously identified with the projected needfulness. Interpersonally, in the therapy, she behaved in such a way that the therapist developed a countertransference feeling of need to be helped by the patient, when he accepted a referral that actually made him a bit too busy. Reflecting upon this irrational feeling and behavior on his part helped the therapist understand the patient's projective identification and her relationships throughout her life. Although drives and oedipal longings associated with the patient's special relationship with her father, her guilt feelings over the paralysis of her mother, and her wish to help as a reaction formation against or reparation for her wish to harm were eventually explored, the patient was unable to do so until projective identification was interpreted, possibly because she had previously been too busy helping the therapist to experience his interpretations as useful to her.

Case 2. Projective Identification

Mrs. B., a 43-year-old woman, suffered from a severe depression with sleeplessness, loss of interest, fatigue, and numerous somatic complaints. B. had held outside jobs for over ten years and continued to work, despite her severe symptoms, because of a strong sense of duty. She and her husband had been married for twenty-two years, raised two daughters—the younger one had just married. B. maintained several long-term friendships, and sang in the church choir, though she did not believe in all the tenets of any denomination.

She was treated with a tricyclic antidepressant and once-weekly psychotherapy. While still depressed, but recovering to some extent, she said she was considering divorce, since she no longer loved her husband, though she had "no reason to divorce." She described her husband as "okay." "If only he would take an interest in something, it doesn't even matter if it is me," she said. "He's become so boring. The same friends, the same restaurants, the same vacations." The therapist found himself stifling a yawn as he listened to the same complaints again. He felt a need to speak to keep awake and to let the patient know he was interested in her. He wondered about his impulse to "act lively."

She went on, saying she had always looked forward to the children growing up so she and her husband could have time and freedom together. Now, the next twenty to thirty years looked bleak. She described a drab life stretching out before her, devoid of excitement.

Patient: My life in the future isn't interesting any more. I don't have any enthusiasm for the future.

Therapist: So you don't love yourself right now any more than you love your husband. You and your husband have that in common.
Patient: You mean I don't love either of us?
Therapist: Yes.

Here, the therapist did not conceptualize himself as addressing the cause of the patient's depression, but its result. Now that she was overwhelmingly depressed and felt bleak, she saw her lack of interest in her own life as her husband's lack of interest and simultaneously identified with it. She wished he would do something to liven up her life. She had also come to the therapist to see if he could help her find some interest in the future, and she was boring him. The therapist figured that the patient was trying to manage her depression in others through projective identification. By saying that she did not love either her husband or herself right now, he was not interpreting *per se,* but was, somewhat paradoxically, clarifying a boundary. She and her husband were two separate people with something in common. This clarification helped her to work on understanding her depression within herself before attempting to make a decision about her marriage.

Splitting

When B. originally came to therapy, she said, "I am not myself. Something has happened to me. I'm usually such a happy person."

After four months of combined pharmacotherapy and psychotherapy, she had a remission of a few weeks. She felt she had her "old self" back. She was able to respond to her husband's affection and could love him again. She prematurely reduced the dose of medication, however, and had a setback at work resulting in a recurrence of depression. She again said she no longer loved her husband or herself and did not know if she ever had. She did not think she would ever recover. Her therapist reminded her: "When you feel this badly, you forget that you have ever felt better and that you will feel better again."

The completeness of the division of the healthy, tolerant, creative self and the depressed, aimless, worthless, unloving, and unloved self is describable as splitting. Her therapist juxtaposed the positive and negative self-images to help her overcome the split (Hamilton 1988). Eventually, Ms. B. recovered from her depression and was happy and constructive between sessions. She spent several months, however, in which her therapy sessions were very painful as she worked through old losses. The first such loss was the death of her father when she was 7 years old. Her mother had become depressed and withdrawn at that time and found it too painful to allow B. to talk about her own sadness. The patient and therapist hypothesized that the mother's understandable inability to empathize with the patient's grief led to her experiencing depressed aspects of herself as a second, split-off self. When her own daughter married and left home, she could not grieve her loss without "becoming someone else."

As B. terminated therapy several months later, she displayed an integration of her previously split depressed and productive self by saying, "Perhaps I will have another episode of depression and need to come back, but at least I know I have some things to be sad about, even while I'm fairly happy. And if I do get depressed again, because of biologic reasons or another loss or whatever, I think I can remember that I previously felt better and that I will feel better again. That will help, so maybe I won't have to come back." This was a new and more integrated view of herself, which profoundly affected her relationships, as well as her mood modulation.

Although Mrs. B. displayed splitting and projective identification in regard to the sad aspects of herself, she was well integrated in other areas. Her ability to successfully raise two children, stay married for twenty-two years, remain stably employed outside the home, and contribute to social organizations suggest an ability to tolerate frustration, delay gratification, empathize, and have commitments.

Case 3. Splitting

Mrs. C., the 42-year-old woman described in Chapter 1, had been married for twenty years and raised three children. She complained of a recurrent nightmare and constriction of her social life, since the divorce. Here, the important elements of transference and countertransference are added.

C. repeatedly dreamed of her ex-husband walking down a hallway toward her. She was happy to see him, as if he were coming home from work. The scene suddenly changed. She saw a "different man" lurching toward her in a menacing way. In a fog, he disappeared, and her weeping would wake her. She wondered why she wept about her ex-husband when she had been "so glad to be rid of him."

After the therapist and patient recognized that she had split off the beloved object-image of her husband from the image of an alcoholic and dangerous husband in order to develop the courage to divorce him, she now began to mourn the loss of her marriage and to regain and reintegrate her capacity to love. The patient and therapist both noticed that the patient had seen the outside world, especially men, as dangerous, and that she had seen therapy as a secret, safe place where she could talk candidly. Within that safe place, the therapist had become a valued object, similar to the private image of her good ex-husband, which she had split off within her. The therapist had not originally recognized the transference because it corresponded so well with the actuality of the therapeutic situation, and, in the counter-transference, it seemed so understandable that the patient should feel safe with him. Thus, splitting had taken place in the transference and the countertransference, as well as within the patient's unconscious fantasy.

THE THERAPEUTIC UTILITY OF INTERPRETING THESE MENTAL PROCESSES

These examples demonstrate the presence of splitting and projec-tive identification in patients with normal or neurotic personality organizations and the therapeutic utility of interpreting or other-wise discussing these mental processes.

The patients were not borderline according to either the *DSM-III-R* (American Psychiatric Association 1987) or Kernberg's (1970, 1975) structural diagnosis. None of these patients showed impulsivity, intense unstable relationships, uncontrolled expres-sion of anger, feelings of emptiness, or self-destructiveness. On the contrary, they all had a capacity for commitment, over-control of anger, tolerance of being alone, and good self-care. Only in the specific area of difficulty did they show splitting and diffusion of self-other boundaries. Furthermore, they benefitted from recognition and discussion of these mental processes in once-weekly psychotherapy.

How, then, is splitting and projective identification different in better-integrated patients than in those with borderline personality organization? The cases suggest that better-organized patients do not use these mental mechanisms pervasively or exclusively. They are combined with whole object relations and other defenses. Thus, therapy with these patients is generally not so stormy and intense. Therefore, countertransference is more subtle and difficult to recognize, as in the case of Mrs. C. Interpretation often results in quick and lasting insight and the therapist's containing function (Bion 1962) is not so taxed as it is with borderline patients.

We still must ask ourselves, if splitting and projective identification are not exclusive to borderline disorders and are pervasive among people with neurotic and normal character structure, when do they take place? The examples provide some clues that combined with theory provide a tentative formulation (Hamilton 1988). Splitting and projective identification may result from overwhelming of the integrative ego functions by affects (B.'s depression), by organic failure of integrative ego functions (specific learning disability or intoxication), by persistent parental failure of containment and empathy in one area of life (B.'s mourning), and from extreme adolescent or adult trauma (C.'s abuse) (Brende 1983, Hamilton 1988).

It is not clear why there has been a delay in applying these concepts to healthier patients. Virtually all other defense mechanisms, beginning with Freud's (1900) recognition of repression in both normals and neurotics, have been applied to healthier as well as more disturbed patients. Loyalties to Anna Freud's versus Melanie Klein's factions (Grosskurth 1986, Hamilton 1988) may have made it important for psychoanalytic thinkers to keep Kleinian ideas of splitting and projective identification (Klein 1946) separate from the defenses as described by Anna Freud (1946). Many of us also tend to discuss "primitive defense" as always antedating and being separate from defenses of the oedipal period to avoid overthrowing Freud's assertion of primacy of the oedipal conflict.

Additionally, in the countertransference, it would be understandable if we should wish to see our own defense mechanisms as entirely different from those of our more disturbed patients, especially when they pressure us with their projective identifications. When we observe splitting and projective identification in our healthier patients, we are next invited to look at them in ourselves (Langs and Searles 1980). Additionally, there is a theoretical issue which has made splitting and projective identification harder to see in healthier patients.

In North America, some authors (Gabbard 1989, Ogden 1982) have defined projective identification so it only exists when there are both interpersonal and intrapsychic components, with emphasis given to the interpersonal, i.e., when the therapist has a marked countertransference reaction. This theoretical stance makes it difficult for therapists to observe subtle variants when the countertransference is less obvious. If the process is interpersonal, therapists cannot observe it through introspection alone, i.e., within themselves. The theoretical and therapeutic utility of retaining Klein's (1946) original intrapsychic definition, as well as a separate but related interpersonal definition of projective identification, has been discussed in detail elsewhere (Hamilton 1988, 1989b).

This chapter illustrates splitting and projective identification among people with normal and neurotic personality organizations. Adding these concepts to the repertoire of analytically oriented psychotherapists does not replace previous theories but adds to them. This approach can be integrated with drive theory and ego psychology in practice, or can be used to supplement the approaches of cognitive or interpersonal therapists.

Not only borderline patients, but all of us, continually need to define and redefine ourselves in relation to others as we grow and change. The concepts of splitting and projective identification can help when that growth process becomes stymied.

REFERENCES

American Psychiatric Association (1987). *Diagnostic and Statistical Manual of Mental Disorders.* 3rd ed. Washington, DC: American Psychiatric Association Press.

Bion, W. R. (1962). *Learning from Experience*. London: Heinemann.

Brende, J. O. (1983). A psychodynamic view of character pathology in Vietnam combat veterans. *Bulletin of the Menninger Clinic* 47:193–216.

Freud, A. (1946). *The Ego and Its Mechanisms of Defense*. New York: International Universities Press.

Freud, S. (1900). The interpretation of dreams. *Standard Edition* 5:373–374.

Gabbard, G. O. (1989). Splitting in hospital treatment. *American Journal of Psychiatry* 146:444–451.

Grosskurth, P. (1986). *Melanie Klein: Her World and Her Work*. New York: Knopf.

Grotstein, J. S. (1981). *Splitting and Positive Identification*. New York: Jason Aronson.

Hamilton, N. G. (1986). Positive projective identification. *International Journal of Psycho-Analysis* 67:489–496.

———— (1988). *Self and Others: Object Relations Theory in Practice*. Northvale, NJ: Jason Aronson.

———— (1989a). A critical review of object relations theory. *American Journal of Psychiatry* 146:1552–1560.

———— (1989b). Intrapsychic and interpersonal projective identification. *Melanie Klein and Object Relations* 7:31–42.

———— (1990). The containing function and the analyst's projective identification. *International Journal of Psycho-Analysis* 71:445–453.

Horowitz, M. (1987). *States of Mind*. New York: Plenum Press.

Kernberg, O. F. (1970). A psychoanalytic classification of character pathology. *Journal of the American Psychoanalytic Association* 18:800–820.

———— (1975). *Borderline Conditions and Pathological Narcissism*. New York: Jason Aronson.

———— (1980). *Internal World and External Reality*. New York: Basic Books.

Klein, M. (1946). Notes on some schizoid mechanisms. *International Journal of Psycho-Analysis* 27:99–110.

Langs, R., and Searles, H. F. (1980). *Intrapsychic and Interpersonal Dimensions of Treatment*. New York: Jason Aronson.

Masterson, J. F., and Rinsley, D. B. (1975). The borderline syndrome: the role of the mother in the genesis and psychic structure of the borderline personality. *International Journal of Psycho-Analysis* 56:163–177.

Ogden, T. H. (1982). *Projective Identification and Psychotherapeutic Technique*. New York: Jason Aronson.

_____ (1986). *The Matrix of the Mind.* Northvale, NJ: Jason Aronson.

Rinsley, D. B. (1978). Borderline psychopathology: a review of aetiology, dynamics, and treatment. *International Review of Psycho-Analysis* 5:45–54.

Sandler, J. (1987). The concept of projective identification. In *Projection, Identification, Projective Identification,* ed. J. Sandler, pp. 13–26. Madison, CT: International Universities Press.

6

Projective Identification and Couple Therapy

David E. and Jill S. Scharff

*D*avid *and Jill Scharff have written extensively about object relations approaches to family, couple, and sex therapy. This selection from their fine book, Object Relations Couple Therapy (Scharff and Scharff 1991), provides an introduction to and a clear description of this new approach. Their work has clearly sprung from the inner source, the insights of individual psychotherapy and psychoanalysis. Yet, it does not sacrifice depth by its application to couples.*

Since one theme of this collection is the overlap and integration of various therapies informed by object relations theories, it seems useful to at least touch on couple therapy, although individual work remains our central focus. Object Relations Couple Therapy is a delightfully written guide to the Scharffs' work with couples. For an overview of object relations family therapies see Foundations of Object Relations Family Therapy (J. Scharff 1989).

Object relations theory is an individual psychology that views the personality as a system of parts in interaction with significant others in the environment. It is an amalgam of the theories of a number of independent British thinkers: Fairbairn, Guntrip,

Balint, and Winnicott. Although their work is generally recognized as influenced by Klein, they form a group that in Britain is quite separate from the group of theorists that gathered around her. In the United States, where we are less concerned with such boundaries, we tend to group Klein with the object relations theorists. Of them all, only Fairbairn systematically developed a clear concept of the personality sufficient to challenge Freud's instinct and structural theories. Thus we rely most heavily on the work of Fairbairn (1944, 1952, 1954, 1963) with some filling in from Winnicott (1958, 1960b, 1968, 1971). Klein's concept of projective identification (1946) provides the necessary bridging concept to extend the individual psychology of object relations theory to the interpersonal situation. We also refer to Dicks's (1967) use of object relations theory in marital therapy, to Bion's (1961) application of the theory to small groups, and to Zinner and Shapiro's extension of that to marital interaction and family dynamics (Zinner 1976, Zinner and Shapiro 1972).

A BACKGROUND OF OBJECT RELATIONS THEORY

Fairbairn: An Individual Psychology Based on Object Relations

Fairbairn (1952, 1963) saw infants as "object-seeking," compelled to reach for a relationship with their mothers so that their fundamental needs for attachment and nurturance could be met. During the long years of absolute, and later relative dependency, human infants develop relationships with their parents and their older siblings. Infant personality is built from the infant's perception of the actual family experience. Feelings of need or frustration color the infant's appreciation of actual events. This mixture of experience, affect, perception, and misconception not only affects the experience and the child's memory of events but, much more important, it determines the child's psychic structure. This structure is seen as one consisting of a system of conscious and unconscious object relationships that crystallize out of the infant's experience of real relationships. In summary, as Bollas (1987) put it, "ego structure is the trace of a relationship" (p. 50).

The endopsychic situation is reinforced or modified in the light of future experience, maturing cognitive abilities, and changes in the quality of the primary relationships at various developmental phases. Not only is the individual child moving through the classic stages of psychosexual development described by Freud (1905) but the family is moving on through the life cycle too, perhaps dealing with death or illness of significant members in the previous generation, a geographic move, a change in life-style or economic circumstances, or the birth of another child.

The individual personality, composed of a system of parts, some conscious and some unconscious, is in dynamic relation to the family system and its parts and to the individual members and their personality parts. Beyond the fixed number of whole person relationships, an infinite number of ever-changing part-to-part relationships is extended as a culture medium for the growth of the child. The resulting personality is complex, reflecting multiple identifications and counteridentifications with parts of others, organized in conscious and unconscious areas of the personality. The conscious parts remain in an open system, flexible and changeable, and able to interact freely with others. The unconscious parts are split off into a closed system, rigid and unchanging under the force of repression, and not available for interaction with others or for learning and change at the conscious level (Sutherland 1963). One of Fairbairn's major contributions was to point out that all these systems and their conscious and unconscious parts are in constant dynamic interaction with each other internally. Needs, frustrations, longings, love, and hate are reexperienced inside the self. These affects characterize the exciting and rejecting object relationships that were internalized and that continue to interact dynamically within the overall personality. These inner relationships are being actively repressed and are equally actively seeking to return to consciousness.

Bion: Containment, Group Assumptions, and Valency

From studies of group communication, thought process, and mother–infant dynamics, Bion (1962, 1967, 1970) postulated that the mother in a special state of thought called "reverie" is able to bear her infant's anxiety and frustration so that her child feels contained. By identifying with the mother as the container, the child develops a secure self capable of thinking through. This kind of identification is an example of *introjective identification,* introduced by Klein (1946) and defined by Segal (1964) as "the result when the object is introjected into the ego which then identifies with some or all of its characteristics" (p. 105). Bion's concept of *container-contained* describes a situation where the infant's projective process can occur without damage to the mother and introjective identification is benign and growth-promoting. This is to be distinguished from Winnicott's (1960a) description of the *holding environment,* which refers to an empathic *psychosomatic* partnership between mother and baby permitting the management of physiological and psychological experiences rather than to a cognitive function of the mother that creates psychological space in the realm of *thought* as Bion intended. Containment is also distinct from Winnicott's (1971) description of the transitional space between mother and infant, the area in which the infant uses an object that represents the mother but is under the infant's control.

Winnicott's description of the holding environment and transitional space refers to the interpersonal process, which expresses much of what the mother has modified and which the infant has then to rework, whereas containment refers to the mother's capacity for introjective and projective identification in fantasy.

As couple and family therapists, we use both terms — container and holding environment — for the provision by the family or the couple of the normal context that facilitates spontaneous mutative, mutual projective identification among family members.

From his study of small group process, Bion (1961) noted that members tended to unite in subgroup formations that expressed and met unconscious needs not satisfied by the leader. The subgroups formed on the basis of members' shared unconscious assumptions about how to find gratification of wishes for dependency, aggression expressed as fight or flight, and pairing to produce a savior for the group in distress. How did individuals self-select to respond to one of these themes? Bion suggested the concept of *valency:* "the capacity for instantaneous, involuntary combination of one individual with another for sharing and acting on a basic assumption. It is instantaneous, inevitable, and instinctive" (p. 153). Most evident in the formation of the couple that falls in love, valency operates between marriage partners and family members and determines future personality development. We return later to consider how valency helps us to understand projective identification.

Dicks: The Introduction of Projective Identification to Marital Studies

Another British theorist, Dicks (1967) grasped the value of Fairbairn's individual psychology for understanding the marital relationship. Dicks studied sets of spouses. He conceptualized each individual personality, in Fairbairn's terms, as consisting of conscious and unconscious object relationship systems. Based on his study of parallel individual psychotherapy of spouses, each partner seeing a separate but collaborating therapist, Dicks noted in the spouses a degree of fit between these systems and their parts at both conscious and unconscious levels. He suggested that marital choice, apparently based on conscious factors, was also determined by a congruence between unconscious object relations. He called the need for this fit "unconscious complementariness." Perceptions of the spouse occur "*as if* the other was part of oneself. The partner is then treated according to how this aspect of oneself was valued: spoilt and cherished, or denigrated and persecuted" (p. 69). As the marriage progressed, this unconscious fit persisted along with a blurring of boundaries between self and other, to the point where the couple developed a "marital joint personality. This joint personality or integrate enabled each half to rediscover lost aspects of their primary object relations, which they had split off or repressed, and which they were, in their involvement with the spouse, re-experiencing by projective identification" (p. 69).

To account for his findings, Dicks invoked Klein's (1946) concept of projective identification. The dynamic relation between parts of the personality described by Fairbairn could now be conceptualized as occurring between the systems involving parts of two personalities uniquely joined in marriage. Projective identification gave Dicks the explanatory link he needed to apply Fairbairn's object relations theory of individual endopsychic structure to marital interaction. But what exactly is projective identification?

SOURCES OF CONFUSION ABOUT PROJECTIVE IDENTIFICATION

Although Dicks referred to projective identification frequently and gave many theoretical descriptions and clinical examples of its occurrence, he did not formally define the concept himself. Like Klein, he tended to demonstrate it in action—in his case, in application to marriage—and to assume that his readers knew about the basic concept already. Those of us with a working familiarity with the term tend to think that we have got the hang of it and talk about it together, not realizing that some of us think of projective identification as an intrapsychic or *one-body phenomenon* and others as an interpersonal or *two-body phenomenon* (Meissner 1987). On the one hand this points to the remarkable flexibility and applicability of the concept; on the other, it demonstrates a lack of conceptual clarity.

We postulate that this confusion is to some extent an inevitable consequence of the ambiguity of the process of projective identification. It has been contributed to by unacknowledged differences in meaning of the term identification in the writings of various authors, following one and ignoring the other aspect of the dual meaning introduced by Segal (1964), because of the difficulty of holding complexity and ambiguity in mind. There have been differences in view as to where in the identificatory process the identification itself is located, either in self or other, in ego or object, in internal object or in external object. On the subject of projective identification, our opinions are influenced toward the intrapsychic or interpersonal dimensions by our personal experience of the relationship between self and other in the early months of life, in other words, by our resolution of the phase Klein called the paranoid-schizoid position, in which projective identification emerges as the major defense. Finally, the lack of conceptual clarity originates with Klein's discursive writing style.

KLEIN'S CONCEPT OF PROJECTIVE
IDENTIFICATION

In her paper on schizoid mechanisms Klein (1946) introduced the concept of projective identification through an illustration of its occurrence in the paranoid-schizoid position during the first months of life. Without formally defining it, Klein mentions projective identification as the name she gives to the mechanism for dealing in fantasy with object relations when the infant is struggling with hatred due to anxiety during the earliest relation to the mother and her breast. Thus in hatred, the anxious infant seeks to rid itself of destructive parts of the self by spitting out or vomiting them out or excreting them in fantasy in its urine or explosive feces and projecting them in a hostile stream into the object residing in the mother's body. Then the infant experiences this part of itself as if it were the mother attacking the infant. The infant identifies with this persecutory maternal object, which further fuels the paranoid-schizoid position.

Klein then qualifies her discussion of projective identification by reminding us that the good parts of the self may also be projected. By identifying with the projected good parts of itself the infant personality can experience good object relations; this is important for integration of the ego. She goes on to say that projective identification occurs in love as well as hate under the influence of the life instinct as well as the death instinct. Splitting, projection, projective identification and introjection are part and parcel of projective and introjective processes characteristic of object relations in the paranoid-schizoid position normally achieved during the early months of life.

Segal (1964), who has given the clearest exposition of Klein, wrote that *projective identification* "is the result of the projection of parts of the self into an object. It may result in the object being perceived as having acquired the characteristics of the projected part of the self, but it can also result in the self becoming identified with the object of its projection" (p. 105). Thus Segal gives a dual meaning to the term. It could mean that the object was misperceived as if it was like the self and/or that the self became like the misperceived object. Segal extends this one-body view to a two-body view when she describes the effect of the projections on the other person: "the external object . . . becomes possessed by, controlled and identified with the projected parts" (p. 14). The link between the two views is provided by the concept of introjective identification, which refers to "the result when the object is introjected into the ego which then identifies with some or all of its characteristics" (p. 105). According to Segal these processes occur only under the influence of anxiety in the paranoid-schizoid position, whereas in normal development, projections return undisturbed and are reintegrated into the self. Modern expositors of Klein agreed in discussions at the present time that in projective identification the external object is affected by the projections into it. In projective identification a state of mind of the self is evoked in someone else (Williams 1981).

OTHER CONTRIBUTIONS: MALIN AND GROTSTEIN, MEISSNER, KERNBERG, OGDEN, SANDLER

A review of the literature on projective identification (Scharff 1992, Jaffe 1968) reveals that many authors tend to use the term projection as synonymous with projective identification, while others expend much energy arguing about the differences between them. For instance, Malin and Grotstein (1966) said that the term projection alone should be reserved for the projection of displaced instinctual drives, whereas projection of parts of the self cannot exist alone but is always accompanied by projective identification when the object receives the projected, disclaimed parts of the self "and then this new alloy — external object plus newly arrived projected part — is reintrojected to complete the cycle" (p. 26). Meissner (1980) deplores the confusion and gives the following distinguishing points:

In *projection,* "what is projected is experienced as belonging to, coming from, or as an attribute or quality of the object."

In *projective identification* "what is projected is simultaneously identified with and is experienced as part of the self." [p. 55]

Meissner then declares that since it involves loss of ego boundaries and taking the object as part of the self, projective identification is inherently a psychotic mechanism, thus contradicting Klein's view of projective identification as a normal developmental process that can only become pathological if the degree of anxiety due to the death instinct is too great to bear. Unlike Freud (1894), who viewed projection as an abnormal mechanism found in paranoia, Meissner sees projection as a normal mechanism, while Kernberg (1987) finds it a normal or neurotic one. Agreeing with Meissner's view of projective identification as always abnormal, Kernberg describes it as a primitive but not inevitably psychotic defensive operation, which, however, is most evident in psychosis and borderline conditions. Kernberg (1987) defines projective identification as follows:

> Clinical experience has led me to define projective identification as a primitive defense mechanism consisting of (a) projecting intolerable aspects of intrapsychic experience onto an object, (b) maintaining empathy with what is projected, (c) attempting to control the object as a continuation of the defensive efforts against the intolerable intrapsychic experience, and (d) unconsciously inducing in the object what is projected in the actual interaction with the object. [p. 94]

Meissner (1980) also addresses himself to a "certain vogue" in using the concept in family dynamics. He agrees that complex projective-introjective processes occur but not projective identification. He agrees with Zinner and Shapiro (1972) that indeed when "the subject perceives the object *as if* the object contained elements of the subject's personality," then truly the term projective identification applies. But he states that that is not often the case except in psychotic interaction. Yet Meissner gives no clinical or research evidence to disprove Zinner and Shapiro's conclusion that it does occur in nonpsychotic interaction. Zinner and Shapiro's argument is, however, based on their documented clinical research.

More recently, Ogden (1982) brought some order to the chaos, attempting a definition of projective identification as he experienced it in clinical situations. He, too, makes a distinction between projection and projective identification:

In *projection,* ". . . the aspect of the self that is in fantasy expelled is disavowed and attributed to the recipient."

In *projective identification,* "the projector subjectively experiences a feeling of oneness with the recipient with regard to the expelled feeling, idea, or self-representation." [p. 34]

Here Ogden elaborates upon identification as a feeling of oneness. He also specifies what is projected: not just a part of the self, it may also be a feeling or an idea. Later in his text, he concludes that he views projective identification as "a group of fantasies and accompanying object relations" (p. 36) in the intrapsychic dimension. These operate in interpersonal interaction in three phases outlined by Ogden (1982) and derived from Malin and Grotstein (1966) (see Table 6-1).

This model of projection, coercion, and reclaiming brings out the interactive sequence. From the intrapsychic perspective of the projector (the one who is doing the projecting), Ogden goes further to ask why the projector goes through all these stages. What are the intrapsychic and interpersonal benefits of projective identification? He finds that there are four purposes of projective identification, summarized in Table 6-2:

Consider Ogden's (1982) opening statement on projective identification:

> The concept integrates statements about unconscious fantasy, interpersonal pressure, and the response of a separate personality system to a set of engendered feelings. Projective identification is in part a statement about an interpersonal interaction (the pressure of one person on another to comply with a projective fantasy) and in part a statement about individual mental activity (projective fantasies, introjective fantasies, psychological processing). Most fundamentally, however, it is a statement about the dynamic interplay of the two, the intrapsychic and the interpersonal. [p. 3]

Table 6-1. Ogden's Phases of Projective Identification

1. Expelling part of the self into someone else, where it takes hold
2. Pressuring the other person to experience it
3. Getting it back from the other person

Table 6-2. Ogden's Four Functions of Projective Identification

1. Defense — to distance oneself from the unwanted part, or to keep it alive in someone else
2. Communication — to make oneself understood by pressing the recipient to experience a set of feelings like one's own
3. Object-relatedness — to interact with a recipient separate enough to receive the projection yet undifferentiated enough to allow some misperception to occur and to foster the sense of oneness
4. Pathway for psychological change — to be transformed by reintrojecting the projection after its modification by the recipient, as occurs in the mother-infant relationship, marriage, or the patient-therapist relationship.

Primarily an individual therapist, Ogden does not refer to Dicks on marital studies. Yet interestingly enough, based on his study of the patient-therapist relationship and its evocation of the primitive processes of infancy, he comes up with the foregoing concept of projective identification that is in the mold of Dicks and certainly just as applicable to understanding marital dynamics.

In later writing, Ogden (1986) has been concerned with explaining the change in the quality of the infant's experience after a projection has been metabolized by the mother and returned to the infant in a more useful or manageable form. Ogden suggests that "in the process of creating the type of emotional linkage that is involved in projective identification" there occurs an actual alteration in the infant, because the "simultaneous oneness and twoness (unity and separateness of mother and infant)" involved in projective identification "creates a potential for a form of experience more generative than the sum of the individual psychological states contributing to it" (p. 36). In his view, both infant and mother, patient and therapist, projector and projectee contribute actively to the process and the infant/patient/projector is changed by it. By including the therapist's elaboration of what has been projected, Ogden explores the two-body projective identificatory system. Although we welcome his expansion, others do not; for instance, Kernberg (1987) deplores such "unwarranted" broadening of the concept (p. 93). Ogden goes beyond Klein to emphasize the interpersonal aspects of projective identification and the importance of the environment that were only implied in her work, but like Klein, he emphasizes the infant's experience. Drawing on Bion (1962), he deliberates upon the effect on the

contained infant (or the "mother–infant" as he prefers to call the
infant in the mother–infant dyad), and the containing function of
the mother rather than upon the formation of altered psychic
structure in the mother. Thus he points us back to the intrapsychic
dimension of the interpersonal process of projective identification.

There is a correspondence between the phases of the interactive
sequence in the process of projective identification described by
Ogden and stages of theory building identified by Sandler (1987).
He noted that the concept had gone through three stages, in which
it was viewed as (1) an intrapsychic process in which the real object
is not affected by the fantasy; (2) an interpersonal process in which
the object is affected by the fantasy (as occurs in countertransference); (3) an interpersonal process in which the object affects the
fantasy when the projected parts are modified by the thought or
reverie (Bion 1967) of the containing mother. (Sandler remains
unconvinced of the validity of this third stage concept.)

CONTRIBUTIONS FROM FAMILY THERAPY: ZINNER AND SHAPIRO

Zinner and Shapiro (1972) applied their understanding of the
intrapsychic process of projective identification to interpersonal
situations in family life. Zinner (1976), having read Dicks (1967),
brought the concept to bear in marital therapy in the United
States. He emphasized that projective identification is an *unconscious* process with defensive and restorative functions. His
emphasis on the unconscious is helpful; other writers describe
projective identification in such tangible terms that it may seem
conscious and sometimes even willful. Zinner writes:

> Projective identification is an activity of the ego that modifies
> perception of the object and, in a reciprocal fashion, alters the
> image of the self." He adds, "Again through projective identifica-
> tion, the individual may locate the object not inside the self, but as
> if it were inside the other partner in a relationship. [Zinner 1976 in
> J. S. Scharff 1989, p. 156]

For Zinner, projective identification is an unconscious intrapsychic process through which conflict can be contained inside the self or projected out into a relationship. He noted, as Dicks had, that this happens in marriage and that the process not only alters how the self perceives the object but actually evokes a collusive response in the object. This fits with Ogden's idea of interpersonal pressuring of the object. But Zinner, like Dicks, goes further to point out that both spouses are involved in processes of projective identification. In modern terms we might say both are simultaneously projectors and projectees. Thus, Zinner describes a marriage as "a mutually gratifying collusive system" (Zinner 1976 in J. S. Scharff 1989, p. 156). Here is projective identification as a mutual process. The goal of marital therapy in Zinner's view is to help each spouse reinternalize these projected conflicts.

Zinner also has a useful concept of projective identification as a process that is both healthy and unhealthy. Depending on the extent of the use of projective identification, the nature of a marriage relationship may fall anywhere on a continuum from normally empathic to frankly delusional:

> The location of a particular relationship along this continuum is determined by the quality and developmental level of internalized nuclear object relations, by the capacity of the spouses to experience each other as separate, differentiated individuals, and by the intensity of the need for defense. To the extent that a spouse uses projective modes less as a way of externalizing conflict and more as an instrument for approximating shared experience, the marital relationship approaches the healthy end of the continuum. [Zinner 1976 in J. S. Scharff, p. 159]

Projective identification as a concept can now be seen to have the power to offer a conceptual bridge between individual and interpersonal psychology. We have seen that marital choice is "motivated by a desire to find an object who will complement and reinforce unconscious fantasies" (Dicks 1967). Thus adult development continues to be strongly affected by projective identification. Family studies by Zinner and Shapiro (1972) go further to show its influence on individual development. They write: "Projective identification leads to authentic and lasting structural

change in the *recipient* of the projections. A prime example of this
phenomenon is the effect of family interaction on the developing
personality of the child" (Zinner and Shapiro 1972 in J. S. Scharff
1989, p. 110).

In contrast to what he wrote then on projective identification in
family interaction, Zinner says in discussion that he now regards
projective identification as entirely an intrapsychic process occurring between parts of self and internal objects inside the projector.
For Zinner, it is a one-body phenomenon. Similar intrapsychic
processes occur in significant others, but Zinner says that the idea
of projecting into another person or vice versa is too mystical for
him to accept. Although in his writing he had emphasized the
interpersonal context, in his teaching now Zinner focuses on the
intrapsychic dimension, on what happens in the individual. So if
projective identification is entirely an intrapsychic process, how
does Zinner account for the process of mutual projective identification, which he has described and to which he still subscribes?
How does he explain the effect on the object? For Zinner, the
missing link is interpersonal behavior. Zinner states that the wife's
intrapsychic operation of projective identification, which affects
her perception of the spouse, leads to changes in her behavior
toward him. Her husband then responds with his own intrapsychic
processes of projective identification and corresponding relevant
behaviors. Zinner does not regard this statement as a shift in his
view but rather as a clarification of precisely where projective
identification occurs.

Integrating the contributions from family therapy research with
our clinical experience as family therapists, we conclude that
multiple individual processes governed by shared unconscious
assumptions about family life eventually lead to the identification
of parts of the family inside individuals. At the same time, the
intrapsychic situation is projected onto the intrafamily group
unconscious. An individual is selected as host for, or object for
projection of, the unwanted or disavowed parts of the central self
of the family. In health, the host role rotates among family
members, but when projective identification focuses and fixes on
one member, a pathological situation has arisen. An index patient
now holds disavowed parts for the other family members, and

stands for a family group problem in metabolizing the unwanted aspects of the family unconscious.

CONTRIBUTIONS FROM SEX THERAPY

In projective identification in the marital dyad, the projection induces a state of mind in the external object. We have tended to think of this happening through the stirring of behavior, thought, or feeling relevant to the received projection. But in the sexual situation, as in infancy, the medium for projection tends to be the body. The projector projects not into the psyche, but into the soma of the projectee, and vice versa in mutual projective identification. Sometimes, in order to protect the other, the projector projects into his or her own body parts directly or indirectly after introjective identification with the returned projection, in either case the object of projection now being located inside the self. Any body part of self or other can become identified with the disclaimed projection, but the erotic zones are particularly likely targets. Conflicts are projected in condensed form on the body screen of the genitalia (D. Scharff 1982). Penis, vagina, and the woman's breasts become the physical locus of the repressed rejecting and exciting object systems. Repressed objects then return directly through contributing to or interfering with physical love in the married state.

CONTRIBUTING CONCEPTS

Valency

In his study of small groups, Bion (1961) had noted the engagement of personalities around unconscious group themes. To account for it, he suggested the concept of valency: the instinctive capacity for instantaneous involuntary combination of one individual personality with another. Bion simply said that valency was "a spontaneous unconscious function of the gregarious quality in

the personality of man" (p. 136). But this does not take us far
enough into understanding how it happens. So we turn to the work
of Racker.

Concordant and Complementary Identification

Racker (1968) described countertransference as the therapist's
reaction to the patient's projections organized as projective identifications occurring unconsciously in the therapist. These identifications might be of two types:

> In *concordant identification,* the therapist identifies with a pro-
> jected part of the patient's *self.*

> In *complementary identification,* the therapist identifies with a
> projected part of the patient's *object.*

We have applied these ideas to the family therapist's experience
of identifying with family group projections (Scharff and Scharff
1987). We can also take Racker's formulation out of its therapeutic context and apply it to the marital relationship where it
helps us to fill out Bion's concept of valency and Dicks's concept
of unconscious complementarity. To put it simply, a wife's self (or
part thereof) may be seen as her husband's object or as a part of
his self, exclusively, alternately, or simultaneously. The result is an
exponential progression involving mutual projection of and identification with parts of self and object in a growing cybernetic
system of unconscious object relationships in the couple and the
family.

Extractive Introjection

We also find helpful Bollas's (1987) concept of *extractive introjection:* "an intersubjective process . . . in which one person
invades another person's mind and appropriates certain elements
of mental life" leaving the victim "denuded of parts of the self" (p.
163). The mental theft may be of ideas, feelings, mental structure
such as superego, and parts of the self. For instance, when a wife
fails an exam for reasons that seem unfair and finds her husband

more upset than she is, she is robbed of her right to outrage. In extreme cases, extraction may be "followed by vaporization of the psychic structure" (p. 164). In other cases, Bollas continues, "as a person takes from another person's psyche, he leaves a gap, or a vacuum, in its place. There he deposits despair or emptiness in exchange for what he has stolen." Thus, "each extractive introjection is accompanied by some corresponding projective identification" (p. 164).

Now we can say that projective identification occurs along with introjective identification and in more violent examples it is associated with extractive introjection. These interlocking processes are the basis for valency. We find that spouses connect through valencies for concordant or complementary identification that determine the "unconscious complementariness" of fit described by Dicks (1967, p. 69). A match in valencies leads to the instantaneous combination of two personalities falling in love. The balance of the projective and introjective processes is determined by the nature of the object relations of each personality and the degree of fit between the parts of self and internal objects of the spouse and the partner. In sickness and in health, valency is determined by inner object relationships seeking expression, repetition, or healing in current life relationships (Scharff and Scharff 1987).

THE STEPS OF PROJECTIVE IDENTIFICATION

Now we will present our own view of projection and projective identification based on this literature, on our experience as analysts, as couple and family therapists, and on previous elaboration of the concept (J. Scharff 1992).

In projection a part of the self—either a part of the ego or of its internal objects, or a feeling or an idea originally connected to the self or objects now split off from them—is expelled from the intrapsychic domain and displaced to an external object during an unconscious mental process. The person doing the projecting (the projector) has no awareness of the projection onto the other person (the projectee), and so has a feeling of separateness from the external object that possesses the expelled part of the self. The object is believed to be invested with qualities that it does not have. The only identification occurring is that of recognizing a quality in that object. The projection does not necessarily fit. This process may be a delusion as in paranoia, a misperception as in neurosis, or a normal momentary expulsion followed by reintrojection.

In projective identification, a number of steps follow. The first step is always a projection. Whether it remains a projection or becomes a projective identification depends on whether the second step of affecting the object occurs. If the only object affected is the internal object, then the process remains an intrapsychic one. When the external object of the projection contributes to the process, either passively or actively, then projective identification has entered the interpersonal dimension. Then the object may simultaneously project parts of itself into the subject in a process of mutual projective identification. If all the steps are completed, the process of projective identification goes beyond its description as a one-body or two-body phenomenon to a multipart-and-object phenomenon, a description that does justice to the recruitment into the process of any number of parts of self and objects of one, two or more personalities in unconscious communication during interaction in family life.

The following steps characterize projective identification in marriage (J. Scharff 1992):

1. *Projection.* The projector spouse expels a part of the self and identifies the external object in the projectee spouse as if it were imbued with qualities that do not pertain to it in fact but that pertain to the self. (This is the original projection. Identification occurs only in the sense of naming or recognizing a quality.)
2. *Object induction.* The projector spouse so convincingly identifies the part of the self in the external object that the feeling state corresponding to that part of the self is evoked in the projectee spouse.
3. *Introjective identification by the object.* At this point the projectee spouse has identified with the projection of the projector spouse through the process of introjective identification at the unconscious level.

4. *Transformation by the object.* Since the projectee spouse has his or her own personality, the projected part of the projector spouse's self with which the projectee identifies is not the same as that part was when still inside the intrapsychic arena of the projector. The part has been transformed by its temporary lodging in the psyche of the spouse, its goodness or badness being confirmed, exaggerated, or diminished.

5. *Valency of the object to receive a projection.* When the projectee spouse has a valency for a certain projection, then the projectee will tend to accept that projection and identify with that part of the other spouse's self. This valent part is not passively inducted but actively seeks parts of another to identify with to the point of stealing part of another person's mind through a process called "extractive introjection" (Bollas 1987, p. 5).

6. *Complementary and concordant identification by the object.* The part of the self projected may, however, be a part of the ego (part of the self representation) or a part of the object. Thus the projectee spouse may be induced to embody the ego in relation to the object that is located in the projector spouse or to embody the object in relation to the projector's ego. This is determined not only by which part of the self is actually projected but also by the projectee's valency to respond in identification with the projector's projected part of self or to respond as the nonprojected part of the self that is in relation to the projected part. In other words, the introjective identification of the projectee spouse may be, in Racker's (1968) terms, concordant or complementary to projector spouse's self or object.

7. *Introjective identification by the self.* The self identifies with or assimilates itself to the reinternalized confirmed or modified part of the self. Then psychic structure is "cemented" or slightly altered. Cementing can be a healthy process if accurately received projections are accurately returned by the external object but it can be unhealthy by not permitting change. Alteration in the range, flexibility, or acceptability of responses can pro-

118   David E. and Jill S. Scharff

mote growth if the modification is slight and is based on
the projectee spouse's unconscious capacity to appreciate
the otherness of the marital partner and to harbor and
return the projected part of the projector spouse without
fundamental distortion.

8. *Mutual projective identification.* The projector that
projects into the projectee is at the same time receiving
projections from the projectee. Projector/projectee marital pairs unconsciously match up based on valencies for
identifying with each other's projections. Thus, projective
identification is a mutual process: husband and wife
connect according to unconscious complementarity of
object relations. Similarly, couple and therapist relate
through the transference and countertransference.

CASE ILLUSTRATION OF OBJECT RELATIONS
COUPLE THERAPY:
THE MANAGEMENT OF IMPASSE

Sooner or later, the marital therapist will be asked to help a couple
of spouses who seem to attack their marriage at every quarter.
Theoretically we know that it is the longing underneath the attack
that keeps such couples together, but in the process of our trying
to help them, they often turn from attacking each other to
assaulting our capacity to provide a therapeutic context. In these
situations, it is finally the capacity to survive that offers any
possibility of a therapeutic change. The work is often painful, but
it offers lessons that are infinitely helpful with less thoroughly
destructive couples whose transferences nevertheless echo the one
to be presented. The experience of impasse and impossibility in the
countertransference that is illustrated here is a central feature of
work with these couples.

Harvey and Anne Van Duren sought help for an impossible situation.
He was a 58-year-old writer, raised in England, and she, at 42, a
scientist of substantial and still growing reputation. They had been
married for only eighteen months, but the marriage had been a stormy
one from the start. They met in a long affair after Harvey had been

invited to do a biography of Anne for a magazine. Both had been married at the time, but had essentially signed out of their marriages, with multiple affairs and little regard for their previous spouses. Harvey said that his first wife had been depressed and unresponsive except to their child, who was now grown. Anne described a marriage to a successful builder who had little interest in the family, and who left her alone with their son and daughter, allowing her to do as she pleased in raising them. Both first marriages had been calm, with no turbulence or remarkable fighting. Harvey had emotionally left his marriage many years before, and for several years had lived in an apartment in a building near his wife's house. Anne had taken the initiative in running her family while getting her emotional needs met elsewhere.

Their affair, though hardly noticed by either of their spouses, was passionate from the beginning. They each said they felt alive as they never had before, and they expended enormous amounts of energy planning to see each other. During the early phase of their romance, when their meetings were brief and surreptitious, the sex went well. But as soon as they declared their love, felt free to date openly, and to have longer times together, Harvey began to have intermittent erectile difficulty. They both explained this as being due to the stress of the relationship in forbidding circumstances, but the sexual difficulty persisted even when both were free to date. After their marriage, Harvey's difficulty with erections increased.

This was what Anne said was the chief reason for her anger. She could no longer face being married without a sexual life. Things were too difficult. She had to face difficulties with her children, who had repeated school troubles. She felt she got no sympathy from Harvey about this, but she could stand that. After all, she had always raised her children alone. What she could not face was that having had to handle everything herself, she then got nothing from him sexually. This she felt as an extreme rejection, and it made her feel uncared for in the way she had as a small child when she had suffered severe burns to her legs and lower body in a fire at the age of 5. She felt ugly and rejected. She could barely remember the fire, but as far back as she could remember, she had to spend long lonely periods in the hospital, times when she felt rejected and uncared for. The repairs to her skin and the related physical therapy had gone on until age 10. Surprisingly, slight scars remained. These ugly feelings came back with the sexual rejection she felt from Harvey. But that was certainly not all. Mainly, she felt he did not care what she had to put up with in her own daily situation. He was not there emotionally when she tried to manage her children, one of whom was anorectic, and the other who, although bright, was constantly defeating himself. The children were demanding, and in addition resented Harvey—and no wonder. He was self-centered and uncaring with them, and when he did tune in on them, he was often provocative or teasing, so that they dissolved into tears. Once the boy had attacked Harvey physically after Harvey had been scathing with him.

While Anne's round face was flushed with anger, Harvey's was pale and immobile. He sat quietly and dispassionately, a bit slumped in the easy chair, until she finished. Then he pulled himself up and began to defend himself. He was as distressed as she was about his impotence. He had intermittent trouble with it earlier in his life, but never as much difficulty as this. He did not feel unsympathetic about her troubles, nor did he feel unsupportive.

He was calm, rational, and well spoken, with a high-bred accent. Nothing about his demeanor would have seemed to warrant the tirade that Anne had launched. He expressed his hope that they could do something, and as quickly as possible, about the trouble with the erections. He would like to make her happy.

THE TREATMENT

Work with Harvey and Anne was among the most difficult and discouraging I [D.E.S.] have done. Early on, Anne reached an equilibrium in which she would refuse to speak for the first part of the session. She was trying to control her rage and to force his participation. At first she said, "I'm not going to speak today. Harvey, you speak!" This soon hardened into a pattern in which he would look to me, and begin with whatever he could muster— an account of the week's activities, the fight that had preceded the appointment, or occasionally, an account of a relatively good week.

Sooner or later, Anne would cut in to disagree with his account. He had not represented her side of it correctly, she would say. Or he had been accurate in his account, but had failed to be understanding of her this time, as usual. The pattern that regularly surfaced was that although he did the talking, nothing he said mattered until she cut in. And the talking that he did by himself was a rational accounting for the time since I had last seen them, for the most part devoid of any emotion.

My job was not made any easier by the fact that I regularly felt my position with them severely skewed. I liked his urbane wit, his upper-class English accent, and his patrician elocution despite his being relatively walled off from feeling. I found her shrewish despite her capacity for psychological mindedness. Overall, I felt that this couple constantly cut me off from my own wish to be neutral between them. I felt inside me the unwelcome wish to side with him and to get rid of her. In my struggle to be true to my principles and regain a position equidistant between them, I felt so frequently frustrated that I often wished to be rid of them altogether.

The first task of the therapy was, on the one hand, to help them settle down enough that they did not burst apart, while, on the other hand, containing the fiery physical fights that had become a feature of their marriage. Neither of them had been involved in fights in previous relationships, but they had been fighting violently and frequently for the past year. The fights were echoed by Anne's flaming eruptions within the sessions when she would scream at Harvey with a ferocity I had not previously heard in couple therapy, even though I have worked with many desperately angry couples. The threat that this would erupt began to permeate every session, although the episodes occurred only every few weeks. At their request, I was now seeing them two to three times a week, and while the intensity of the rages seemed to have increased, they were now contained inside the therapy.

At first the couple gave me the impression that they were largely verbally abusive to each other. Because they felt trusting enough to tell me, it eventually became clear that the fights actually included physical abuse to each other. I found out that Harvey's social drinking was more than moderate. He reluctantly agreed when I suggested that this could be exacerbating their lack of control. I advised him to stop drinking—which would also remove alcohol's depressant effect on his erections—and said they both had to agree to stop the physical aspects of their fights. I immediately took the position that they had to stop hitting each other, because of the threat to fundamental survival, and without a measure of physical safety we could not work. They were able to virtually stop the physical fighting, with only a few recurrences over the next few months. This brought the strength of the difficulties all the more pressingly into the hours. Anne spoke for the brunt of the upset, while Harvey was the patient, but spare stoic. When they were at peace, they had a relationship where love was expressed through mutual teasing and sarcasm at an admirable level of wit and erudition. George Bernard Shaw might have written their lines of mutual cynicism about the human condition and each other's contribution to our common catastrophe. Their relationship was a constantly humbling experience for anyone who wished to remain optimistic about the possibility of humane marriage in a humane world.

A new pattern now developed in therapy hours. While either Harvey or I was speaking, Anne would declare without warning that she had had all she could take. She would start to cry, promptly leave the room, and slam the door. On the first such occasion, Harvey stayed and we tried to make some sense of what he had done to contribute to her retreat. But after the hour, she said that his staying had left her burning with anger, hurt, and fundamentally mistrustful of me. She could only assume he and I were ganging up against her. If that happened again, she really would never come back.

This declaration paradoxically gave me some hope for them, because until then I had felt that her leaving the room was close to her quitting the therapy. Her ultimatum let me know that she left when she was beyond words, but that she did not intend to end the work.

After that, when Anne left, Harvey would stir himself in a languid way, and, nodding at me in resignation, follow her out. Sometimes they returned together after a few minutes, and sometimes not until the next hour. On some occasions, Anne's departure would occur in the midst of expressing doubt about continuing the process at all. Then Harvey would have to leave lest Anne feel we were ganging up on her—and I would be left alone and often somewhat perturbed. But usually, when they returned for the next appointment, it was as though nothing had happened.

When they walked out, not knowing whether they would return, I felt shaken every time. I felt diminished, incompetent, and contemptible. I felt I was not smart enough for him nor steady enough for her. I began to hate them for making me feel this way and so there was also some relief each time they left. I could only work on this countertransference feeling by myself, because my attempts to use it in discussion of the transference to me were frustrated.

When I spoke with them about the way in which they left me shaken and wondering if there would be a tomorrow, only to return as though everything was fine, or at least no worse than the usual doom and gloom, Anne could be counted on to lecture me about Harvey's failures and unreliabilities. He was, she assured me, a truly terrible man, full of aggression and a bane to all who tried to be close to him, including his child and first wife. She felt sympathetic to his first wife, since he was so horrible.

I felt that it was unsaid that I was not far behind Harvey in my human failings, especially if I were measured by my failure to help them. I could tangibly feel her disappointment in me from her feeling, which I shared, that I failed to understand the depth of her unjustified suffering at his hands.

And yet Anne could also work in the hours with a capacity that Harvey could not manage. She drew on her previous psychoanalysis to link the marital difficulty and her role in it both to her early childhood and to her concerns as a parent of two adolescents. She clung closely to her children, she thought, out of her aloneness. In her previous empty marriage, when she had retreated to the children, her former husband had been glad to have her off his back.

Early and late in this therapy I felt controlled by Anne's rages and subsequent nonchalance. I felt buffeted and turned on my head like a puppet with no brain. I often felt that my attempt to discern a truly shared contribution to the troubling relationship was merely lip service to my belief. I thought Harvey did contribute to their difficulties, but I could not find out how, because Anne's rages and demandingness were so ascendant. I tried to work with Harvey on the underlying issues in his treatment of her but always felt frustrated by a well-meaning but shallow compliance in his attempts.

He would talk about his family history, but with little feeling. He told of his father, who was a high-level failure, a politician who had a startling early career, but who had suffered subsequent defeat. Although his father eventually became a widely respected elder statesman, he had always carried a sense of failure and disappointment with him, which Harvey had absorbed. Harvey's mother had become alcoholic during his adolescence, and she deteriorated, especially after the death of his father when Harvey was 18. He had an older brother and a younger sister. The brother was the father's favorite. It was the sister, however, with whom Harvey had the more problematic relationship. She had had encephalitis at the age of 3, and the subsequent attention from the family had left Harvey feeling both responsible for her and jealous of the attention she received from his parents.

Harvey could make the intellectual connections. He could say that Anne represented his unsatisfiable or unavailable mother and made him feel like his revered but failed father. He could agree that he was trying to goad her into a better opinion of him. But I never had the satisfaction of things hitting home with him. He admitted his affective disconnection. He lamented it. But he could not change it.

Nevertheless, things continued to improve slowly. From time to time, the couple began to report periods of well-being when life together was more tolerable.

Then Anne reintroduced the demand that something be done about their sex life. The lack of sex in a marginal marriage was more than she felt she could live with. Since thorough evaluation had established that Harvey's impotence did not have an organic cause, and Harvey said he was willing to work on their sexual relationship, we switched to sex therapy, in which I assigned homework. They did the assignments dubiously, and reported on them with their typically contemptuous wit. Still, they made progress with them, and Harvey began having more reliable erections. The previous erectile incapacity could now be understood: it served to suppress rage at Anne as a controlling mother, while protecting her from the rage that would have been located in an invading penis. But at the end of three months of this work, they refused to "play by rules" and plunged ahead to full intercourse before I thought it wise. They told me they assumed that I had set up "my rules" so that they could triumph over me by breaking them.

I found it of interest, intellectually rising above my sense of being abused, to see what was possible therapeutically now that I felt treated by the two of them together the way they habitually treated each other. I told them this was happening, and while they took in my confrontation, they did not change. For some time they continued to have successful intercourse over my therapeutic dead body, and then the sex fell away again as their competitive rage resurfaced.

Now a new crisis emerged. Anne felt betrayed when Harvey took a drink while out with a mutual friend, an old girlfriend of Harvey's by whom Anne had always felt mistreated. Harvey had been effectively off alcohol for more than six months, and he said that he felt healthier, calmer, and considerably relieved. But on this occasion he had given in to their friend's urgent tender of a drink.

Harvey admitted that part of his motivation for taking a drink had been annoyance with Anne, and he explored his angry wish to get back at her through it, but nothing would satisfy her. She moved steadily away from him, berating him in almost every session. Her silent demand that he begin the sessions was stronger than ever. My interventions seemed to make less and less difference, because she now felt any focus on her was a weapon used against her, whether Harvey or I was talking. Because of this insistence, any focus on Harvey assumed a false air of being carried out simply to appease her.

In this situation, all I could do was openly discuss my countertransference position. The couple had seemed impossible and now therapy seemed impossible too. I talked about feeling that I was helpless to make a difference, and I reflected on Anne's now avowed intention to end the marriage. I addressed the relentless spoiling I felt she led with that also was a characteristic of their marriage which, outside the sessions, both of them carried out. I spent many hours feeling I had nothing to offer. On these occasions, Anne would turn to me and say, "Why don't you talk, Dr. Scharff? What do you think about us?"

I would say, "I don't have any new thoughts about you. I'm not sure there is anything I have to offer because I can't say what I think." Having said that, I then was able to face what I thought, which was that Anne had the controlling lead in forbidding thought

*or feeling. I felt hamstrung, particularly by her, even though she
had told me that was just what she could not stand hearing.*

Over time, Anne was hit by my confrontation. The first time I
said this, not surprisingly, she walked out of the hour. I felt better
mainly because I thought the agony of the work with this couple
was likely to be over soon. But Anne came back with Harvey in the
next hour, and acted as though everything was better. I said I was
sure that Harvey did contribute to the problem fully, as she had
said. But I knew from my experience of feeling hampered by her
control on my thoughts that until she let Harvey off the hook, he
would not be free to work. I noted that although she said he was
impossible and that the marriage was not salvageable, she stayed.
And I concluded that if she meant to stay, she would have to stop
spoiling and blocking the work. Otherwise we would not be able to
understand his contribution. Her fearfulness, for all the reasons
we understood and many we did not, was keeping her from
allowing Harvey to really speak despite her insistence that he fill
the time. And her determination that it was not safe was the
controlling factor, like it or not. She certainly had the right to end
the marriage. But if she did not want to end the marriage, or if she
did want to invest in the therapy, she would have to let go. She
would have to make that decision.

They stayed, and after another four months, things began to
yield. Almost imperceptibly, Anne softened and began to admit
that Harvey was capable of standing by her on occasions. After
my repeated confrontation, she rarely had to leave the room after
I spoke, and so, with trepidation, I could mention that things were
reported as better. During these months we could discuss the
factors that threw them over the cliff so that we were not confined
to experiencing the fall over and over without any added capacity
for understanding.

And finally Anne began, now with full affect that caught my
sympathy, to tell the story of feeling so abandoned by her parents
during her long bout of recovering from her childhood trauma.
The fire had happened in the night when she was asleep. She
awoke screaming with her bed on fire. Really she had been lucky
it was only her lower body that was badly burned, but what she
chiefly remembered was the time in the hospital afterward. The

burn had been excruciating, and required painful dressing and redressing. She had multiple surgical procedures, and to this day had bodily scarring. She found her nude body painfully ugly, although residual scarring was minimal. But most painful to her was the feeling that her parents had abandoned her to the care of the hospital. Later while she was healing, her father told her she would never fully recover — which to her had meant that she would never recover their affection. She felt that her treatment by doctors and nurses had gone on in the absence of her parents, who had apparently stayed away a good deal in reaction to their own fear and turmoil. That feeling had made her insistence that the treatment itself was a trauma all the more heartfelt, since the more searing the couple's therapy was, the more it reminded her of the fear and pain of the treatment for her burns.

But this time, her review of this material meant more to both Anne and Harvey. Although the reasons are not entirely clear, I think that my talking about my helplessness addressed her situation as a child, and that my confrontation about her leaving sessions and slamming doors against Harvey and me may have spoken to a childhood wish to scream at her parents for leaving her alone. I could now understand the shaken feeling I had when she walked out of the hour as representing how she had felt when left alone by her parents in the hospital to face the painful "assault" of the doctors and nurses.

Harvey thought of his concern as a boy for his sister, who similarly had a physically painful childhood hospitalization with his wish to take care of Anne. Now he lived out the same ambivalence about taking care of Anne that must have existed then about his sister: he both wanted to take care of her, and he was wordlessly envious of the care she received, even from himself.

A SESSION WITH SHIFTED DEFENSIVE STRUCTURE

Finally, after just two years, their defensive structure shifted. On the day I am going to describe, they sat next to each other on the same couch, a configuration I had not seen in at least a year.

Separated still by the middle seat in the couch, Harvey teasingly reached across to Anne and poked her in the ribs from time to time. Finally she said the poking really bothered her. Harvey smiled and said that he knew she really liked it, at which she shot him an ambiguously sweet grimace. Harvey began, as was still the mandatory procedure, by filling me in on the situation. They had a good week, despite extraordinary stress. Anne's son had been arrested mistakenly by the police, and her daughter had been in an automobile accident and taken to the hospital. Although she was all right, that had not been clear at first. And there was a house full of visitors including the daughter's live-in boyfriend. Nevertheless, Anne had been able to cope, supported by Harvey. Anne said that she did not know quite what accounted for the improvement.

I was having the feeling of walking again on thin ice, having tried so often to speak to the forces of destructiveness that led them to spoil periods of good feeling. Yet I felt a bit flushed with some late-inning success. So I elected, in a way against my better judgment, to push on in this positive view, glad that today a new kind of work seemed possible.

For the first time in two years of work, Harvey seemed able to respond. Anne took the lead in introducing the topic of Harvey's son Bill's recent request for financial support from them so that he could have psychotherapy. Harvey was disposed to give it to him, but he felt mildly abused by the request from a self-supporting 30-year-old. This led Anne to discuss Harvey's dreadful relationship with his son. Harvey agreed it was awful, but in the intellectually distant way he agreed about anything. In my experience of him, he was always emotionally out of touch with what he was agreeing to. His tendency to erupt irrationally at home in the enormous fights with Anne had not been betrayed in the hours, where even his anger would seem most reasonable.

But today, something yielded. Harvey said that he thought he felt resentful of his son because, in large part, he would like to give him so much. When Bill called, Harvey felt himself in the role of his father, the man he had longed to turn to when he had felt isolated or rejected. So the request from Bill stirred the urge to give to him, as he longed to be given to. Then the underlying sense of rejection loomed when, on the other hand, he felt he should not give to Bill because the request was unreasonable.

But another issue was nearby, one to do with his mother. Somehow, he said, he had a sense that she interfered between him and his father. How was it that she came between them? Here Anne chimed in to ask if it was his mother's alcoholism. Harvey thought not because she wasn't alcoholic until later, probably when he was already in his teens. But there was something in the way with his father, and he couldn't identify it, try as he might.

I said that although he could not find the information in his memory at present, perhaps he could learn about it from his interaction with Anne, in which he participated in and initiated relentless, recurrent fighting to which both of them were quite attached. I recalled what I had noted so often: whenever things were quiet, they seemed to share an urge to have some noise, and the quickest way to quiet the anxiety about peace was to fight. Their way of expressing intimacy was often to prod each other, just as Harvey had physically prodded Anne early in this hour.

Harvey, looking thoughtful, seemed to be following me. I thought he might find something to connect back to his parents' relationship and his difficulty in reaching his father. I continued saying that Harvey frequently prodded Anne verbally. Anne protested that she did not like that prodding either. Although she was a partner in the acerbically witty exchanges, I accepted her statement, and prepared to continue my review of their relationship. But Anne was off and running. She said that however much this might be a part of her, she did not relate this way with anyone else. She could see that it expressed her resentment. The resentment was an old one that we had discussed frequently, stemming from the period of her childhood convalescence when she was so resentful of the pain and the expectations of her, and especially, she now added, of the insult added to the injury when her father said to her that since she was scarred and no longer beautiful, she had better develop her brain in order to get along in this life. This was the father she was trying to reach, even while resenting him, when Harvey was busy prodding her. But, she noted, here we were in the hour focusing on her again. And she resented that. She resented it that Harvey could duck out, partly to be sure, because she was so ready to pick up the work and focus it on herself. But she was tired of that.

> *I agreed, I thought that this was an example of the two of them working to take the emotional focus off Harvey, just when he had begun to move into it. I was feeling that the slender thread of their working together without Anne wading in or storming out would break in my grasp — or perhaps that I had no hold on it at all. It was in their hands. It was as if the thread had wound around me, not enough for me to pull on it helpfully, but only enough for them to pull on it and spin me around in the process. Feeling here today that they were beginning to work, I felt again the sense of therapeutic helplessness and of being only one step away from their familiar maelstrom. On the other hand, I would see that she was right on the theme of connecting their relationship to the problem of reaching for a parent, in her case the father and, in the transference, me.*

I now wondered aloud how Harvey and Anne had joined to keep Harvey from continuing to investigate something about his early life with his parents. Perhaps it was something painful to both of them that threatened to emerge at the point they had switched away from Harvey. Could he go back to that?

In his evenhanded and overly reasonable way, Harvey said that he would try. It was a dim impression, but he thought his mother must have made demands on him by which he felt constrained. Many times his father would be trying to placate his mother, when he could not, therefore, get his father's attention.

I wondered if things were not rougher in the early relationship with his mother than he had been thinking. The evidence in the relationship with Anne was that he was extraordinarily wary, and yet at the same time he was prodding her. That behavior, so destructive of what he said he wanted with her, was a persistent and repeated pattern. Anne was busy nodding from her chair, about to speak and challenge him herself. I imagined she would do so aggressively, and so I asserted myself and continued my direct work with Harvey to model a check on *her* prodding of him.

> *I was countertransferentially experiencing the mutual prodding that was a feature of the way they, with their anxious holding relationship, experienced calm or peace to be absence and rejec-*

tion. Mutual prodding was their attempt to get compliant surrender or a nonthreatening sign of life from each other. My heightened activity occurred without my quite being aware of it, in order to substitute my empathic questioning for her invasive relationship.

This sense let me suggest to Harvey that his mother may well have been, in her depression when he was 4 or 5, difficult for him to get to. In his attempt to bring her to life, and to focus on him, he must have had to prod her, and must have been willing to do so even at the expense of angering her.

"I think that's true," he said. "I can remember her being depressed. Probably she did drink some then, maybe more than I remember, just as I used to drink more than I thought. As we talk about this, I do have a distant feeling, one of loneliness, a quiet without walls, stretching in front of me and all around. It's eerie. And this relates to my father somehow. To a feeling that if I could just get to him, I could get some comfort. So even right now, I have a sense of missing him terribly. But where is he? And then, there is the sense that he's a failure. And the one way I can be with him is to risk being a failure myself. But I think the failure here is not just about the failures he felt in the later years, which were many. Yes!" he said, his eyes unexpectedly filling with tears, "Here, I think it's mainly the failure to help me with my mother, and the sense of sorrow that he, too, could not breathe life into her."

The room was quiet, in an unusually sad and full way. I felt we had given birth to something. Since it was close to the end of the hour, I turned to Anne to ask her response.

Anne said that she felt moved. There was something tentative, perhaps grudging in her acknowledgment, but she did not interrupt, and she looked concerned for Harvey. It made sense, she said, of his prodding her, as though she were the depressed, rejecting mother who he had to jolly into life, but with whom it was preferable to fight if that's what it took to get through to her. She could see the loneliness behind it. Until today, she had never felt she could penetrate the fog that always seemed to separate Harvey from her and in which he blamed her for nearly everything. But this helped. And challengingly, at the end, she added that she hoped there would be more of it.

HANDLING THE COUPLE'S ASSAULT ON THE
THERAPIST'S CAPACITY

We chose to present this work because it illustrates the therapist's struggle in the face of the couple's assault on the therapist's capacity to provide a therapeutic context that stems directly from the couple's devastatingly flawed holding. They attempted to compensate for their fears for themselves and for each other. For Anne, there was the fear that she would be engulfed in the flames of her original burn and abandoned to pain without support. In the face of this she became enormously controlling of Harvey and the therapist. Harvey's experience with a depressed and later volatile mother and an absent father had led him to be rigidly walled off. His controlled personality felt like a continual, maddening rejection to Anne, so they came together mostly in aggressive outbursts, at which times they felt closest.

We have outlined the way in which the countertransference reflected the couple's flawed holding capacity, expressed in their dubious contextual transference. Both of them had internalized the experience of enviable but rejecting parents. Harvey and Anne had somewhat different constellations of exciting and rejecting parents. Both were focused on their fathers as exciting figures. For Anne, father was also the rejecting figure. She had few thoughts of her mother at all: functionally, no mother seemed to exist, leaving her with little model for an accepting mother. For Harvey, good and bad were mainly split between father and mother, but the cost of identification with his father was the internalization of the failed father—probably as reinforced by his mother's accusations. For both of them, however, the parental couples had been disappointing and yet envied.

In the countertransference, the therapist was often absorbed in his own doubts and feelings of failure as a therapist. It was a daily experience of feeling deskilled and dismissed, separated from his own operating principles and self-esteem, and joined with them in a style that he felt attracted to, and yet which gave him considerable self-loathing.

It was through being willing to absorb this couple's destructiveness, their mutual spoiling and envy, their condescension and contempt, and through becoming someone he did not like in small ways, that the therapist was able to understand their internal experience of trying to reach each other in endlessly frustrating ways. With them he felt that he was in the presence of enviable but persecuting parents, ones who would not let him in. What resonated in him was his own rejecting internal couple, just as it was in sharing a projective identification of rejecting internal couples that the couple so badly abused each other.

This therapy demonstrates, more than anything, the power of survival of the therapist. Here the holding and the experience of trying to provide the holding has none of the softness or mutuality of the mother and the baby. It has the immediacy of coping with assault by an automatic weapon that fires repeatedly at point blank range. It is the therapist's duty to survive the aggressive attacks just as parents must. The triumph of survival is therapeutic because that is what the couple's relationship cannot do until the partners experience it with us.

Meanwhile, it is not fun. The spoiling in the holding between the couple has to be fully, and emotionally, leveled at the therapist, and probably felt quite fully inside the therapist, before it can finally be taken back inside the couple. Without this kind of work, couples like this face a life of continued mutual battering. Some of them may choose to separate, while others will stay together. Certainly, in the middle of therapy it seems that they would be better separated. A therapist is tempted to advise them to separate in the middle of the storm, but it is not up to us to cut their options. Many such therapies do indeed founder before a turning point of the kind described here, but some turn the corner to a different kind of relationship.

In the middle of this, we may decide *we* can go no further with a given marriage, but we cannot make the decision that such a couple should not be together. Barring the case of continued physical abuse or threats of death, it is not up to us to decide which marriages are over and which are not. Those decisions are too important to be decided by the therapist, who in the end does not have to live with the consequences of the decision.

Therapeutically transforming this experience was a longer, slower haul than for many couples. It often felt beyond the outer limits of possibility as the therapist frequently felt overwhelmed with hopelessness! But it is precisely such couples who make the point that this kind of difficulty can only be worked with if one is willing to absorb and suffer the inner objects, the mutual projective identifications, and then to slowly work one's way out of them. It is a most uncomfortable process, for these aggressive and hating couples have almost given up on being loved for themselves, and they can do no other than bring this difficulty to us.

THE COUNTERTRANSFERENCE OF IMPASSE

The turning point of this case centered around the therapist's absorption of the sense of impossibility from the couple — a thorough introjective identification that accumulated through the months of work. It was not a conscious decision but a feeling there was nowhere else to turn that led to his sharing the countertransference with them. Only then could the destructiveness of their work be understood and worked with as deriving from their shared early experience of unreachable parents, absent holding, and anger in place of loving support.

For us, this experience of hopelessness in the countertransference is not uncommon. We have learned that it is often the central experience in couples who use massive splitting and repression, and who fear confrontation with their own mutual destructiveness. Work with such countertransference cannot be "faked." Therapists cannot interpret it until they experience it in cases at hand. They must have absorbed it in the current clinical experience for such interpretation to be honest and effective. But they can be on the lookout for such countertransferences when they encounter difficult couples — and for milder similar versions of countertransference with many couples.

REFERENCES

Bion, W. R. (1961). *Experiences in Groups*. New York: Basic Books.
_____ (1962). *Learning from Experience*. London: Tavistock.
_____ (1967). *Second Thoughts*. London: Heinemann.
_____ (1970). *Attention and Interpretation: A Scientific Approach to Insight in Psycho-Analysis and Groups*. London: Tavistock.

Bollas, C. (1987). *The Shadow of the Object*. New York: Columbia University Press.

Dicks, H. V. (1967). *Marital Tensions: Clinical Studies towards a Psycho-analytic Theory of Interaction*. London: Routledge and Kegan Paul.

Fairbairn, W. R. D. (1944). Endopsychic structure considered in terms of object relationships. In *Psychoanalytic Studies of the Personality,* pp. 82–135. London: Routledge and Kegan Paul, 1952.

———— (1952). *Psychoanalytic Studies of the Personality*. London: Routledge and Kegan Paul. Also published as *An Object Relations Theory of the Personality*. New York: Basic Books.

———— (1954). Observations on the nature of hysterical states. *British Journal of Medical Psychology* 27:105–125.

———— (1963). Synopsis of an object-relations theory of the personality. *International Journal of Psycho-Analysis* 44:224–225.

Freud, S. (1894). Unpublished draft G. *Standard Edition* 1:206–212.

———— (1905). Three essays on the theory of sexuality. *Standard Edition* 7:135–243.

Jaffe, D. S. (1968). The mechanism of projection: its dual role in object relations. *International Journal of Psycho-Analysis* 49:662–677.

Kernberg, O. (1987). Projection and projective identification: developmental and clinical aspects. In *Projection, Identification, Projective Identification,* ed. J. Sandler, pp. 93–115. Madison, CT: International Universities Press.

Klein, M. (1946). Notes on some schizoid mechanisms, *International Journal of Psycho-Analysis* 27:99–110.

Malin, A., and Grotstein, J. (1966). Projective identification in the therapeutic process. *International Journal of Psycho-Analysis* 47:26–31.

Meissner, W. W. (1980). A note on projective identification. *Journal of the American Psychoanalytic Association* 28:43–67.

———— (1987). Projection and projective identification. In *Projection, Identification, Projective Identification,* ed. J. Sandler, pp. 27–49. Madison, CT: International Universities Press.

Ogden, T. H. (1982). *Projective Identification and Therapeutic Technique*. New York: Jason Aronson.

———— (1986). *The Matrix of the Mind*. Northvale, NJ: Jason Aronson.

Racker, H. (1968). *Transference and Countertransference*. New York: International Universities Press.

Sandler, J., ed. (1987). *Projection, Identification, Projective Identification*. Madison, CT: International Universities Press.

Scharff, D. (1982). *The Sexual Relationship: An Object Relations View of Sex and the Family.* Boston: Routledge and Kegan Paul.

Scharff, D., and Scharff, J. S. (1987). *Object Relations Family Therapy.* Northvale, NJ: Jason Aronson.

_____ (1991). *Object Relations Couple Therapy.* Northvale, NJ: Jason Aronson.

Scharff, J. S., ed. (1989). *Foundations of Object Relations Family Therapy.* Northvale, NJ: Jason Aronson.

_____ (1992). *Projective and Introjective Identification and the Use of the Therapist's Self.* Northvale, NJ: Jason Aronson.

Segal, H. (1964). *Introduction to the Work of Melanie Klein.* London: Heinemann.

Sutherland, J. D. (1963). Object relations theory and the conceptual model of psychoanalysis. *British Journal of Medical Psychology* 36:109–124.

Williams, A. H. (1981). The micro environment. In *Psychotherapy with Families: An Analytic Approach,* ed. S. Box et al., pp. 105–119. London: Routledge and Kegan Paul.

Winnicott, D. W. (1958). *Collected Papers: Through Paediatrics to Psychoanalysis.* London: Tavistock, 1958, and Hogarth Press, 1975.

_____ (1960a). The theory of the parent–infant relationship. *International Journal of Psycho-Analysis* 41:585–595. Also in *The Maturational Processes and the Facilitating Environment,* pp. 37–55. London: Hogarth Press, 1965.

_____ (1960b). Ego distortion in terms of true and false self. In *The Maturational Processes and the Facilitating Environment: Studies on the Theory of Emotional Development,* pp. 140–152. London: Hogarth Press, 1965.

_____ (1968). The use of an object and relating through cross-identification. In *Playing and Reality,* pp. 86–94. New York: Basic Books.

_____ (1971). *Playing and Reality.* New York: Basic Books.

Zinner, L. (1976). The implications of projective identification for marital interaction. In *Contemporary Marriage: Structure, Dynamics, and Therapy,* ed. H. Grunebaum and J. Christ, pp. 293–308. Boston: Little, Brown. Also in *Foundations of Object Relations Family Therapy,* ed. J. S. Scharff, pp. 155–173. Northvale, NJ: Jason Aronson, 1989.

Zinner, L., and Shapiro, R. (1972). Projective identification as a mode of perception and behavior in families of adolescents. *International Journal of Psycho-Analysis* 53:523–530. Also in *Foundations of Object Relations Family Therapy,* ed. J. S. Scharff, pp. 109–126. Northvale, NJ: Jason Aronson.

II

THE THERAPIST AND THE RELATIONSHIP

Part I focused on the patients to whom object relations theories are applied. Part II looks more closely at the therapist and the clinical theorist.

Examining countertransference is not a new direction in psychotherapy. Freud began with self-examination. What is new is the comfort with which authors are beginning to discuss the therapist in relation to the patient at a deeper and more sensitive level. The object relations concepts of projective identification and containment and the self psychology understandings of empathy and selfobject function make this direction of study more fruitful.

Clinical theory is becoming a way of understanding oneself and one's patients, rather than a tool for determining the best technical intervention as a thing in itself. Perhaps because of this shift, there is an increasing recognition that different therapists need slightly different theories with their various patients. Even the same clinician may need different theories at different times. Thus, there seems to be a new tolerance for and even encompassing of divergent viewpoints.

As theoretical diversity becomes a valued necessity, there arises a dangerous temptation to use tolerance in avoidance of legitimate debate. Psychotherapists and clinical theorists are a sufficiently contentious lot, however, so there is little fear that any ecumenical tendency will go too far.

The Selfobject Function of Projective Identification

Gerald Adler and Mark W. Rhine

Gerald Adler is a pioneer in understanding and treating narcissistic and borderline disorders. He freely crosses theoretical boundaries, drawing widely from ego psychology, object relations theory, and self psychology. Throughout his work, he has emphasized the personal relationship aspects of treatment, along with transference and countertransference.

In this chapter, Adler and Rhine illustrate how both the self psychology concept — empathy — and the object relations concept — projective identification — can be useful. Because the two terms and implied theoretical approaches have slightly different nuances, using both has helped Adler and Rhine to more thoroughly understand the patient as a whole human being. Using both terms allows the therapist to more fully understand himself in relation to the patient.

Object relations theory is the study of what is within the boundary of the self, what is outside the boundary of the self, and what is in between. Between therapist and patient, hopefully, there is a certain common human relatedness, something that is increasingly attended to by the newer therapies. In this chapter, there is also consideration given to what is within the theoretical boundaries of self psychology,

*what is within the boundaries of object relations theory, and
what is in between the two—a recognition that the boundaries between self and other are semipermeable and, optimally, not entirely clear.*

*Adler's creative and human approach is reflected in
Borderline Psychopathology and Its Treatment (Adler
1985).*

Therapists' and analysts' attempts to understand their patients
are limited by theoretical frameworks. Although clinicians may try
to maintain an openness to new data, their choice of theory
restricts their ability to integrate clinical material from patients. If
their theoretical perspective fails to address issues that patients are
experiencing and discussing, the richness of the patients' communications may not be understood and used by the therapist or
analyst.

Recent interest in psychoanalytic or psychoanalytically oriented
treatment of more primitive patients—that is, those with schizoid,
borderline, or narcissistic personality disorders—has led to a
growing literature that expands both theoretical and clinical
understanding of these patients and the process of change during
treatment. However, inevitably, the contributors to this literature
tend to use frameworks that at times polarize rather than integrate
attempts to develop a broader metapsychology that encompasses
more of the data these patients provide.

In our treatment of primitive patients, we have found it
necessary to incorporate contributions from numerous workers to
conceptualize data from our patients. Sometimes we have had to
acknowledge the contradictory nature of these different frameworks. At other times, we have found that different theories,
although somewhat contradictory, struggle with the same issues in
a complementary fashion. Sometimes we have been able to
integrate aspects of these approaches to enrich our understanding
of our patients both clinically and theoretically, and to help define
further some of the curative factors in psychotherapeutic and
psychoanalytic treatment.

In this chapter, we will present the case of a patient who helped
us bridge the gap between object relations and self psychology
theories. Specifically, we determined how this patient used her

therapist* as a selfobject who accepted her projections and interpersonal provocations to help her work effectively and change in psychotherapy. Although clinicians who describe the concept of projective identification usually do not use a framework that stresses Kohut's formulations of selfobject functions and selfobject transferences (1971), we found that bringing together these concepts enriched our understanding of this patient's psychopathology, the role of projective identification in the treatment, and the nature of some curative factors in psychotherapy and psychoanalysis.

Because the specifics of this patient's treatment vividly illuminate the nature of her disorder and the quality of her interaction with her therapist (M.W.R.), we will present the clinical work in detail. In addition, because the therapist's countertransference feelings, fantasies, and responses are crucial in understanding the patient's problems and their impact on both therapist and patient, we will use a more personal style in describing the treatment and present data usually not revealed in clinical case reports.

CONTAINING THE PATIENT'S PROJECTIONS AND PROVOCATIONS

Ms. T., a 22-year-old single college graduate, was working as a file clerk when she was referred for psychoanalysis because of a chronic sense of feeling subhuman and getting no pleasure from life. She felt unable to get involved with people because she feared rejection; she was also depressed and preoccupied with suicidal thoughts.

She was the second of four children raised in a Roman Catholic family that appeared successful and happy. Her father was a hardworking small-business man who, having only a high school background himself, very much wanted all his children to be educated. The patient thought she was the "dumb one" and the black sheep of the family. Her grades were average, but the other children were all exceptional; they never understood the patient's perception of what was going on in the family. Although the father was a driven man who

---

*Although the treatment consisted of psychotherapy and psychoanalysis, we will refer to "the therapist" for simplicity when we discuss his role as both therapist and analyst.

at times had beaten her during her childhood, Ms. T. felt closer to him than to her mother, whose impulsivity and unpredictability frightened her. The patient's developmental history remained vague; the parents thought that other than her "temper" and her fear of being left behind, the patient had had a "normal" early life with unremarkable milestones and a good adjustment to school and peers. It was never clear whether they had been poor observers or whether the patient had adapted superficially and had managed to hide her inner suffering.

In her third session, Ms. T. handed me (M.W.R.) an essay and waited apprehensively as I read it:

I remember when your hand came forward, confident that when it came to rest on my arm it would touch warmth and solidness. I watched its faith extending from your body and your humanness, unaware that it would be contacting a structure that contained space itself. There was no place inside for the warmth of the sun, piercing, in the late autumn afternoon. As your hand came closer, its warmth, like the sun, dropped behind the mountains, changing in the extended shadows from red to blue to gray, till all was cold and colorless in the stillness of twilight. Your innocence was to be shattered by entering a void where it would be shivering for warmth, left gasping at the horror that God would allow anything that terrifying to exist. Wanting to warn you, my screams traveled, reverberating in the emptiness, becoming echoes debilitated in the vastness, suspended and lifeless.

I saw the confidence crash from your hand when it touched. Jolted back into your pocket, it quivered from the disgust of touching my remoteness and vileness. Without looking at your face, both of us knowing I no longer had the right, I knew of the repudiation that existed in your eyes, reflected by your hand.

There was a time when I, too, was oblivious of my alienation. You were not the first to react with disgust. There were others, invoking God as their witness, saying that I contained no soul. At first I rejected their claims. Then I watched the words come out of their mouths, terrifying in their lucidity, transform into darkness as they inundated my inner being. Patiently and continuously, they taught me to accept their gospel. Before the food could reach my mouth, they would spit in it and dash it to the ground. I learned I no longer hungered. At night when I tried to run from their truth, they would gather around my bed, tearing at me with their God. I learned there was no need for sleep. In the morning I would try to escape down the hall, only to be captured by their ropes cutting into my body. I learned that I could no longer feel. Then I returned, only to be locked out, left staring at the shafts of light emanating from inside, stopping at my feet, my body blocked by the unforgiving door. I learned I wasn't human.

Today, upon your request, I entered into your house. The rooms were torn apart in the violence of life. Glass shattered against the wall, out at my feet as I approached the back of your chair. You turned to me and I saw the blood. It streamed from your eyes, onto your face, and fell from your cheeks. Your lap was a receptacle receiving each life-giving drop. Through the redness you gazed at me and I could tell by the way you pressed the injured hand down into your lap, immersing it with blood, that you had not forgotten what I was.

Then I knew why you had commanded me before you. You needed help and there wasn't a soul on earth you could turn to. No one was to see the violent life dropping out of you. You knew my space, pleading with me to lose your pain in my gray vastness. I was the emotional vacuum swallowing your hatred and your fears, plunging them deeper until they, too, would become lost and you could be at peace with your soul.

"Is this a warning?" I asked. She nodded in agreement. I often wondered later in the treatment about the grandiosity of my determination to persevere in the face of such an admonition. Many times in the following years I wondered why I had chosen to work with this patient, questioned my ability to help her, wondered if she were treatable, and dreaded seeing her during the lengthy treatment that often left both of us confused, angry, hurt, bewildered, despairing, and feeling as if each of us was going stark raving mad because of the other.

Although Ms. T. had been referred for psychoanalysis, she wanted to come three times a week and sit up during the sessions. She stated that it was important to see my face; she was afraid she would lose control of her anger if she were lying down. In addition, she feared that if she could not see me, I would not be there for her in her head when she went back to her apartment.

However, six months later she decided to have four sessions a week and use the couch. On the one hand, she felt more rested on the couch and could talk with more emotion. On the other hand, she was more alone with her feelings; she was concerned that I would attack her and beat her up as her family did. At the same time, she said she knew that I despised her even though she had no evidence of it.

She consistently used the couch for slightly more than one year. During the next six months, she described the room becoming frighteningly smaller for her when she talked about her increasing anger at me; she also feared both feeling engulfed by and falling in love with me. Gradually, she began to experience me as "the Gestapo" and thought that I was more and more angry with her. During this period, she alternated between sitting in a chair and lying on the couch. Finally, she was too frightened to trust me not to be in a rage at her, and for the final four years of treatment, she sat up. At the time when she quit using the couch, she also became action-oriented in her treatment.

One day when she was even afraid to sit in the chair, she asked that we take a walk and hold our session outside. I attempted to explore her suggestion, her fantasies about the walk, and her motivations. She reacted with rage. She wanted to *go* for a walk, not *talk* about it. She reminded me of what I had said at the beginning of treatment when she had wondered what she was supposed to talk about, and I had replied, "It's your therapy — you can talk about whatever you'd like." She now wanted to know if I really meant what I said. Was this really *her* therapy? If so, she wanted to go for a walk. In her family, talk was cheap; they said and promised everything, but never meant a word. If this therapy were to be merely a repetition of her family experience, she was quitting. I was flooded with fantasies: To go outside was fine now during the springtime, but what if this were to continue into the winter? I imagined the opprobrium of my colleagues if I were to be seen, as well as the envy of my other patients who would all demand to go on walks. I would never be able to sit in my office again. Only later was I to understand that these fantasies of being overwhelmed, controlled, and humiliated were exactly what Ms. T. was experiencing with me. When I finally relented, we took three very pleasant walks and then returned to my office for the rest of her therapy.

The issue of walks never came up again, but I began to feel more harassed by the patient. She insisted that I open the hour by talking first; to be comfortable, she needed to determine my mood. As a child, she had been terrified when she came home from school, never knowing whether her unpredictable mother would beat her or give her cookies when she stepped into the kitchen; similarly, with me she needed to prepare herself. I was used to patients starting the hour (so I could find out where they were) and found this demand disconcerting. As usual, Ms. T. left me no choice but to comply. Initially puzzled as to what I should say, I would often pick up where the last session had ended, but as time went on I began to free associate more about what she might have done between sessions, about a song or news item I had heard on the car radio. Another problem for me was the fact that although Ms. T. would allow me to make hypotheses about the meaning of her behavior, I was not permitted to retract or change anything I had said, no matter how speculative I might have considered it. For her, these were all statements of fact. Again, this perspective derived from her family, where nothing was ever forgotten, and items from the distant past might be dredged up to insult or mortify. If you say it, you mean it, and you cannot take it back. Once when she had been genuinely impressed by my forbearance, she asked what it would take to get thrown out of treatment; by now I had learned that it was fruitless to ask for her fantasies, so I was obliged to reply. I stated that I guessed she could say anything, but that if she were to wreck my office, I wouldn't put up with it. She was furious: Since I had had this thought about her, it meant that she was capable of such an outrage; furthermore, I expected it of her and she would have to do it. Understandably, I became terrified of saying anything else (again, I later realized that this was exactly what was frightening her); to her, talking was not, as it was to me, trial action; it was the equivalent of action. Furthermore, talking was of no use if it did not result in action.

On another occasion, having decided to quit therapy, Ms. T. demanded that I give her medical records to her. We became embroiled in another fight, this time about whose records they were. I felt invaded and violated; they were my records, because I had written them. She countered — just as baffled by my posture as I was by hers — that they were hers, since they were about her. I had fantasies about how she would use the records to embarrass me, but eventually I gave them to her. She quit therapy for only a few days, and a month later she returned the records to me, having carried them in the trunk of her car without ever looking at them. She apologized for a minute water stain on the manila folder. This apology showed another side of her, a tremendous compassion for me and for what was mine. Interestingly, although I felt harassed by her in the office, she had a great respect for my time and my private life, and she rarely intruded on it. She asked the same consideration from me, and once became enraged at me early in the treatment when she had a dream in which I appeared. She told me in no uncertain terms to keep out of her dreams in the future.

As time went on, the patient increasingly berated and harassed me. She belittled my competency, pointing out that she was no better than when she started. These complaints were quite painful to me, but I initially responded with forbearance. I consoled myself that she needed to attack and humiliate me and that I should not interfere with the transference, but as her behavior continued, I wondered if it would ever stop. I did not question my technique, but my patient eventually did. She would ask how I felt about her remarks. I would respond, for example, that I felt sorry she held me in such contempt. Or she would threaten to quit therapy and ask how that made me feel. I would often reply, as neutrally as possible, that although I would like for her to continue, I would respect her decision about what was best for her. After such replies, she would then ask, "How does it *really* make you feel?" Again and again I replied with some platitude, which I honestly thought was what I was experiencing, but the patient knew better. Her attacks increased until one day, exasperated, I finally pleaded that she was being unfair, that I might well have shortcomings that disappointed her, but that she was leaving out all the things that I was doing right, and that it was quite painful to be berated continuously. Her response surprised me: She hastened to reassure me that it wasn't *me* she was berating, it was *herself;* she needed to know what a human being would feel and do under such attack; she needed me to speak for a part of her that had never spoken up, that was terrified and didn't know how to be human. She related it to a part of her that had endured beatings and humiliation from her parents in silence.

Much of the therapy that followed consisted of my attempts to be as honest as possible about what was going on within me. My negative feelings toward the patient made this effort particularly difficult. I was aware of her vulnerability and felt guilty about my anger. I began to feel inhuman myself as I became aware of my guilt about how much I detested this anguished human being, and I felt like a sadistic Nazi torturer. I therefore denied my hatred of her, although she was, of course, well aware of it because I expressed it indirectly. It was a significant moment when I could finally admit to her how much I hated her when she belittled and attacked me and how much I dreaded her hour. Rather than disintegrating as I had feared, she was relieved that I was finally being honest. Not long afterward, she hesitatingly told me about her eight-year history of bulimia, a symptom so disgusting that she was certain I would be repelled. She needed to know that I was truly in touch with my feelings and not afraid to express them; only then could she tell me of the bulimia. If I were disgusted, as she anticipated, she needed me to be truthful about it. She noted that we had both survived my anger and hers, although she had thought we would both disappear.

She told me that everyone in her family was "perfect." They never acknowledged any errors or limitations and repeatedly denied what they were feeling. It was important to her to find out if I believed that I was perfect. She would then show me that I was not, as part of learning what it was like to be human, that is, imperfect. She was constantly frantic about whether her parents would accept her. She could never understand what she had done to make her capricious mother angry. It was crucial for her to understand that with me. She pleaded, "Just tell me that *something* is going on. If you don't want to tell me what it is, you don't have to."

She never knew who she was, even when performing mundane tasks. She was a chameleon, constantly trying to discover what would please her mother and her therapist. (In retrospect, I realized how much I had striven to discover what would satisfy *her.*) She had to try a number of personalities to please her mother, hoping that her mother wouldn't realize that she was still the same person. She became whomever she was expected to be, hence her response to my remark about her wrecking my office. Her own hatred terrified her; she believed that it was "not-me," yet knew it was a part of her. She would sit up through the night, dissociated, screaming, her mind in "85,000 parts," pleading, "Please don't destroy me for having done wrong." It was crucial, she implored, that she know what I, a human being she respected, felt and thought. I was touched and amazed to hear this comment, for by this time I was convinced that I was inhuman myself, since I felt cruel, callous, and sadistic. When she complained, "You are not helping me," she meant, "I don't know how you are feeling." When she left town for a consultation with a nationally known expert, arranged by her parents, who were becoming as discouraged as she was with her seeming lack of progress, my initial, rather neutral, reaction of pleasure that we might get some help with our impasse was not useful to her. But when I could finally acknowledge my envy of the consultant who knew more than I, my sense of inferiority at not being enough for the patient, and my anger at her for leaving me (both for the consultation and, perhaps, to find a new therapist), she found this knowledge quite helpful. She needed to know that it was alright to say such things, that humans had such feelings.

As time passed, Ms. T.'s therapy became almost another personal analysis for me, as I allowed myself to free associate in her presence. I was surprised that she didn't hurt me or take advantage of me. I was able to get in touch with how painful I found her threats of leaving and how my "neutral" position (that she had to do whatever she thought was in her best interest) was mere camouflage. I acknowledged to her that I was ashamed of my feelings, that they didn't seem professional, and that I did not want her to leave. She responded that she loved me and could tell me so, now that she knew my feelings; otherwise she would have to forget me. Now she could leave and remember me. She needed to know how she affected people; how did she drive them away? Her only means was to find out how she made me feel, but I often didn't know how I felt. When earlier in treatment I said that I cared for her, she had experienced it as mere words, but now I was being candid with her. She had felt that she was in quicksand at times, and I had just wanted to talk to her about it or give her some interpretation. She needed me as a sounding board: How did she make me feel; how would I like to be treated? This input helped her see how she was feeling. She also needed to have me figure out why I repeatedly seemed to hurt her. When I could finally admit that I often seemed to hurt her in retaliation for her hurting me and that at other times I detested her neediness, which threatened to devour me, she hugged me and told me that I was one of the most beautiful men she had ever known.

She then declared that in addition to my true feelings, she needed to hear my perspective. She taught me how to treat her, telling me that if I were feeling that something was a crisis, I should be aware that she was probably feeling that herself; it was then helpful for her to be told that it might not be a crisis—she didn't know that. It was useful to her to realize that she didn't have to act on a feeling. She always thought that she had to kill herself because she was feeling suicidal; only toward the end of therapy did she realize that a feeling was not a requirement to act. She taught me that if I felt the need to act, I should recognize her sense of urgency and immediacy. I should then point out that she did not necessarily want to do what she said, and she could then reflect. Her first human contact with me as someone not godlike and infallible was when she learned that I had limits, at the time I told her what it would take for her to be thrown out of therapy; she was sorry to learn that, but it gave her a clearer concept of me.

In the later phase of treatment, Ms. T. learned to deal further with the lack of perfection in herself and in me. My increasing ability to talk about my own perfectionistic needs and how I often felt inadequate for her, my pain at not being able to alleviate her suffering or to permit her to feel safe with me, and my anger when she exposed my inadequacy enabled her to clarify how she was feeling. Eventually, after many months of Sturm and Drang, which culminated about six and one-half years of treatment, she was able to terminate, feeling she could see both of us no longer as parts but as whole human beings with our respective strengths and weaknesses. Typically, she brought up termination by remarking that I no longer seemed to need her and that she could now move on. I experienced this statement as a playful acknowledgment of our interaction over the years which I did not question or interpret. We had an appropriate period to say good-bye, with much mutual sadness.

Discussion

This clinical material can be used to discuss many issues about the diagnosis and treatment of severely disturbed patients. We will focus here on how the patient used her therapist as a selfobject who allowed projective identification to flourish as a creative experience, and the implications from these data for understanding some of the curative factors in psychotherapy and psychoanalysis. However, this patient's treatment can be viewed in many ways that also illuminate an understanding of the interaction and the process of change that occurred. The therapist's sensitivity to this patient's need for a flexible, nondefensive therapist who could be in touch with her pain helped her acknowledge it, bear it, and put it into perspective (Semrad 1969). His ability to meet her level of regression (Myerson 1964, 1976) and maintain an empathic stance in the face of her devaluation, rage, pain, and longings (Adler 1985) were significant factors in her capacity to grow. We believe that our emphasis on the selfobject function of projective identification, which we shall also relate to transitional phenomena, can add to our understanding of the process of change in treatment.

In the essay she brought to her third session, Ms. T. predicted the course of the treatment to follow. She defined the therapist's expectation of finding his patient a warm, solid person with a self, and his beginning sense of confidence and faith. Instead, she believed that he would find a cold void that could freeze and possibly destroy his own warmth. Her inner space consisted of emptiness, worthlessness, terror, and feelings of annihilation, violence, and death, and she expected to see her therapist feel repulsed, repudiated, and rejected in return. She then described her understanding of the childhood origins of her difficulties: She had felt rejected by the important people in her life. At first she repudiated their views of her, but then she succumbed. She believed that there was no escape except to withdraw or to be a false self. In therapy she entered a new situation, but saw violence as well as blood in her therapist's face, with his lap a receptacle for each "life-giving drop." Yet her therapist did not forget what she was, that is, a malevolent, destructive person. She then described why he wanted to see her: He needed her because he had his own pain, hatred, and fears.

We thought that in her essay the patient was defining the severity of her emotional disorder, how she coped with it, and the treatment she needed if she were to grow. She had retreated to a schizoid position, superficially complying to survive. A false self covered enormous pain, emptiness, and rage. She thus was describing herself as someone in the severe schizoid-to-borderline part of the continuum that we conceptualize (Adler 1985) as extending from psychotic through borderline, then narcissistic personality, to neurotic disorders. She was also defining the complex mechanism of projective identification that she used, as well as her exquisite sensitivity and compassion. She warned her therapist about what he would go through with her, and saw his repudiation and rage as well as his emotional pain.

How much of what she saw as the therapist's repudiation, rage, and pain was her finely tuned perception and capacity to cogently observe what was latently present in the therapist? Or how much of it was a defensive manifestation of projective identification, which to exist must have a participatory part involving a patient–therapist interaction? In her formulation, her blood and her therapist's blood would mix, that is, both would experience unbearably murderous feelings of intermingled hatred. What her therapist would do with his emotional pain and hatred, which at the same time was hers, would determine the outcome of the treatment and the possibility of her emergence from a schizoid and false self-existence. In addition to bearing and trying to understand the patient's and his own pain, can the therapist accept the ambiguity of the situation and not rapidly have to differentiate their pain and rage? Can he also understand that she requires a person to tolerate this pain and ambiguity without retaliating, and without interpreting aspects of it prematurely? The central question in this view of the treatment is whether the therapist can function as a selfobject for her, whether he can accept, bear, contain, and help her integrate intolerable aspects of herself as she involves him in projective identification.

To discuss the changes made by the patient in her treatment, we will first define and describe the concepts of projective identification and the selfobject that we use in our theoretical framework.

PROJECTIVE IDENTIFICATION

The term *projective identification* was first used by Melanie Klein (1952). Since then, many contributors have clarified the concept and defined it in detail. Kernberg (1975) described the projection onto the other person of parts of the self that a person wants either to preserve or get rid of. The person who projects then must maintain a relationship with the other person to control those projected parts through controlling that person. Other workers (e.g., Grotstein 1981, Malin and Grotstein 1966, Morrison 1986, Ogden 1979, Shapiro 1978, 1982a, 1982b, Zinner and Shapiro 1972) emphasized the interpersonal component of projective identification first noted by Bion (1962). In these authors' association of projection with interpersonal provocation, the projector attempts to induce in the receiver the behavior that is consistent with the projected aspect. It is especially important for the receiver of the projection to have a part of himself or herself that can be provoked (Shapiro et al. 1977). For the part of the receiver to be readily provocable, it must be conflictual, or unacceptable, and therefore repressed, split off, or repudiated by the receiver.

Since the person who projects and provokes has found a ready target in a receiver whose feelings are certain to resonate with the feelings or issues projected and provoked, the outcome depends on the way the receiver of the projection contains (Bion 1962) or responds to the projection. For example, when patients project their rage as part of a self-representation or introject and provoke their therapists to kill them, therapists who are aware of these feelings will certainly experience the rage. However, if the expressions of rage toward the patients consist of some annoyed and curt comments at the height of the patients' most intense provocations, the projections are relatively successfully contained. Ideally, rage is best contained through the capacity to bear and interpret it; this successful containment modifies the projections.

Once contained, projective identification then reinternalizes the now-modified projected part so that it can be "assimilated" by the projector (Ogden 1979, Shapiro 1982b), who takes it back through introjective identification. The reinternalization process, as part of the entire experience with projective identification, provides the opportunity for change in internal structure in psychotherapy and psychoanalysis.

Projective identification is not only a pathological defense in primitive patients. It is ubiquitous in everyone, and is especially manifest in interpersonal situations with an ill-defined structure. For example, Bion (1961) described the emergence of projective identification in groups where the work task is lost. There is also a literature that defines projective identification in couples (Morrison 1986) and families (Zinner and Shapiro 1972). What distinguishes projective identification in healthier people is their greater capacity to reality test and "own" the projection, as well as the fact that the projection is less closely linked with primitive impulses and conflicts. At its highest level, projective identification may be related to empathy.

SELFOBJECTS

We will now integrate some relevant concepts of Kohut's self psychology with the concept of projective identification. A central construct in Kohut's (1971, 1977, 1984) work is the selfobject, which he defined as someone who performs a needed function for another person and is experienced, at the same time, as a part of the person requiring the function. Although Kohut first employed the concept to describe the incompleteness issues of patients with narcissistic personality disorders who formed selfobject transferences in therapy and analysis, he later defined the selfobject needs of all people. Narcissistic patients require selfobjects largely in the area of their feelings of low self-esteem. In fact, their establishment of relatively stable selfobject transferences as the major transference, especially for self-esteem regulation, defines the narcissistic personality disorder in Kohut's formulations. Kohut also described the use of selfobjects by all people throughout life, stating that as they develop greater maturity, they choose more mature selfobjects. In addition, self-esteem regulation is not the major issue in the selfobject needs of mature people.

PROJECTIVE IDENTIFICATION AS A SELFOBJECT FUNCTION

The self psychology literature has not systematically delineated the many selfobject functions possible between self and selfobject. Wolf (1980) has described the variety of selfobject needs of people along a developmental continuum. Although the selfobject function of projective identification was not specifically mentioned in his paper, he did define the selfobject role of the therapist or analyst as an antagonist in treatment. Since Wolf did not work in a framework using contributions from the object relations literature, he did not relate the antagonist selfobject role specifically to the projection, provocation, and reinternalization aspects of projective identification that seem to have contributed significantly to the interaction he describes. The use that patients make of their therapists and analysts can certainly include the bearing and containment of projective identification as an important selfobject function provided by therapists and analysts.

One conceptual problem with Kohut's self psychology that makes it more difficult to integrate with object-relations theory relates to his use of transmuting internalization as a major mechanism for taking in aspects of the other person. Transmuting internalization specifically describes the internalization of *functions* rather than introjects or object representations. However, projective identification is usually conceptualized to mean the projection of affects associated with a self- or object representation. Thus, in this regard, Kohut's theory would not readily allow for a view that defines the details of what is projected, provoked, contained, and reintrojected beyond its specific functions, although Grotstein (1981) and Morrison (1986) have described the role of projective identification in defining the relationship of the self to its self-objects. Yet Kohut's theory helps clarify the need for the therapist or analyst to function as a selfobject to bear, to contain, and, when appropriate, to analyze the experience of projective identification.

One could argue that there is a basic incompatibility in attempting to bring together projective identification, which uses a theoretical framework involving the primacy of drives, and self psychology, which stresses the frustration of the needs of the child and the adult. However, in this chapter, we are defining the *clinical utility* of joining these two frameworks. We also wish to note Ogden's (1979) observation that projective identification is a fantasy that is projected, followed by an interpersonal interaction. The emphasis on fantasy helps bridge the gap between two seemingly incompatible frameworks and makes less crucial the role of drives and impulses in them.

IMPLICATIONS FOR THERAPY

Much of Ms. T.'s treatment can be explained by examining it from a variety of vantage points. We have chosen to discuss her use of projective identification and its selfobject function to amplify some aspects of therapeutic change. At the point of significant regression in her treatment, certain interactions between her and her therapist suggested the existence of projective identification. Her insistent wish to go for a walk aroused intense feelings in her therapist, who felt overwhelmed, controlled, and humiliated. Only later in the therapy did he learn that the patient had identical feelings. The insistent quality of her requests and demands indicated the nature of the process. And the therapist's fantasies and impulses, which he later learned were the same as the patient's, were his responses to her projections and provocations.

As treatment continued, the intensity of the provocations increased, involving the patient's escalating attacks on the therapist's competence. It was only when the therapist could acknowledge, at the patient's insistence, what he *really* felt, that therapy moved ahead significantly. When the therapist could painfully and with shame define his hate, helplessness, and despair, the patient could then clarify that she was not berating the therapist, but rather herself. In essence, she was explaining that she had projected important parts of herself onto the therapist and had provoked him to feel those feelings in himself that related to those parts of herself, so that she could learn about those parts. Until then, those parts of herself had been buried and silent. In our analysis of this material, we believe that the patient was explaining that she needed her therapist to function as a selfobject who would accept her projections and provocations and then put into words the feelings elicited in him as an aspect of his selfobject function. The fact that the therapist would verbalize his feelings nonsadistically instead of acting on them destructively implies that he was also containing the projections as part of his self-object function. This process then allowed the patient to reinternalize what she needed from the experience, helping her ultimately to acknowledge and "own" feelings associated with the parts of herself that had been buried. As part of the transmuting internalization aspect of the process, she internalized not only a modified part of herself but also a part of the therapist's function in which he helped her modify the projection through his containment (Dan H. Buie, personal communication, 1986).

Our definition of the selfobject needs of this specific patient, which required the therapist to put into words what he was experiencing in response to his interaction with her, should not be seen as our advocacy of such a therapeutic technique with all patients. This patient was a schizoid woman with a false self who engaged her therapist in the way she needed to become alive. We believe that the treatment would have been stalemated if the therapist had not responded as he did. The more honest he could be in a nonsadistic way about his responses to her, the more alive she became, and the greater was her capacity to relate to him as a whole person who could love and show concern and compassion.

However, as the therapist revealed, the task for him was enormously painful. It meant acknowledging both to himself and to the patient aspects of himself that aroused guilt and shame and that he had repudiated. In effect, his growing capacity to acknowledge those unacceptable feelings and parts of himself allowed her to develop similar capacities in herself. She gradually became a whole person by integrating affects with the self-representations, object representations, and introjects that either were tenuously present or were hidden or split off within her. These were combined with the modified reinternalized projections as well as with new introjects and functions internalized from her interaction with her therapist in the experience of his containment of her projections and provocations; ultimately she developed a much more cohesive self.

The final phase of Ms. T.'s treatment dealt with her and her therapist's needs for perfection. At that point, the schizoid and false self issues appeared significantly resolved; she was able to acknowledge to the therapist what she felt and who she was. The perfectionist issues seem related to the narcissistic personality disorder problems of grandiosity and self-worth. In her characteristic fashion, she terminated when she felt that her therapist no longer seemed to need her. We believe that at this point the patient was using an ambiguous aspect of projective identification in which she left unclear how much she was projecting and how much she still saw as arising from her therapist's needs. The therapist chose not to interpret this ambiguity. He believed that she was demonstrating her comfort with her playfulness and sense of humor by telling him that she did not need him any longer.

IMPLICATIONS FOR CURATIVE FACTORS

That therapists and analysts must survive the rage and devouring orality of borderline patients has been well described in the psychoanalytic literature (Adler 1985, Frosch 1970, Kernberg 1975, Winnicott 1969). The same experience can also be viewed from the perspective of projective identification. From this perspective, the patient's projections and interpersonal provocations are contained by the therapist; the modifications of the projections are then reintrojected by the patient, leading to structural change in treatment. Rather than a dreaded aspect of psychotherapy, the therapeutic work with the inevitable experience of projective identification becomes a core aspect of the curative process in treatment, and the role of the therapist as someone who allows it to occur, contains it, and appropriately analyzes it defines the self-object function of the therapist.

Another aspect of projective identification is its relationship to transitional phenomena (Adler, 1989). The transitional space that Winnicott (1953) defined with the small child, in which spontaneity, illusion, play, and creativity can occur, can also be applied to adults, including their treatment. Psychoanalysis and many psychotherapies are structured to allow for ambiguity and a space between participants that leaves unanswered how much emanates from the therapist and how much from the patient, and how much is related to the past and how much to the present. In psychoanalysis, the use of the couch, free association, and the analyst's style of responding to maintain the ambiguity foster the transitional space. As Winnicott described, the mother does not ask the small child with the transitional object: Did you provide it or was it given to you? In clinical situations where such ambiguity is allowed, both transitional phenomena and constructive projective identification can flourish and are almost identical; the one difference is the interpersonal provocative aspect of projective identification. In contrast, with transitional phenomena the patient's only wish is for the therapist to allow the creative process and to not destroy the transitional space between them. With destructive projective identification, the increasing intensity of the interpersonal provocation makes it much more difficult for the therapist or analyst to contain the projection and not be provoked into a destructive countertransference response. The interaction between patient and therapist, and the therapist's capacity to bear and ultimately to analyze it, can determine to what extent projective identification is a creative or destructive experience in psychotherapy and psychoanalysis. Both transitional phenomena and the creative use of projective identification can facilitate significant structural change in the patient.

With more disturbed patients, such as the one discussed here, aspects of the treatment situation that allow ambiguity sometimes must be modified by the therapist. These patients may be unable to tolerate, without clarification or interpretation, a response from the therapist that leaves ambiguity about how much emanates from each person. However, therapists who are totally honest with themselves often have doubts about how much belongs to them and how much to their patients. It is an unending task for therapists to attempt to be in touch with repudiated aspects of their own personalities as well as the complexities of who is doing what to whom in the charged interactions in psychoanalysis or psychotherapy. Thus, when therapists feel compelled to clarify or interpret, they do so based on what they *think* is happening. To the degree that they can acknowledge to themselves a lack of certainty, they can say something to their patients that allows for the possibility that they may not be correct. That is, there is something ambiguous or uncertain in their own minds about what is happening, even when they attempt to clarify issues about how much is transference and how much is the real relationship. For example, patients may ask whether their therapists are angry in a situation where therapists feel that a response is required. Therapists who believe that they are not angry at their patients can state that they are *not aware* of being angry. This response maintains the possibility that they *could* be angry and not know it. The ambiguity and transitional space are thus preserved between therapists and patients. In contrast, a response of certainty from therapists that they are not angry can destroy the transitional space. The therapist's stance of certainty (Adler, 1989) is similar to that examined in Shapiro's work (1982b) with families, in which he described pathological certainty manifested in some disturbed families as a lack of curiosity.

Ms. T.'s therapist learned to respond with honesty to her requests for information about his responses to her. On the one hand, this response removed some of the ambiguity that we associate with the technical handling of the treatment that allows the transference to flourish in healthier patients. The therapist's role with this patient provided the selfobject function of allowing the creative use of projective identification that she required. On the other hand, the therapist's response retained the aspect of ambiguity and uncertainty for the therapist, which he experienced as part of his countertransference response. It was not always clear to him who was doing what to whom and whether both of them could survive the treatment situation. He did not attempt to interpret what he thought came from him and what came from the patient in projective identification until she herself made those distinctions. He also did not try to remove the ambiguity of her termination, which she explained as her therapist not needing her anymore. Thus we believe that ambiguity in the therapeutic situation exists along a continuum; the degree to which it is allowed to remain in the treatment setting is based on the patient's health and capacity to use different degrees of ambiguity creatively. With active projective identification, the therapist's capacity to contain the experience of ambiguity, which the patient may be projecting, is another aspect of the selfobject function.

We have discussed only a sector of the many curative factors involved in successful treatment. We did not explore the importance of such issues as transference and its interpretation, the quality of the real relationship in successful treatment, or the therapist's capacity to respond flexibly and empathically to the level of the patient's regression. However, there is a connection between those areas and the selfobject function of projective identification, the maintenance of transitional space in treatment, and the importance of ambiguity and uncertainty. In fact, we believe that a treatment setting that allows transitional phenomena, creative projective identification, and an analyzable transference requires a milieu in which ambiguity and uncertainty are experienced by both parties. Change that occurs in successful treatment is accompanied by the relatively constant uncertainty that is never fully clarified: how much comes from the therapist, how much from the patient, how much from the past and how much from the present, how much is transference and how much is the real relationship.

REFERENCES

Adler, G. (1985). *Borderline Psychopathology and Its Treatment*. New York: Jason Aronson.

———— (1989). Transitional phenomena, projective identification, and the essential ambiguity of the psychoanalytic situation. *Psychoanalytic Quarterly* 58:81–104.

Bion, W. R. (1961). *Experiences in Groups and Other Papers*. New York: Basic Books.

———— (1962). A theory of thinking. In *Second Thoughts: Selected Papers on Psychoanalysis,* pp. 110–119. New York: Jason Aronson, 1967.

Frosch, J. (1970). Psychoanalytic considerations of the psychotic character. *Journal of the American Psychoanalytic Association* 18:24–50.

Grotstein, J. S. (1981). *Splitting and Projective Identification*. New York: Jason Aronson.

Kernberg, O. F. (1975). *Borderline Conditions and Pathological Narcissism.* New York: Jason Aronson.

Klein, M. (1952). Notes on some schizoid mechanisms. In *Developments in Psycho-analysis,* ed. J. Riviere, pp. 292–320. London: Hogarth Press.

Kohut, H. (1971). *The Analysis of the Self: A Systematic Approach to the Psychoanalytic Treatment of Narcissistic Personality Disorders.* New York: International Universities Press.

_____ (1977). *The Restoration of the Self.* New York: International Universities Press.

_____ (1984). *How Does Analysis Cure?* Chicago: University of Chicago Press.

Malin, A., and Grotstein, J. S. (1966). Projective identification in the therapeutic process. *International Journal of Psycho-Analysis* 47:26–31.

Morrison, A. P. (1986). On projective identification in couples' groups. *International Journal of Group Psychotherapy* 36:55–73.

Myerson, P. G. (1964). *Discussion of "The theory of therapy in relation to a developmental model of the psychic apparatus" by E. R. Zetzel.* Paper presented at the meeting of the Boston Psychoanalytic Society and Institute, Boston, MA, January.

_____ (1976). *The level of regression and the therapeutic work.* Paper presented at the 11th Annual Tufts Symposium on Psychotherapy, Boston, MA, April.

Ogden, T. H. (1979). On projective identification. *International Journal of Psycho-Analysis* 60:357–373.

Semrad, E. V. (1969). *Teaching Psychotherapy of Psychotic Patients: Supervision of Beginning Residents in the "Clinical Approach."* New York: Grune & Stratton.

Shapiro, E. R. (1978). The psychodynamics and developmental psychology of the borderline patient: a review of the literature. *American Journal of Psychiatry* 135:1305–1315.

_____ (1982a). The holding environment and family therapy with acting out adolescents. *International Journal of Psychoanalytic Psychotherapy* 9:209–226.

_____ (1982b). On curiosity: intrapsychic and interpersonal boundary formation in family life. *International Journal of Family Psychiatry* 3:69–89.

Shapiro, E. R., Shapiro, R. L., Zinner, J., and Berkowitz, D. A. (1977). The borderline ego and the working alliance: indications for family and individual treatment in adolescence. *International Journal of Psycho-Analysis* 58:77–87.

Winnicott, D. W. (1953). Transitional objects and transitional phenom-
ena. In *Collected Papers: Through Paediatrics to Psycho-Analysis,*
pp. 229–242. New York: Basic Books, 1958.
————— (1969). The use of an object. *International Journal of Psycho-
Analysis* 50:711–716.
Wolf, E. S. (1980). On the developmental line of selfobject relations. In
Advances in Self Psychology, ed. A. Goldberg, pp. 117–135. New
York: International Universities Press.
Zinner, J., and Shapiro, R. L. (1972). Projective identification as a mode
of perception and behaviour in families of adolescents. *International
Journal of Psycho-Analysis* 53:523–530.

The Containing Function and the Analyst's Projective Identification

N. Gregory Hamilton

This chapter extends the idea of projective identification further by applying it to the everyday function of the psychoanalyst and even to the context or frame in which he or she works. Those who equate projective identification with severe pathology and intense and obvious affects may be uneasy with this application. The notion that a psychoanalyst would have an active, if sometimes unconscious, intention to influence or to insinuate an aspect of his or her own self-experience into the patient, even while adopting a neutral and interpretive stance, goes further in the direction of acknowledging that the therapist is always an active presence, even when he or she is quiet.

In discussions of the container and contained (Bion 1962), the patient's projective identification has been emphasized as central (Hamilton 1988). Concerning the psychoanalyst's role, introjection and modulated, integrated thinking have been considered primary. The place of the psychoanalyst's projective identification in containing has been implied, but not delineated in detail. This chapter describes the analyst's normal and necessary projective identification as part of his or her containing function. How this viewpoint compares to previous understandings of the analytic relationship is briefly discussed.

THE CONTAINER AND THE CONTAINED

Bion (1957) initially elaborated his concept of the container and the contained in regard to psychotic patients; he also clearly stated that projective identification and containing apply to normal adults (Bion 1959), as well as to children. In his view, infants become overwhelmed by extreme and unmodulated affects. They project these feelings, along with split-off self-images and object images, into the parent. The attentive parent takes in these projected aspects, modulates them, transforms them, gives them meaning, and returns them to the baby in a form that can be assimilated. The child eventually internalizes this process and learns to perform his own containing function. What the child receives back is not only the contained and transformed contents, but the very process of containing that the parent has performed for him.

In psychoanalysis, the framework of quiet listening, uninterrupted hours, and modulated and interested responses provides a containing function. There need be no break from the interpretive mode for this to take place. The analyst listens, reflects, and formulates an interpretation, thereby transforming and giving meaning to what he has heard. This takes place both with fairly well-integrated neurotic patients and those who are more chaotic.

PROJECTIVE IDENTIFICATION

As did Klein (1946), Bion (1957) considered projective identification to be the mental mechanism whereby the subject attributes an aspect of the self and attendant affects to the object, while retaining some conscious or unconscious awareness that the projected aspect pertains to the self. He described in graphic and concrete terms this phenomenon whereby the patient may split off an unwanted persecutory or demonic aspect, project it into the object, then try to control it in the container. In the most extreme examples, the subject attempts to get under the object's skin, invade his body cavities, infiltrate his tissues, take over control. The analyst thereby becomes the container of split-off part self-representations and object representations for the patient. Thus, projective identification is the mode by which what is contained passes from the subject to the object.

Although the concept of projective identification has been widely elaborated, the above definition corresponds with Klein's (1946) original usage and is compatible with other conceptualizations (Adler 1986, Bion 1957, Gabbard 1986, Grotstein 1981, Hamilton 1986, 1988, 1989, Kernberg 1965, Malin and Grotstein 1966, Ogden 1979, Rosenfeld 1983, Sandler 1987, Spillius 1983).

Klein considered projective identification to be an internal, mental phenomenon. Subsequently, interpersonal, as well as intrapsychic, projective identification has been discussed. Building on Bion's work, Ogden (1979, 1982) pointed out that while the patient internally attributes aspects of the self to the object, he behaves in such a way as to elicit from the analyst the experience of "pressure to think, feel, and behave in a manner congruent with the projection" (Ogden 1979, p. 12). He conceptualized the intrapsychic and interpersonal processes as necessary and stated, "Projective identification does not exist where there is no interaction between projector and recipient" (p. 14). Ogden made an important contribution by emphasizing the interpersonal, as well as intrapsychic. Other authors (Hamilton 1986, 1988, 1989, Sandler 1987), however, have discussed projective identification in terms which allow for a distinction between the internal and external. For these authors, mental and social projective identification are parallel and often simultaneous, but not necessarily equivalent. If one assumes that emotions cannot cross personal boundaries without behavioral communications as an intermediary, they are at least theoretically distinguishable. That is, the subject in his own private thoughts may wish to, and even try to, insinuate an aspect of himself into the other, but may not behave in such a way that the other person has any conscious or unconscious awareness of the subject's projected aspects. This definition has the benefit of being dependent only on the subject's intentions, and not necessarily on his overt behavior or on the recipient's openness to influence. An example of intrapsychic projective identification without a concomitant external, interpersonal process has been provided in previous publications (Hamilton 1986, 1989).

Although Klein (1946, 1952) originally discussed projective identification in terms of both good and bad aspects of the self, clinical papers have often emphasized projective identification of destructive aspects and associated aggressive drives (Spillius 1983). Several authors have provided a corrective for this one-sided focus, pointing out that benign aspects of the self and attendant loving feelings can be involved (Grotstein 1981, Hamilton 1986, 1988, Ogden 1982). This chapter deals primarily with the projective identification of competent and creative aspects of the self.

Many authors have observed that this mental mechanism is used by normal or neurotic patients (Adler and Rhine 1988, Grotstein 1981, Hamilton 1988, Ogden 1979) and may play a necessary part in all communication (Bion 1959, Grinberg 1965) and in empathy (Sandler 1987). The opposing viewpoint is expressed by Meissner (1980) and Kernberg (1987).

THE CONTAINING FUNCTION AS PROJECTIVE IDENTIFICATION

As container, the analyst, according to Bion's formulation, is not a passive recipient of the patient's projective identification. In his or her analytic reverie (Bion 1967), he reflects upon and gives meaning to the projections he has introjected. He then offers his understanding to the patient in the form of an interpretation. The patient reintrojects the now transformed aspects of himself and modifies his internal self-images with this new understanding. Bion did not emphasize the analyst's projective identification. I am elaborating his theory by making explicit that just as what the therapist introjects from the patient is the patient's projective identification, what the patient introjects from the analyst is the analyst's projective identification. What is conveyed to the patient is both the transformed, original projection from the patient and an aspect of the analyst's self—the containing aspect of the analyst, the analyzing function itself—which he wishes, however benignly and gently, to insinuate into the patient so as to influence him.

Money-Kyrle (1956) suggested, concerning the analyst's transient identification with the patient, that "when all is going well, this identification seems to oscillate between its introjective and projective forms" (p. 364). While he did not refer specifically to the container concept, his comment clearly implies that the analyst's normal projective identification plays a role in therapeutic endeavors.

As an example, Pick (1985) commented in relation to a disturbing patient, "I needed to work through the experience of being an overwhelmed mother threatened with disintegration by an interaction with the baby. . . . This, in my view, enabled me to help the patient to feel that these contradictory intense feelings could be endured" (p. 164). This being able to "help the patient to feel" that they can endure, as the analyst endures, suggests a benign and normal projective identification on the analyst's part. As an element of her containing function, the analyst attributes her own enduring self-image to the patient, while retaining it as her own, and behaves in such a way as to elicit congruent self-images and attitudes in the analysand.

Pick's fine paper on working through in the countertransference makes explicit attitudes which can be seen throughout the literature. As Hans Loewald (1986) has said, "In analyzing patients who have chosen to come to us, we choose to enter into their psychodynamics and conflicts and archaic mental states and recognize in them variations of our own" (p. 286). Jaffe, referring to Noy (1984) in his discussion of the analyst's empathy, states that for empathy to function, the analyst must have "a tendency to project oneself into the self of others" (Jaffe 1986, p. 231).

CLINICAL EXAMPLE: THE THERAPIST CONTAINING HIS OWN ANXIETY

Rather than further elaborating such examples, I will provide an illustration with more detail. Since it is the therapist's projective identification while containing which is being discussed, the following vignette[1] will report more of his thinking than is common in such reports.

A 34-year-old woman, Ms. A., came to her appointments day after day appearing anxious and exhausted. She had a demanding job with a large international trading company and was a single parent. In her early 20s, she had had a brief, but severe depression and required a two-week hospitalization. She had not needed medication or hospitalization since that time, despite her considerable anxiety and frequent depressions. One session she looked particularly fatigued. She began the hour describing how overwhelmed and harried she was. She felt so distraught she feared she was on the verge of a psychotic episode—perhaps she needed to go into the hospital, she said. She wanted to give up and have someone take care of her.

"I am very upset, and I wish you would talk to me a little more."

The psychotherapist felt concerned that his patient might have a psychotic regression or become suicidal. As he listened quietly, he mulled over his anxieties about the patient. In the space of a few moments, he thought that if he were to hospitalize her, as she suggested, or give her medication or even break with his technique by chatting with her, he would implicitly be agreeing with her that neither he nor she could tolerate her affects. He would be acting on his own countertransference anxiety rather than using it constructively. He remembered that he considered this patient a sound and resourceful woman who could tolerate the anxiety of and benefit from analytic work. He assumed that he was tempted to break with his technique because the patient had elicited in him the kind of anxiety she experienced. He decided that he needed to contain and modulate his own affects and let the patient know that he had heard her. He recalled from earlier times his own analyst's words, supervisor's comments, discussions with colleagues, fragments of papers, and more recent discussions of the containing concept. He consciously assumed that if he contained the anxiety his patient elicited in him, she in turn would eventually internalize his containing function. He did not have the more scientifically correct thought that she would not actually internalize his containing function, but that his analyzing behavior would lead to the activation of her potentially available, or at least partially developed, self-containing function. His thought at that moment was metaphoric, that she would take in his containing.

---

[1]Some elements of this case were previously discussed in a separate publication (Hamilton 1988).

"You have a difficult time soothing yourself," he said, "and you would like me to soothe you by talking to you. As you have described, in your early life, you were expected to be a reasonable and responsible little girl at a very young age. Perhaps this problem of not being able to settle yourself interferes with your going to sleep. You look tired today."

Ms. A. calmed enough to go on, "Well, I have that problem, too, but last night it was my son. I couldn't help him fall asleep. He kept waking me up. I got mad and shouted at him and sent him back to bed, but he kept crying and telling me he was scared about nightmares. I felt terribly guilty. Finally, I thought it would be easier to let him sleep in my bed. I know I shouldn't do that. Everybody has told me he will get used to sleeping in his own bed in a few nights, but he doesn't. What am I supposed to do?"

The therapist again felt a slight, anxious impulse to switch from an analytic modality and to do parent counselling. He sat quietly considering what was best, while the patient stared at him with a facial expression which demanded his immediate response.

"I'm not sure why you've asked for my advice," he said, "when you've just let me know you didn't heed the advice you have already gotten from others. What do you make of it?"

"I don't know. What do you make of it?" she said rather testily.

"Perhaps you would like me to demonstrate that I care about you by giving you advice. You may wish me to make a special exception for you so you won't feel so alone, the same way your son does with you. When I leave you to handle it on your own, you become irritated and protest even louder that you can't do it."

This comment was intended to convey a containing of affect more than to interpret. It seemed to allow the patient to return to the analytic mode. For the rest of the hour she sorted through memories of how her parents expected her to act more mature than her age. She recalled that she had felt abandoned and full of rage about not having dependency needs gratified. When her son was born, she was determined to care for him the way she wished her parents had cared for her. She overindulged him until she was exhausted. Despite this insight and work during the middle forty minutes of the session, she returned to her anxious demanding just before the end of the hour. She again wondered if she might become psychotic. She asked if she should go into the hospital.

"What should I do? I can't stand it."

"Our time is up," the therapist said. "I will see you Friday." The patient smiled and departed.

At the next session, the patient appeared more rested. Her facial expression was bright and confident. Her son had slept through the last two nights for the first time in months.

"When he came into my room saying he had had a nightmare, I got up, took him back to his room, and told him to tell me about it. After he finished, I told him it was just a dream and he would be all right. If he had another dream, he could tell me about it at breakfast in the morning, but for now, he was a big boy and could sleep in his own bed."

Although there is much to discuss in any clinical vignette, this one is intended to illustrate that when an analyst or other psychotherapist intends to provide a containing function, it can be considered a projective identification, whether conscious or unconscious, on the part of the analyst. This may also apply to the empathic, self-object function performed by analysts influenced by Kohut's (1971) thinking.

In this example, the therapist developed anxiety when the patient described herself as being on the verge of psychosis. Through interpersonal projective identification, she had elicited an anxiety equivalent to her own in him. He was empathically receptive to experiencing this anxiety in the countertransference, as used in the broad sense of the word (Kernberg 1965). Once he internalized her expressed anxiety, it was no longer her affect alone; it was also his own (Hamilton 1988). He contained and modulated his own affect by reflecting about it. Once he had transformed his concerns, which had been stimulated by the patient's projective identification, he developed the conviction that the patient, too, could calm herself. That is, he attributed his self-image of being capable of containing and modulating anxiety and persisting with the analytic mode to the patient. Since he attributed a self-image to an object image, while simultaneously retaining it as a self-image, this mental operation was intrapsychic projective identification.

He then displayed his calm understanding of the patient's anxiety, thereby influencing her to calm herself and to continue with the analytic work. Since he was now behaving in such a way as to elicit his calm confidence in the patient and to influence her, however subtly and gently, he was engaging in interpersonal projective identification.

The patient responded by calming herself and continuing with the analytic work. She later confirmed that she had internalized the therapist's projected containing function when she described how she had effectively contained her son's anxiety in parallel with how the therapist had responded to her.

It is not suggested that the analyst's projective identification is a sufficient agent of change. In this session, an interpretation was made concerning the transferential perception of the therapist as being unable to help her understand and tolerate her affects, as she had experienced her parents being unable to empathize with and help modulate her feelings. Anger in the transference was also related back to early life experiences. The therapist's containing function and his benign projective identification helped the patient return to a mode of thinking which allowed her to benefit from such interpretation.

Discussion

The noun for the process *projection* is linguistically related to the noun *projectile* — something sharp and intrusive. Containing is related to the noun *container* — something open and receptive. It is at first counter to our intuition to think of projecting something open and receptive, actually surrounding, into someone.[2] Nevertheless, those of us who use the concept of performing a containing function for the patient and expecting the patient to internalize that function are projecting a container into the patient, who now becomes the container of our benign projective identification. This is an intrapsychic process which takes place in the analyst. Interpersonally, we do not project anything into the patient, any more than they project anything into us. We behave in such a way as to elicit an affect and image which corresponds with our own internal affects and images.

This view is consistent with the understanding and many clinical examples Ogden (1982) has provided. He stated, "The perspective of projective identification neither requires nor excludes the use of verbal interpretation. The therapist attempts to find a way of

---

[2]In Bion's (1962) notation, this would be $\sigma \rightarrow \varphi_2$, where $\sigma = \varphi_1$.

talking with and being with the patient that will constitute a
medium through which the therapist may accept unintegratable
aspects of the patient's internal object world and return them to
the patient in a form that the patient can accept and learn from"
(p. 42). This "returning" to the patient through a way of talking
and being has all the elements of interpersonal projective identification. Ogden goes on to describe how the mother, like the
analyst, initially serves as a container for the infant's projective
identifications and later the infant "internalizes aspects of the
mother's personality structure by introjecting aspects of her
unconscious projections, that is, by functioning as the recipient of
her projective identifications" (Ogden 1982, p. 70). The infant
contains the mother's projected containing. Ogden has not yet
explicitly stated, though I believe he would agree, that what the
patient introjects is the analyst's projective identification.

One must ask, however, if the therapist in this case illustration
had a complementary countertransference (Racker 1957) in which
he identified with the patient's internal parents and expected her to
be grown-up so she acted grown-up? This would have resulted in
a flight into health, or perhaps superficial modelling which may
have obviated further analysis, though it may have provided a
useful kind of supportive psychotherapy. Evidence that this might
be taking place is found in the patient's statement about her son's
nightmare, "It was just a dream," as if dreams are insignificant.
She never did describe her son's nightmare, so we are left in doubt
as to its content, but in the next few sessions she began, for the
first time, to describe her own nightmares. Those dreams had to
do with an aspect of her experience with which neither she nor her
parents could cope. The therapist apparently had made contact,
perhaps by projective identification, with those aspects of the
patient which were more competent so she could begin to address
her own fears. It is a bit speculative, but possible, that the patient's
increasing ability to contain and talk about her own nightmares
may have allowed her to stop eliciting them in her son, thereby
decreasing the likelihood of his nightmares.

While the concepts of projective identification and containing
help in examining the interactive aspects of any analysis, it
remains possible to examine the same material from a drive-
conflict viewpoint as well. In the example above, the patient was

a single parent who was looking not only for an analyst, but also for a partner. By wanting to go into the therapist's hospital, in which his office was located, she may have been asking to go into his bed because of her wishes for physical and sexual closeness. By demanding tangible help and reassurance, she asked that he move beyond the bounds of the analytic situation as it had been defined in this treatment. It is possible that his retaining an analytic approach reassured her that there would be no acting out of sexual fantasies within the treatment, and it may have disappointed her, too. Her little boy probably represented her male partner, as well as the frightened, small child aspects of herself.

These issues came to the fore with more clarity and directness in the transference a year later and required interpretation in terms of oedipal conflicts, as well as envy. In ego psychological terms, making this material conscious and resolving these infantile conflicts frees up psychic energy which now becomes available to add to the strength and structure of the ego.

The theoretical issue of whether conflict resolution or internalization of relationship is a more important curative factor remains unresolved. I would suggest that the issue will never be resolvable because interpretation and the internalization of relationship always take place simultaneously in the analytic situation. Although it is more clear with the analyst's use of the concept of the container and the contained, it is probably also true that any interpretation is made with some intent of the comment entering into the patient and changing him, or at least eliciting something from him. One thing elicited is the patient's identification with the analyst's analysing function. Thus, any analysis can be conceptualized as having within it a mutual and reciprocal process of projective identification between the analyst and the analysand. Thus, the only possible resolution of the issue as to whether conflict resolution or internalization of relationship is a more important curative factor would be to consider both factors helpful.

What I am calling the analyst's projective identification in the containing function is linked historically to discussion about the analytic relationship. What is seen here is the application to the analyst of the term *projective identification,* which implies an *intention to influence.* The active role of the analyst's personality and intentions in treatment has often been separated out and seen as needed only to establish the analytic situation. Freud (1913) suggested that the analyst must exhibit "a serious interest" in the patient and adopt an attitude of "sympathetic understanding" (p. 140) in order to "attach him to the person of the analyst" (p. 139) in the beginning of treatment. Freud's description of this relationship aspect of the treatment is such that it seems outside of technique (Lipton 1977). Loewenstein's (1958) "creation of initial rapport," Waelder's (1960) "procedures necessary to establish and maintain an 'analytic situation' " (p. 237), and Schafer's (1983) "respectful affirmative attitude" (p. 12) are but a few examples of numerous descriptions of how analysts influence patients by modulating their own attitudes. What is described as incidental to establishing an analytic situation, however, can be seen as an attempt to induce a similar attitude of rapport in the patient, that is, projective identification on the part of the analyst, which is actually central to the therapeutic task. Calling it the establishment of an analytic situation, rather than a dynamic and interpersonal event in which the analyst is one agent, makes what is personal and dynamic seem impersonal and static, which I doubt is really the case.

It has long been known that the patient introjects or identifies with aspects of the analyst (Bibring 1937, Blatt and Behrends 1987, Glover 1937, Strachey 1937), particularly the analysing functions. This emphasis upon the patient's receptivity to the analyst has not been paralleled by an equal emphasis on the analyst's intentions. As Stone (1961) has said, there has been a rather slow general acceptance of the "bilateral personality involvement of the analytic process" (p. 15) and there still is.

That slowness is probably warranted. As a part of the analyst's containing (Bion 1962), creating a "holding environment" (Modell 1976, Winnicott 1960) establishing the analytic situation (Bibring 1937, Freud 1913, Stone 1961), and even interpreting itself, there is much room for the analyst's conscious or unconscious intention to influence the patient to adopt aspects of the analyst's own attitude. Such an intention would suggest projective identification on the part of the analyst. And projective identification can be a very treacherous tool, as we can see so clearly in our patients. For example, purposely adopting an attitude or role outside the analytic stance to provide a corrective emotional experience (Alexander 1950) may lead the patient to identify with falseness rather than with the subtleties of what the analyst really is, his or her inner state communicated unconsciously (Nacht 1962). Also, focusing on the analyst's projective identification as being overly important might discount the patient's central initiative in his own life, thereby devaluing the patient. On the other hand, seeing one's self, as an analyst, as neutral in the sense of remaining equidistant from the id, the ego, the superego, and external reality (A. Freud 1936) probably helps many of us convey our quiet confidence that the patient, like us, can tolerate external reality, can tolerate himself, and can grow from his own inner resources. In this sense, "neutrality" can be conceptualized as a broad term, which often implies an intrapsychic and interpersonal stance which conveys an attitude with which patients identify. Paradoxically, then, the concept of neutrality serves as a vehicle for our appropriate containment and therefore projective identification. Although the concept of neutrality is a bit illusory, it should not be lightly discarded. The examination of our own intrapsychic and interpersonal contribution to the analytic process, including our own projective identifications, should proceed, but without pressure to change a very useful procedure and style of helping our patients.

Like any conceptual tool, the idea of the analyst's projective identification can be more grossly misused (Ogden 1982). This probably takes place most often when the analyst's or psychotherapist's projective identification is extreme and his or her internal images of himself and the patient do not sufficiently correspond with the external object, the patient. In the case illustration provided above, if the therapist's view of himself and his patient being able to contain her despondency in the analytic context had been wrong, the result could have been disastrous (i.e., she may have deteriorated into psychosis or suicide). The analyst's projective identification can be employed to defend against countertransference frustration, helplessness, or hostility, or to deny countertransference fear of the patient's aggression. This mechanism could be invoked in naive attempts to magically cancel out or neutralize the patient's destructiveness with "goodwill." A more thorough scrutiny of the adverse effects of the analyst's maladaptive projective identification would be of interest.

It is not the purpose here to defend the use of projective identification by the analyst, but to suggest that it is used when the concept of the container and contained is invoked. It may also be involved whenever any interpretation is made and even when the analytic situation is established. While the ideas of projective identification and of containing are not new in themselves, what is new and therefore controversial in this chapter is the contention that the analyst is not only experienced by the patient as doing something, but that the analyst intends to do something to the patient, psychologically, if only as a receptor-interpreter, that is a container. Here, the "intention" is attitudinal and internal. It is this author's viewpoint that containing takes place in all analyses, regardless of the analyst's orientation, or conscious view of him- or herself as neutral, or otherwise. What the analyst returns to the patient as a part of the containing function always has attached to it a bit of the analyst's self and of his own internal world.

The concept of the container and the contained in psychoanalysis describes a process whereby the patient's projective identifications are internalized by the analyst, transformed, given meaning, and returned to the patient in a useful fashion. In this chapter, it is suggested that what the analyst gives back, and what the patient receives, is the analyst's projective identification. The containing function itself can be transmitted to the patient via this mechanism. All interpretation, from whatever theoretical viewpoint, has an element of containing and therefore projective identification on the part of the analyst. Paradoxically, neutrality itself can be considered a vehicle for projective identification. Previously, the role of the therapist's projective identification in the containing process has been implied, but not discussed.

REFERENCES

Adler, G. (1986). *Borderline Psychotherapy and Its Treatment*. Northvale, NJ: Jason Aronson.

Adler, G., and Rhine, M. W. (1988). The self object function of projective identification. *Bulletin of the Menninger Clinic* 52:473–491.

Alexander, F. (1950). Analysis of the therapeutic factors in psychoanalytic treatment. *Psychoanalytic Quarterly* 19:482–500.

Bibring, E. (1937). Symposium on the theory of the therapeutic results of psychoanalysis. *International Journal of Psycho-Analysis* 18: 170–189.

Bion, W. R. (1957). Differentiation of the psychotic from the non-psychotic personalities. *International Journal of Psycho-Analysis* 38:266–275.

———— (1959). Attacks on linking. *International Journal of Psycho-Analysis* 40:308–315.

———— (1962). *Learning from Experience*. London: Heinemann.

———— (1967). *Second Thoughts*. London: Heinemann.

Blatt, S. J., and Behrends, R. S. (1987). Internalization, separation-individuation, and the nature of therapeutic action. *International Journal of Psycho-Analysis* 68:279–297.

Freud, A. (1936). *The Ego and the Mechanisms of Defence*. London: Hogarth Press, 1937.

Freud, S. (1913). On beginning the treatment. *Standard Edition* 12:121–144.

Gabbard, G. O. (1986). The treatment of the "special" patient in a psychoanalytic hospital. *International Review of Psycho-Analysis* 13:333–347.

Glover, E. (1937). Symposium on the theory of the therapeutic results of psychoanalysis. *International Journal of Psycho-Analysis* 18:125–132.

Grinberg, L. (1965). Contribucion al estudio de las modalidades de la identification projectiva. *Revista de Psicoanalisis* 22:263–279.

Grotstein, J. S. (1981). *Splitting and Projective Identification*. New York: Jason Aronson.

Hamilton, N. G. (1986). Positive projective identification. *International Journal of Psycho-Analysis* 67:489–496.

———— (1988). *Self and Others: Object Relations Theory in Practice*. Northvale, NJ: Jason Aronson.

———— (1989). Intrapsychic and interpersonal projective identification. In *Melanie Klein and Object Relations* 7:31–42.

Jaffe, D. S. (1986). Empathy, counteridentification, countertransference. *Psychoanalytic Quarterly* 55:215–243.

Kernberg, O. F. (1965). Notes on countertransference. *Journal of the American Psychoanalytic Association* 13:38–56.

———— (1987). Projection and projective identification: developmental and clinical aspects. *Journal of the American Psycho-Analytic Association* 35:795–819.

Klein, M. (1946). Notes on some schizoid mechanisms. *International Journal of Psycho-Analysis* 27:99–110.

_____ (1952). Some theoretical conclusions regarding the emotional life of the infant. In *Developments in Psychoanalysis,* ed. J. Riviere, pp. 198–236. London: Hogarth Press.

Kohut, H. (1971). *The Analysis of the Self.* New York: International Universities Press.

Lipton, S. D. (1977). The advantages of Freud's technique as shown in his analysis of the Rat Man. *International Journal of Psycho-Analysis* 58:255–273.

Loewald, H. W. (1986). Transference-countertransference. *Journal of the American Psychoanalytic Association* 34:275–287.

Loewenstein, R. M. (1958). Remarks on some variations in psycho-analytic technique. *International Journal of Psycho-Analysis* 39:202–210.

Malin, A., and Grotstein, J. S. (1966). Projective identification in the therapeutic process. *International Journal of Psycho-Analysis* 47:26–31.

Meissner, W. W. (1980). A note on projective identification. *Journal of the American Psychoanalytic Association* 28:43–67.

_____ (1987). Projection and projective identification. In *Projection, Identification, Projective Identification,* ed. J. Sandler, pp. 27–49. Madison, CT: International Universities Press.

Modell, A. H. (1976). "The holding environment" and the therapeutic action of psychoanalysis. *Journal of the American Psychoanalytic Association* 24:285–307.

Money-Kyrle, R. E. (1956). Normal counter-transference and some of its deviations. *International Journal of Psycho-Analysis* 37:360–366.

Nacht, S. (1962). The curative factors in psychoanalysis. *International Journal of Psycho-Analysis* 43:206–211.

Noy, P. (1984). The three components of empathy: normal and patho-logic development. In *Empathy I,* ed. J. Lichtenberg, M. Bernstein, and D. Silver, pp. 167–199. Hillsdale, NJ: Analytic Press.

Ogden, T. H. (1979). On projective identification. *International Journal of Psycho-Analysis* 60:357–373.

_____ (1982). *Projective Identification and Psychotherapeutic Technique.* New York: Jason Aronson.

Pick, I. B. (1985). Working through in the countertransference. *International Journal of Psycho-Analysis* 66:157–166.

Racker, H. (1957). The meanings and uses of countertransference. *Psychoanalytic Quarterly* 26:303–357.

Rosenfeld, H. (1983). Primitive object relations and mechanisms. *International Journal of Psycho-Analysis* 64:261–267.

Sandler, J. (1987). The concept of projective identification. In *Projec-*

tion, Identification, Projective Identification, pp. 12–26. Madison, CT: International Universities Press.

Schafer, R. (1983). *The Analytic Attitude.* New York: Basic Books.

Spillius, E. B. (1983). Some developments from the work of Melanie Klein. *International Journal of Psycho-Analysis* 64:321–332.

Stone, L. (1961). *The Psychoanalytic Situation.* New York: International Universities Press.

Strachey, J. (1937). Symposium on the theory of therapeutic results of psychoanalysis. *International Journal of Psycho-Analysis* 18:139–145.

Waelder, R. (1960). *Basic Theory of Psychoanalysis.* New York: International Universities Press.

Winnicott, D. W. (1960). The theory of the parent–infant relationship. *International Journal of Psycho-Analysis* 43:585–594.

Intersubjectivity in Psychoanalytic Treatment

Robert D. Stolorow, Bernard Brandchaft, and George E. Atwood

T his important contribution takes yet another look at what is between patient and therapist. The approach is markedly different in emphasis and tone from the previous chapter, which describes clearly distinct individuals with an avenue for profound, if subtle, communication and some exchange of self and object experiences between them. By contrast, the emphasis in this chapter is on shared experience, an immersion in directly perceived intersubjectivity. Stolorow and his colleagues write about this highly abstract concept in a way that allows not only a ready understanding, but also a feeling for and sense of the intersubjective viewpoint.

Differences in the nuances of relatedness in this chapter and the two preceding ones probably do not reflect disagreement about universal psychological principles. What is universal must take into account all these understandings. The differences probably derive more from the personalities of the authors and the ways in which they are most comfortable being with other people and seeing themselves in relation to their patients when they write. What is most similar in the viewpoints is that the primary focus is on the emotional context for both patient and therapist over and above the specifics of technique. There is an increasing awareness among psychotherapists influenced by object relations theory and self psychology that there must be tolerance for subtle differences in clinical theory, which take into account the therapist's basic experience of him- or herself in relation to others, without discarding theory altogether. There is an increasing diversity within the unity.

Winnicott (1960) once remarked, "There is no such thing as an infant" (p. 39n), meaning that infant and maternal care together form an indivisible unit. Our analytic work has led us to a similar viewpoint with regard to the "difficult patient." We have observed that the difficulty in such cases does not reside solely within the patient. It arises, rather, *between* the patient and the analyst and must be viewed, therefore, as a difficulty in the more inclusive patient–therapist system. This observation serves as a starting point for some broad reflections on the nature of psychoanalytic therapy. Our clinical focus in this chapter will be on the analysis of patients whose archaic states and needs often lead therapists to believe that they are "difficult to treat."

Our thesis, in its most general form, is that psychoanalytic treatment seeks to illuminate phenomena that emerge within a specific psychological field constituted by the intersection of two subjectivities—that of the patient and that of the analyst. In this conceptualization, psychoanalysis is not seen as a science of the intrapsychic, focused on events presumed to occur within one isolated "mental apparatus." Nor is it conceived as a science of the interpersonal, investigating the "behavioral facts" of the therapeutic interaction as seen from a point of observation outside the field under study. Rather, psychoanalysis is pictured here as a science of the *intersubjective,* focused on the interplay between the differently organized subjective worlds of the observer and the observed. The observational stance is always within, rather than outside, the intersubjective field or "contextual unit" (Schwaber 1979) being observed, a fact that guarantees the centrality of introspection and empathy as the methods of observation (Kohut 1959). Psychoanalysis is unique among the sciences in that the observer is also the observed (Stolorow and Atwood 1979). In this chapter we shall examine the implications of this curious intersubjective situation for four issues that are of critical concern in psychoanalytic treatment in general and in the analysis of "difficult patients" in particular: the nature of transference and countertransference, the explanation of "negative therapeutic reactions," the psychoanalytic understanding of psychopathology, and the conceptualization of the therapeutic action of psychoanalysis.

TRANSFERENCE AND COUNTERTRANSFERENCE

The intersubjectivity concept proposed here is a direct outgrowth of the psychoanalytic understanding of transference and countertransference. The concept of transference may be understood to refer to all the ways in which patients' experiences of the analytic relationship become organized according to the configurations of self and object that unconsciously structure their subjective universes. Countertransference, in turn, refers to how the structures of the analysts' subjectivity shape their experience of the analytic relationship and, in particular, of their patients' transference.

Two basic situations repeatedly arise from the continual interplay between transference and countertransference: intersubjective conjunction and intersubjective disjunction (Stolorow et al. 1978). The first of these situations is illustrated by instances in which the configurations of self and object that structure patients' experiences give rise to expressions that are assimilated into closely similar central configurations in the psychological lives of their analysts. Disjunction, by contrast, occurs when analysts assimilate the material expressed by their patients into configurations that significantly distort that material's actual subjective meaning for the patients. Repetitive occurrences of intersubjective conjunction and disjunction are inevitable accompaniments of the analytic process and reflect the interaction of differently organized subjective worlds. Clinical examples of each of these intersubjective situations can be found in Stolorow et al. (1978, 1981).

Whether or not these intersubjective situations facilitate or obstruct the progress of analysis depends in large part on the extent of the analyst's reflective self-awareness and capacity to decenter (Piaget 1970) from the organizing principles of his or her own subjective world and thereby to grasp empathically the actual

184 Robert D. Stolorow, Bernard Brandchaft, and George E. Atwood

meaning of the patient's experiences. When such reflective self-awareness on the part of the analyst is reliably present, then the correspondence or disparity between the subjective worlds of patient and therapist can be used to promote analytic understanding. In the case of an intersubjective conjunction which has been recognized, for example, the analyst's self-knowledge can serve as an invaluable adjunctive source of information regarding the probable background meanings of the patient's expressions. Disjunctions, once they have become conscious from a decentered perspective, may also assist an analyst's ongoing efforts to understand the patients, for then the analyst's emotional reactions can serve as potential intersubjective indices of the configurations actually structuring the patient's experiences.

In the absence of decentered self-awareness on the part of the analyst, such conjunctions and disjunctions can seriously impede the progress of analysis. The most common situation in which conjunction leads to an interference with treatment is when the region of intersubjective correspondence escapes analytic scrutiny because it reflects a defensive solution shared by both patient and analyst. In such instances, the conjunction results in a mutual strengthening of resistance and counterresistance and, hence, in a prolongation of the analysis.

Even more damaging, however, are the interferences with treatment that arise as a result of protracted, unrecognized intersubjective disjunctions. In such instances, empathy is chronically replaced by misunderstanding, as the therapeutic interventions are repeatedly directed toward a subjective situation which, in fact, does not exist. Such persistent disjunctions contribute to the formation of vicious countertherapeutic spirals, which serve to intensify rather than alleviate a patient's suffering and manifest psychopathology. It is in these spirals that analysts can find the source of what they have euphemistically termed "negative therapeutic reactions."

NEGATIVE THERAPEUTIC REACTIONS

The concept of a "negative therapeutic reaction" was created by analysts to explain those difficult situations in which interpretations they presumed to be correct actually made patients worse rather than better. Typically, such untoward reactions to an analyst's well-intended interpretive efforts were attributed exclusively to intrapsychic mechanisms, such as an unconscious sense of guilt, a need for punishment, and primal masochism (Freud 1923, 1937), narcissistic character resistances (Abraham 1919), a need to ward off the depressive position through omnipotent control (Riviere 1936), or unconscious envy and a resulting compulsion to spoil the analytic work (Kernberg 1975, Klein 1957). We contend, by contrast, that such therapeutic impasses and disasters cannot be understood apart from the intersubjective context in which they arise. They are most often the product of prolonged, unrecognized transference–countertransference disjunctions and the chronic misunderstandings that result from them (Brandchaft 1983, Stolorow et al. 1981, Stolorow and Lachmann 1980).

Kohut's (1971, 1977) concepts of selfobject and selfobject transference have immeasurably deepened our understanding of human intersubjectivity, of the psychoanalytic situation, and of so-called negative therapeutic reactions. In the selfobject transferences, patients revive with their analysts the early idealizing and mirroring ties that were traumatically and phase-inappropriately ruptured during their formative years, and upon which they rely for the restoration and maintenance of a sense of self and for the resumption and completion of arrested psychological growth. In our experience, exacerbations and entrenchments of patients' psychopathology severe enough to be termed "negative therapeutic reactions" are most often produced by prolonged, unrecognized intersubjective disjunctions wherein the patients' selfobject transference needs are consistently misunderstood and thereby relentlessly rejected by their analysts. Such misunderstandings typically take the form of erroneous interpretations of the revival of an arrested selfobject tie or need as an expression of malignant, pathological resistance. When patients revive an arrested selfobject tie or need within the analytic relationship, and their analysts repeatedly interpret this developmental necessity as if it were merely a pathological resistance, the patients will experience such misinterpretations as gross failures of empathy. These traumatic, repeatedly inflicted narcissistic injuries are similar in their impact to the pathogenic events of the patients' early lives. Such chronic, unrecognized disjunctions, wherein vital developmental requirements revived in relation to the analyst meet with consistently unempathic responses, constitute the intersubjective context in which negative — often dramatically negative — "therapeutic" reactions are produced. This finding, we believe, holds the broadest implications for the psychoanalytic understanding of psychopathology in general and of "difficult-to-treat" cases in particular.

THE PSYCHOANALYTIC UNDERSTANDING OF PSYCHOPATHOLOGY

We contend that from a psychoanalytic perspective — a perspective derived from empathic-introspective observations within the psychoanalytic situation — psychological disturbances can no longer be viewed as resulting solely from pathological mechanisms located within the mental apparatus of patients. Like "negative therapeutic reactions," psychopathology in general cannot be considered apart from the intersubjective context in which it arises.

In another paper, two of us (Brandchaft and Stolorow 1983) exemplify this thesis with respect to so-called borderline psychopathology. After we critique the view that the term *borderline* refers to a discrete, stable, pathological character structure rooted in pathognomonic instinctual conflicts and primitive defenses, we demonstrate that clinical evidence cited for the centrality of such conflicts and defenses is actually evidence of needs for specific modes of relatedness to archaic selfobjects and of the empathic failures of such selfobjects. We propose that the psychological essence of what is called *borderline* is not that it is a pathological condition located solely in the patient. Rather, it refers to phenomena arising in an intersubjective field — a field consisting of a precarious, vulnerable self and a failing, archaic selfobject.

Furthermore, we claim that when the archaic states and needs of patients who have been called borderline are correctly understood and accepted, these patients can be helped to form more or less stable selfobject transference relationships and, when such relationships are formed, these patients' so-called borderline features recede and even disappear. As long as their selfobject ties to their therapists remain intact, their treatment will bear a close similarity to descriptions of analyses of narcissistic personality disorders (Kohut 1971). In contrast, when the patients' selfobject ties to their therapists become significantly disrupted by empathic failures, the patients may once again appear borderline. Whether or not a stable selfobject bond can develop and be maintained— which, in turn, shapes both the apparent diagnostic picture and the assessment of analyzability—will depend not only on the extent of impairment and vulnerability of the patients' nuclear self. It will be codetermined as well by the extent of the therapists' ability to decenter from the structures of their own subjectivity and by their ability to comprehend empathically the nature of each patient's archaic subjective universe as it begins to structure the microcosm of the transference.

We believe that further psychoanalytic research will show that the concept of borderline as phenomena arising and receding within an intersubjective field applies to all forms of manifest psychopathology, ranging from the psychoneurotic to the overtly psychotic. However, the intersubjective context of psychopathology is demonstrated most readily in the treatment of patients who rely on archaic selfobject ties to maintain the basic structural integrity and stability of their sense of self and to prevent its structural dissolution. We shall illustrate this viewpoint by the following case example of a patient with transference psychosis.

CLINICAL EXAMPLE: TRANSFERENCE PSYCHOSIS

When the patient entered treatment at age 25, his florid manifest psychopathology included many features that typically are termed *borderline*. He suffered from severe, agitated, lonely depressions, and experienced a desperate, devouring hunger for closeness and physical contact with women, whom he perceived as awesome in their idealized qualities. At the same time, his relations with others, especially women, were extremely chaotic and sadomasochistic, marked by violent rage, envy, and destructiveness directed both against objects and the self. He frequently engaged in bizarre, ritualized enactments of a sadomasochistic and sexually perverse nature.

After several months of treatment, the analyst began to focus his interventions on what seemed to be the patient's unmistakable pattern of phobic avoidance of intimate contact with women. The analyst consistently interpreted this pattern to the patient as reflecting his intense fear of women, based on his images of them—including the maternal prototype—as terribly powerful, sadistic, and dangerously destructive. The patient's fear of women was well documented in the analytic material. Indeed, the patient had disclosed that he consciously pictured the sexual act as a situation of mutual destruction and mutilation, in which his penis would inflict damage to the woman's body, and her vagina, lined with razor blades, would cut off his penis in retaliation against him.

The patient reacted to repeated interpretations of his phobic defense and underlying fears and fantasies by becoming intensely paranoid within the transference. He began to believe, with increasing conviction, that the analyst's sole motivation in making interpretations was to humiliate him, lord it over him, and ultimately destroy him. As a result, the patient became obsessed with fantasies of revenge and wishes to attack and destroy the analyst. In fact, at times during the sessions he seemed about to enact his fantasies. The analyst's interpretations of projective mechanisms only exacerbated the patient's belief that he was being victimized, which eventually became entrenched in the form of full-fledged persecutory delusions.

This paranoid transference psychosis persisted for several weeks and was alleviated in large part as a consequence of two serendipitous circumstances. The first was an incident that occurred when the patient inquired about a day hospital program with which he knew the analyst was familiar. The therapist responded spontaneously and nonanalytically, saying that he believed the patient was "too together" for this particular program. The patient became utterly elated and revealed that he experienced the analyst's comment as an unexpected vote of confidence, a longed-for expression of approval. Shortly thereafter, he reported a highly illuminating dream.

> I was telling people I was going to jump from a very high altitude, off a building or window sill. I wasn't going to commit suicide; I was going to jump and *live!* It would have been the first or second time in the history of the world! Then the big day came. I crawled up on the window sill and I looked down. I was scared. I couldn't jump. I saw a rope ladder and couldn't even go down that. It was incredibly humiliating, telling people I could do something and then being too scared to do it.

The second fortunate circumstance occurred because the analyst was becoming acquainted at this time with Kohut's early papers on the understanding and treatment of archaic narcissism. This material made a deep, personal impact on the analyst and enabled him to expand his reflective self-awareness to include a greater knowledge of his own narcissistic vulnerabilities and needs. This expanded awareness, in turn, made it possible for him to find in his own psychological history analogues of the patient's archaic states. As a result, he began to understand the nature of the patient's selfobject transference needs and the intersubjective situation in which the transference psychosis had developed.

The patient's sense of self had been extremely vulnerable and subject to protracted fragmentations. Indeed, the analyst later understood that the principal purpose of the patient's sadomasochistic, perverse enactments was to restore a tenuous sense of integrity and stability to his crumbling self-experience. What the patient needed was an opportunity to solidify a more cohesive sense of self around archaic images of perfection and omnipotence. What he needed most in the transference was to know that the analyst appreciated and admired the grandeur of this brittle archaic self. In this specific context, as the dream implies, the patient experienced the analyst's repeated interpretations of his fears of women as unendurable mortifications. The transference psychosis developed as a result of a prolonged, unrecognized intersubjective disjunction in which the therapist's interpretive approach persistently obstructed the archaic mirroring tie that the patient urgently needed to sustain the organization of his precarious sense of self. When the analyst recognized and clarified the disjunction and replaced it with an empathic comprehension of the nature of the patient's selfobject transference needs, the transference psychosis dissipated, never to recur during the long course of the treatment.

THE THERAPEUTIC ACTION OF PSYCHOANALYSIS

If "negative therapeutic reactions" and psychopathology cannot be understood apart from the intersubjective field in which they occur, neither can the therapeutic action of psychoanalysis. Freud's (1914, 1937) explanations of therapeutic action emphasized intrapsychic processes, such as the patient's renunciation of infantile wishes liberated through the analysis of transference resistance. Some other analysts, however, who have attempted to account for the therapeutic action of psychoanalysis, have alluded to the importance of the intersubjective. For example, Strachey (1934) introduced the concept of the introjection of the analyst into the patient's superego functioning, and Loewald (1960) stressed the patient's discovery of new modes of object relationship with the analyst. Two of us (Atwood and Stolorow 1980) emphasized the intersubjective quality of the process of structural change. We proposed that the analyst's repeated interpretive clarification of the nature, origins, and significance of the patient's psychological configurations into which the analyst is assimilated, together with the repeated juxtaposition of these structures of subjectivity with the patient's experiences of the analyst as a new object to which these structures must accommodate, invites the synthesis of alternative modes of experiencing the self and object world. Such structural transformation in the patient does not require the analyst to play out any artificial parental or "corrective" role. The analyst's "newness" as an object is insured by the consistency of his or her observational stance — the dedication to the use of introspection and empathy to gain and provide understanding of the meaning of the patient's subjective experiences.

Kohut's (1971, 1977) conceptualizations of the selfobject transferences, and of the central role of the analyst's empathic understanding in establishing and working through these transferences, have brought the intersubjective context of psychoanalytic cure into bold relief. He describes how understanding and working through disruptions of the selfobject bond that has been permitted to develop can result in a process of psychological structure formation. An aspect of this process that we especially wish to underscore is the patient's gradual internalization of the analyst's observational stance, whereby the quality of empathic understanding, formerly perceived to be the property of the analyst as selfobject, becomes an enduring feature of the patient's own self-experience (Atwood and Stolorow 1980). To the therapeutic action of such transmuting internalizations, we would add the mutative power of correct empathy itself. Structure-forming articulations of experience are directly promoted in the facilitating medium of the analyst's empathic communications. Thus, the cumulative experience of being understood in depth leads both to the crystallization of a sense of the self that has been comprehended and to the acquisition of the capacity for empathic self-observation.

It has been a conceptual error, we believe, to use the term *selfobject transference* to refer to a *type* of transference characteristic of a certain type of patient. Instead, we prefer to use the phrase to refer to a *dimension* of transference—indeed, of all transference—which may fluctuate in the extent to which it occupies a position of figure or ground in the patient's experience of the analytic relationship (Stolorow and Lachmann 1980). Kohut's work illuminates the unique therapeutic importance of understanding and working through those transference configurations in which the selfobject dimension is figure—that is, in which the restoration or maintenance of self-experience is the paramount psychological purpose motivating the patient's specific tie to the analyst. However, even when other dimensions of experience and human motivation—such as conflicts over loving, hating, desiring, and competing—emerge as most salient in structuring the transference, the selfobject dimension is never absent. As long as it is undisturbed, preserved in the medium of the analyst's empathy, the selfobject dimension operates silently in the background, enabling the patient to dare to confront frightening feelings and painful dilemmas.

Consider, from this standpoint, the intersubjective situation in which a traditional resistance analysis takes place. Experienced analysts know that clarifying the nature of a patient's resistance has no discernible therapeutic result unless the analyst also is able to identify correctly the subjective danger or emotional conflict that makes the patient believe that the resistance is necessary. Only when analysts show that they know their patients' fear and anguish, thereby becoming established to some degree as calming, containing, idealized selfobjects, do their patients begin to feel safe enough to relax the resistance and allow their subjective lives to emerge more freely. Every mutative therapeutic moment, even when based on interpretation of resistance and conflict, derives its therapeutic action from the intersubjective field in which it occurs.

We have sought to demonstrate that, from a psychoanalytic perspective, clinical phenomena such as transference and counter-transference, negative therapeutic reactions, psychopathology in general, and the therapeutic action of psychoanalysis cannot be understood apart from the intersubjective contexts in which they take form. Maintaining this intersubjective point of view is especially important for therapists treating patients whose archaic states and needs often lead therapists to designate them as "difficult to treat." In our view, there is no such thing as a difficult patient. There are only difficulties that arise in the unique intersection of two subjectivities which constitutes the psychoanalytic situation.

REFERENCES

Abraham, K. (1919). A particular form of neurotic resistance against the psychoanalytic method. In *Selected Papers of Karl Abraham, M.D.,* trans. D. Bryan and A. Strachey, pp. 303–311. London: Hogarth, 1927.

Atwood, G. E., and Stolorow, R. D. (1980). Psychoanalytic concepts and the representational world. *Psychoanalysis in Contemporary Thought* 3:267–290.

Brandchaft, B. (1983). Negativism, negative therapeutic reaction, and self psychology. In *The Future of Psychoanalysis,* ed. A. Goldberg, pp. 327–359. New York: International Universities Press.

Brandchaft, B., and Stolorow, R. D. (1983). The borderline concept: pathological character or iatrogenic myth? In *Empathy,* ed. J. Lichtenberg, pp. 333–357. Hillsdale, NJ: Analytic Press.

Freud, S. (1914). Remembering, repeating, and working through. *Standard Edition* 12:147–156. London: Hogarth, 1958.

———— (1923). The ego and the id. *Standard Edition* 19:12–66. London: Hogarth, 1961.

———— (1937). Analysis terminable and interminable. *Standard Edition* 23:216–253. London: Hogarth, 1964.

Kernberg, O. F. (1975). *Borderline Conditions and Pathological Narcissism.* New York: Jason Aronson.

Klein, M. (1957). *Envy and Gratitude: A Study of Unconscious Sources.* New York: Basic Books.

Kohut, H. (1959). Introspection, empathy, and psychoanalysis: an examination of the relationship between mode of observation and theory. In *The Search for the Self: Selected Writings of Heinz Kohut: 1950-1978,* ed. P. Ornstein, pp. 205-232. New York: International Universities Press, 1978.

——— (1971). *The Analysis of the Self: A Systematic Approach to the Psychoanalytic Treatment of Narcissistic Personality Disorders.* New York: International Universities Press.

——— (1977). *The Restoration of the Self.* New York: International Universities Press.

Loewald, H. W. (1960). On the therapeutic action of psychoanalysis. *International Journal of Psycho-Analysis* 4:16-33.

Piaget, J. (1970). *Main Trends in Psychology.* London: Allen and Unwin, 1973.

Riviere, J. (1936). A contribution to the analysis of the negative therapeutic reaction. *International Journal of Psycho-Analysis* 17:304-320.

Sander, L. W. (1975). Infant and caretaking environment: investigation and conceptualization of adaptive behavior in a system of increasing complexity. In *Explorations in Child Psychiatry,* ed. E. J. Anthony, pp. 129-166. New York: Plenum.

Schwaber, E. (1979). On the "self" within the matrix of analytic theory — some clinical reflections and reconsiderations. *International Journal of Psycho-Analysis* 60:467-479.

Stolorow, R. D., and Atwood, G. E. (1979). *Faces in a Cloud: Subjectivity in Personality Theory.* New York: Jason Aronson.

Stolorow, R. D., Atwood, G. E., and Ross, J. M. (1978). The representational world in psychoanalytic therapy. *International Review of Psycho-Analysis* 5:247-256.

——— (1981). Transference and countertransference in the analysis of developmental arrests. *Bulletin of the Menninger Clinic* 45:20-28.

Stolorow, R. D., and Lachmann, F. M. (1980). *Psychoanalysis of Developmental Arrest: Theory and Treatment.* New York: International Universities Press.

Strachey, J. (1934). The nature of the therapeutic action of psychoanalysis. *International Journal of Psycho-Analysis* 15:127-159.

Winnicott, D. W. (1960). The theory of the parent–infant relationship. In *The Maturational Processes and the Facilitating Environment: Studies in the Theory of Emotional Development,* pp. 37-55. New York: International Universities Press, 1965.

Psychotherapy of the Narcissistic Personality Disorder Patient: Two Contrasting Approaches

Gerald Adler

*T*his chapter directly discusses the relationship between *clinical theory and personality of the author. It is the next step in looking at the relationship between therapist and patient. Here, Adler does not repeat epistemological arguments about subjective bias, how we know things, and the validity of psychoanalysis. His point is that clinical theory is colored in such a way as to be most useful to the therapist in relation to his patients. Similarly, all clinicians prefer theories that fit their own relatedness to their patients.*

Adler does not contend that there are no hard and fast facts in therapy or that all theories are equally correct and none is wrong. He merely reminds us that we must always take the self aspect of the self–other relationship into account, whether we are with a patient, writing about our work, or reading about clinical theory.

It is difficult to address the personality characteristics of our colleagues, especially since we primarily know them in a professional context, which has both collegial and competitive aspects. This kind of discussion can easily deteriorate into an indulgence of self-serving, ad hominum arguments, something that the psychoanalytic community has not been above enjoying. I believe that Adler is both delicate and even-handed in his discussion, though he may be a little hard on both Kohut and Kernberg in that he discusses them at all.

This chapter is not included to tell us who Kohut was and who Kernberg is. Rather, it is included as an invitation for us to look at ourselves, at what these two authors represent within us. In regard to the aggression issue, for instance, when we emphasize Kohut's empathy as sufficient, might we be needing to avoid recognizing aggression in our patients or ourselves for some important reason? When we emphasize the confrontation of hostility in the patient, as Kernberg does in his papers, might we be overlooking the patient's pain or loss at some break in our empathic understanding, our selfobject function? Adler invites us to ask, when we emphasize one approach or another and attribute it to a prominent author, what that tells us about ourselves in relation to a particular patient at a particular time. That question may be as helpful in the asking as in the answering.

The clinician who wishes to use current psychodynamic theory to treat patients with narcissistic personality disorder faces a series of problems. Not only is the theory complex, but the major contributors to it disagree with each other's formulations and, therefore, with the clinical interventions necessary for successful treatment. In addition, the relationship of narcissistic personality disorder to borderline and psychotic disorders is not clear, and there is disagreement on this issue among contributors to the literature. In this brief review of the treatment of narcissistic personality disorder patients, I have chosen to focus on the writings of Kernberg (1975, 1980) and Kohut (1971, 1972, 1977), whose contributions have raised stimulating questions about our understanding and treatment of these patients. The controversy that their formulations cause can add clarity to our knowledge, for it forces us to weigh their theoretical contributions on the scale of our own clinical experiences. Such an effort also requires us to look at the complex interaction of clinical observations, theoretical constructs, treatment implications, and the role of the personalities of theoreticians and clinicians in this interaction. Finally, I shall discuss specific psychotherapeutic techniques based on this complex theoretical work, as well as the role of psychotherapy and psychoanalysis in the treatment of patients who have a narcissistic personality disorder.

Other important contributors to our knowledge of these patients whose work cannot be examined in this brief chapter are Modell (1963, 1976), Masterson (1981), and Rinsley (1982). Modell's contributions, which use theoretical ideas of Winnicott and Kohut, define the "holding environment" aspects of treatment and the interactions between patient and therapist that ultimately move the treatment forward. Masterson and Rinsley both use object relations theory (derived from Kernberg and others) and developmental theory (e.g., Mahler and Winnicott) to describe a theoretical and clinical approach to both borderline and narcissistic personality disorder patients. The work of these contributors deserves careful study by the reader who wishes to enlarge his or her understanding of these patients.

DESCRIPTION OF THE NARCISSISTIC PERSONALITY DISORDER PATIENT

Kernberg and Kohut significantly differ in their theoretical understanding of narcissistic personality disorder patients and the treatment implications derived from this understanding. They are in less disagreement about the descriptive features of these patients (Kernberg 1971), which also closely parallel those in *DSM-III,* although I shall question whether they are ultimately comparing similar patient populations. These patients tend to be extremely self-centered, often needing praise and constant recognition in order to feel momentarily good about themselves. Rather than feeling a sense of their own worth or value, they require repeated bolstering from the outside. In their relationships with people, they tend to be exploitive and insensitive to the feelings and needs of others. Their behavior can be superficially charming on one hand or indifferent and arrogant on the other. They may expect special privileges from those around them without giving anything in return, yet they can feel very easily humiliated or shamed and respond with rage at what they perceive to be criticisms or failure of people to react in the way they wish. Some may alternate between letting people see their vulnerabilities and an aloof distancing, while others maintain their arrogant exterior much more consistently. Many describe their inner world as empty and feel that they are "fakes." Some also have frequent episodes of hypochondriacal symptoms. Many can elaborate active fantasies about magnificent success in love, sex, beauty, wealth, or power. They often devalue people they have previously idealized and tend to "split," i.e., see people as either all good or all bad, or alternate between these extremes.

THEORETICAL UNDERSTANDING: KERNBERG AND KOHUT

Kernberg

Kernberg (1975, 1980) views this descriptive complex of the narcissistic patient as the manifestations of a person with a borderline personality organization who has a specific patholog-ical self organization. Thus, both narcissistic personality disorder and borderline personality disorder have a borderline personality organization, with differences that will be elaborated. Kernberg stresses pathological internal object relations in his formulations: abnormal combinations of self and object images and positive or negative affects associated with them, in complex relationships to self, ego, and superego structures.

Using Jacobson's (1964) schema, Kernberg first distinguishes between psychosis and borderline personality organization. Someone who is psychotic does not have the solid capacity to keep his self images and object images separate. When self and object images fuse under stress, the patient experiences a blurring of where he ends and the other person begins, as well as the terror of totally losing his sense of separateness. Patients with a borderline personality organization have successfully traversed this develop-mental stage, except for very transient regressions (the brief psychotic episodes that borderline patients can experience). A major difficulty in the internal object relations of patients with a borderline personality organization, according to Kernberg, is their inability to synthesize self and object images that have a positive affective valence with self and object images that have a negative affective valence. This defense structure is the essence of "splitting," which accounts for these patients' inability to feel ambivalence, i.e., simultaneous love and hate, for the important persons in their lives, which is also at the core of their defenses of projective identification and primitive idealization. When these defenses, which contribute to the ego weaknesses of these patients, are added to their nonspecific ego weaknesses — symptoms such as diffuse anxiety, multiple phobias, obsessive-compulsive manifestations, and hypochondriasis, as well as a preponderance of pregenital aggressive impulses — we have some of the major features of Kernberg's borderline personality organization.

The internal object relations of the narcissistic personality disorder patient keep him within a borderline personality organization, but specific differences distinguish him from someone with a borderline personality disorder. According to Kernberg (1975), the narcissistic patient has a pathological fusion of aspects of his ideal self, his real self, and his ideal object. Clinically, this conceptualization can be understood by picturing a person who has combined everything he wants from an ideal other person and all he grandiosely wants for himself with aspects of his real self. Under these circumstances, such a person has within himself everything he needs from others and everything he himself ever wanted for himself. He therefore requires nothing from another person and is totally self-sufficient.

Kernberg stresses the narcissistic personality disorder patient's need for a position of self-sufficiency as a central part of the disorder, and the pathological internal object relations that Kernberg describes allow the patient to feel self-sufficient; under these circumstances he does not have to acknowledge the separate existence of the other person and his feelings of helplessness, envy, and rage about that person. A central aspect of Kernberg's formulation is that the narcissistic patient cannot tolerate his envy and rage toward the person with whom he is involved. His pathological internal world allows him to deny his needs, envy, and rage which would be present in a relationship with that person, who is separate from him and whom he cannot control. Rage and devaluation also protect the patient from acknowledging his intense needs for the other person. Of course, he pays a huge price for such a defensive structure. His inner emptiness, boredom, restlessness, intermittent social withdrawal, and lack of "empathy" for others, coupled with his simultaneous need for admiration from the outside and only transient satisfactions from relationships and work, are well-known aspects.

Kernberg emphasizes the importance of the pathological grandiose self in narcissistic personality disorder (made up of the ideal self, real self, and ideal object). This grandiose self is projected onto the other person, who can then be seen as omnipotent and someone to be idealized. Thus, the idealization in Kernberg's formulation is viewed as defensive—a projection of the patient's own pathological grandiosity. It can serve to protect the patient against his own early self-devaluation and helplessness and the acknowledgment of the other person's separateness.

Kohut

The essential feature of narcissistic personality disorder, according to Kohut, is the person's need for "self-objects" to help him regulate his self-esteem and feel complete (Kohut 1971, 1977). The self-object is someone who performs a necessary function for the person, while being experienced as part of him. Kohut stated that all people need self-objects throughout life; however, for narcissistic personality disorder patients the self-object is crucial because of deficiencies in their internal structure. The vicissitudes of the patient's relationship with the self-object become the core of both the diagnosis of narcissistic personality disorder and the treatment experience. Kohut related self-object needs to childhood experiences with parental figures: a child requires parents who can provide phase-appropriate "mirroring" as well as be available as figures to be idealized, so that the child can "merge" with the soothing qualities of the idealized parent. Mirroring consists of the parents' recognizing the emerging aspects of the child's self and responding appropriately to them. In normal development, Kohut described mirroring as the "gleam in the mother's eye" when she responds to the child's exhibitionistic displays. When appropriate, the parent is sensitive to the child's grandiose self and his need to have this emerging self confirmed. The grandiose self of the child is gradually transformed into the healthy ambitions of the adult through parental responses that take into account the phase-appropriate needs, capacities, and vulnerabilities of the child. In addition, the child develops aspects of his self by taking in functions he needs from the idealized self-object through the process of transmuting internalization, a process involving the internalization of *functions* that the other person has and that the child (or patient) needs. (I believe it is Kohut's emphasis on the taking in of functions that allowed him to leave undefined the inner world of narcissistic personality disorder patients. It explains in part the different emphases of Kernberg and Kohut. When the emphasis is on the internalization of missing functions, there is little need to define self and object representations, and pathological amalgamations of them, as Kernberg does in great detail.)

Implied in the importance of intense self-object needs is the tenuous self-cohesiveness of the narcissistic personality disorder patient. When the self-object disappoints the patient through some "empathic failure," i.e., failure to understand or respond in the way the patient may wish or need, the patient may "fragment" as a manifestation of the problem with self-cohesiveness. The symptoms of fragmentation or lack of solid self-cohesiveness can include hypochondriacal complaints and feelings of bodily disconnection or awkwardness or be behaviorally evident in the patient's aloofness and arrogance.

Kohut's definition of the narcissistic personality disorder included data based on the predominant transferences the patient forms, i.e., self-object transferences involving mirroring and idealization. Although other patients show evidence of these transferences at different points in therapy, the emergence of these transferences as the core transference issues distinguishes the narcissistic personality disorder patient from other patients. These self-object transferences emerge in the treatment of the narcissistic personality disorder patient if the therapist does not impede their development through his countertransference difficulties.

Kohut felt that the "mirror transference in the narrower sense," akin to the gleam in the mother's eye, is the only mirror transference that is similar to the normal mirroring function in the growth of the healthy child and his relationship to his parents. In narcissistic personality disorder, there are two other varieties of mirror transference: twinship, or alter ego, and merger. The former is manifested in the patient who experiences the therapist as identical to himself, i.e., as a twin. In the latter, the patient feels that the therapist has merged with him. (The term "merger" is confusing when one is attempting to understand Kernberg and Kohut. For Kernberg, it means the breakdown of self and object images and, therefore, psychosis. Kohut's use of merger implies intactness of ego and self boundaries except in the area of the "merged" self-object function. A useful conceptualization can be that of viewing two separate people as two circles which overlap only at the area of merged self-object functions. Thus, too great an overlap can approach psychosis and account for the extreme vulnerability to psychosis of some narcissistic patients.) The only time the patient and therapist may be aware of this merger is when it is disrupted, for example, by a perceived empathic failure by the self-object therapist. At that point, the patient in the merger mirror transference can experience fragmentation and "narcissistic" rage.

Kohut emphasized the importance of his contributions of empathic listening and vicarious introspection. He felt that too much clinical work is based on viewing the patient from the outside, rather than the therapist immersing himself in the patient's inner world. He argued that the mechanistic formulations of classical theory tend to be "experience far" rather than "experience near" in their clinical explanations. He defined the exquisite sensitivity of patients who feel misunderstood and the particular vulnerabilities of narcissistic personality disorder patients to empathic failures. He explained that the latter does not mean that the therapist has to be perfect but that everyday failures to understand the patient can have profound meanings and be perceived as empathic failures by narcissistically vulnerable patients.

PSYCHOANALYSIS OR PSYCHOTHERAPY?

Before addressing the clinical relevance of Kernberg's and Kohut's theoretical differences, it is important to clarify the role of psychoanalysis and psychotherapy in the treatment of narcissistic personality disorders. Both Kernberg and Kohut have tended to write about the psychoanalytic treatment of these patients. Kernberg feels that narcissistic personality disorder patients are the one group with borderline personality organization that can most successfully be treated by psychoanalysis. The only exception is the narcissistic patient who is functioning on an overt borderline level, that is, with significant ego weakness including an inability to bear anxiety and a tendency toward impulsivity. Kernberg sees some of these more vulnerable patients as requiring "supportive psychotherapy" if their ego weakness is considerable. Although this group of more vulnerable patients receiving psychotherapy may have the most symptomatic relief when compared with those in psychoanalytic treatment, their pathological self structure is only minimally modified, since it is not the focus of interpretive work in the transference.

Kohut's experience with narcissistic personality disorder patients came largely from his analytic work with patients who had had unsuccessful first psychoanalyses because, in his view, the self-object issues that I have described were not addressed in that treatment. For him, psychoanalytic treatment was the treatment of choice for these patients when the nature of the narcissistic psychopathology was understood and analyzed.

Although the issue of psychotherapy for narcissistic personality disorder patients by psychodynamic psychotherapists has been minimally addressed by Kernberg and Kohut, many clinicians have had experiences that support the efficacy of psychotherapy which uses the principles both workers have described. The phenomena that Kernberg and Kohut have elaborated can be seen in once-to-three-times-weekly psychotherapy, and the work they defined in psychoanalytic treatment is possible in psychodynamic psychotherapy. This does not mean that there are not some patients who need psychoanalysis four to five times per week on the couch. Sometimes a psychotherapeutic trial and the advice of a consultant are needed to determine whether psychoanalysis is necessary when psychotherapy seems to be ineffective. The question is particularly difficult because the narcissistic personality disorder patient's defensive style and/or "fragmentation" present countertransference difficulties that make treatment seem stalemated under the best of circumstances.

THEORETICAL DIFFERENCES BETWEEN
KERNBERG AND KOHUT AND THEIR RELEVANCE
TO PSYCHOTHERAPY

Kernberg and Kohut made formulations of narcissistic personality disorder that can explain many of the clinical manifestations of these patients, yet there are some sharply differing aspects of their theories, which they both based on their clinical experiences. I shall enumerate some of them.

For Kernberg, the patient's idealization of the therapist is primarily defensive and is a projection of his grandiosity onto the therapist. Kohut, on the other hand, saw the idealization as a reactivation in the transference of previously unsuccessful idealization of parents in childhood. Thus, for Kernberg, the idealization—which is seen as a defense against the patient's helplessness and envy of the therapist upon whom he cannot depend and whom he cannot control—ultimately has to be understood and interpreted as a defense. In Kohut's view, these transferences must be allowed to unfold, for they are the basis for understanding some of the parental failures in childhood as well as for transmuting internalizations.

Kernberg stresses the pathological internal object relations of the narcissistic personality disorder patient and in his writing says that Kohut did not have a theory of pathological development that goes beyond fixation. Ornstein (1974) has pointed out that Kohut did distinguish between fixations involving the mirror transference in the narrower sense and the pathological twinship and merger transferences.

Another difference that has only been implied thus far is the role of aggression in these theories. For Kernberg, aggression is one of the two primary drives; problems with oral aggression are a major determinant of narcissistic personality disorder pathology and are therefore important in borderline personality organization. Though at times defensive and coupled with devaluation of the therapist, oral aggression is also at the core of the disorder and partially responsible for the pathological self formation. Kernberg emphasizes that the narcissistic personality disorder patient fears his hatred and envy, feeling that they would destroy his relationship with the therapist and the hope he has of being helped.

Kernberg also faults Kohut for his position in *The Analysis of the Self* (Kohut 1971) in which he took up only the libidinal aspects of narcissistic pathology. Although Ornstein (1974) has argued that Kohut did address aggression later (Kohut 1972), there is a basic difference between the two: Kohut saw aggression as secondary to the patient's disappointment in the failing self-object therapist. With such a formulation, the therapist would tend to focus on the meaning of the empathic failure and its relationship to the patient's past. Kernberg stresses the importance of experiencing the aggression and envy and the analysis of it as it emerges in the patient who struggles to deny the separateness and independence of the therapist. Kernberg also views the patient's use of "disappointments" as defending against his envy and anger. Kohut analyzed these disappointments as a central core of the work in the transference and in understanding the roots of these disappointments in childhood. However, both Kernberg and Kohut have described the progress in the narcissistic personality disorder patient who experiences anger later in treatment.

Kohut and Kernberg have differing views of the relationship between narcissistic personality disorders, borderline personality disorders, and psychosis. As already discussed, Kernberg sees the narcissistic personality disorder patient as having a special constellation within borderline personality organization, a category which also includes borderline personality disorder. Borderline personality organization patients have their major difficulty with splitting issues, in contrast to psychotic patients, who cannot keep their self and object images apart. Kohut, on the other hand, viewed borderline and psychotic patients as close together, both having problems with protracted fragmentation of the self, in contrast to the transient fragmentation of the narcissistic patient. Kohut's formulations tended to place borderline patients out of the realm that uses his self psychology principles of treatment. In contrast, Kernberg links the self pathology of the two groups, since he views both of them as having a borderline personality organization. I (Adler 1981) have attempted to address some of these issues by defining a continuum of borderline to narcissistic personality disorder, describing it diagnostically and clinically, through which the patient moves in successful treatment.

Kohut emphasized the ease with which the narcissistic personality disorder patient can feel humiliated when the self-object bond is transiently severed as part of his feeling misunderstood. Both Kernberg and Kohut have pointed out the tendency of these patients to feel criticized. However, Kernberg describes the primitive guilt, often projected, that plays such a prominent role in the treatment of some narcissistic personality disorder patients. The concept of such guilt is largely absent in Kohut's writings.

Although both Kernberg and Kohut have stressed the interpretations of the transference, they differ in their understanding of it. Kernberg (1975) points out that Kohut's tendency to reconstruct parental failures from the past can deflect the "here and now" negative transference to "blaming" the parents. He criticizes Kohut's emphasis on "disappointments" in the therapist, which would miss the significance of aggression, especially oral aggression. Kohut (1977) explained that he was neutral, blaming neither the parents nor the patient, but analyzing whatever material the patient presented. He also was willing to look at the patient's anger when it did appear. Whether these differing approaches influence the emergence of anger and the nature of the transference will be discussed further.

THEORIES AND THE PSYCHOTHERAPIST

What is the clinician to do when exposed to two theoretical positions that have many similarities and yet profound differences? Even in an important area of agreement between Kernberg and Kohut — that the grandiose self be allowed to emerge in treatment and be analyzed — each meant something different by such a statement. For Kernberg, the grandiose self consists of the pathological amalgam of the ideal self, real self, and ideal object. In contrast, for Kohut the grandiose self was developmentally stunted because of parental self-object failures in the patient's childhood. Kernberg's formulation emphasizes the defensive need of the patient to be self-sufficient and thus avoid his envy of and anger toward the separate therapist, leading to a clinical approach that analyzes these defenses and the pathological grandiose self. Kohut's formulation of parental self-object failures encouraged the therapist to examine "empathic failures" in the emerging self-object transferences.

It is useful for the clinician facing these two opposing formulations to examine some of the complexities of theory formation in relation to the interaction between the clinical experiences and beginning theoretical frameworks of therapists and the personalities of the workers who propose these theories. In addition, it is important to question whether Kernberg and Kohut were describing the same group of patients. If a therapist believes that a primary issue for the narcissistic personality disorder patient is his inability to deal with the fact that his therapist is a separate, independent person whom the patient would envy and hate in acknowledging such a reality, the therapist will focus on clarifying, interpreting, and, at times, confronting these defenses. Such an approach, since it tends to confront something the patient does not want to examine, is likely to elicit anger if it is present. Of course, the therapist may argue that he confronts these issues because they are present and at the core of the disorder. The theoretical framework with which he begins his work may support an approach that stresses an examination of, for example, aggression, especially oral aggression in patients with primitive personality organization. If oral aggression is indeed a major problem for the narcissistic personality disorder patient, the confrontation about independent aspects of his therapist that he is avoiding will tend to make the aggression manifest. The beginning theory and the clinical approach which makes use of it are then likely to confirm that aspect of the theory in patients treated according to the theory. Of course, critics could then debate whether the emerging clinical issues are of primary or secondary importance or even iatrogenic (Brandchaft and Stolorow 1984). Similarly, the theory which develops around the "glue" that attaches people to each other, the failure of these attachments, and the missing structures that must be repaired because of failures with these attachments is likely to lead to a clinical approach that is less confronting, since it does not emphasize facing issues that the patient is avoiding, such as the fact of the therapist's separateness. The clinical data derived on the basis of this formulation will be less likely to elicit aggression, even if it does exist in the patient, and also will be likely to confirm its theoretical beginnings and elaborate them. Thus, beginning theory implies a clinical approach that leads to data collection, which tends to confirm the theory and encourage further clinical work, which supports the theory even more.

Another important aspect of clinical practice and its relation to theory formation is the basic personality and style of the clinician-theoretician, as well as whatever remnants of unresolved personal issues exist in him. The personality of the clinician-theoretician will play a role in determining (1) which aspects of his patients he is more likely to observe, respond to, be empathically available to, and use in his formulations, (2) which aspects he is more likely to ignore or (3) respond to on the basis of his own unresolved difficulties, and (4) the degree of activity, aggression, confrontation, warmth, and support he brings to a clinical situation even as he attempts to monitor his interactions according to his formulations. Thus, the personality of the clinician-theoretician becomes another important factor that may determine his particular interest in certain theories at the beginning of his work and the nature of the clinical data he elicits and collects, all in a complex, circularly reinforcing manner.

Can we argue that we are seeing different aspects of the narcissistic personality disorder patient when we study the contributions of Kernberg, Kohut, and others? And does the uniqueness of their personalities, as well as their theoretical beginnings, determine the specific aspects that each elicits in his clinical work? I believe that such a view is valid and useful. In addition, Kernberg and Kohut may have been treating different patient populations, each of which shows different parts of the narcissistic personality disorder patient (Spruiell 1974). Kernberg, with his background of work in a hospital setting with patients who have a primitive personality organization, not only may be able to view certain features of narcissistic patients more clearly but may also treat patients who have more primitive narcissistic personality disorder issues. Kohut, working primarily as a psychoanalyst with the reanalyses of patients who had had unsuccessful first psychoanalytic treatments, may have been seeing another spectrum of narcissistic personality disorder patients. Although these statements may be partially correct, Kernberg's clinical illustrations include both healthier and more primitive narcissistic personality disorder patients. The answer, then, is unclear. In addition, it does appear that there are narcissistic patients who present issues closer to those described by Kernberg, which involve problems of envy, aggression, and guilt, while others present issues closer to the self-object failures defined by Kohut.

Returning to the dilemma of the psychotherapist treating narcissistic personality disorder patients, we are now able to make a few statements that can be helpful. Since current theories support opposing views of these patients and are derived from the complex interactions of the factors described, the clinician can view himself as being in an enviable position. He can understand these theories and make his own observations. He can also observe himself with his patients and attempt to determine what role his own personality style, countertransference difficulties, and theoretical constructs play in his work with narcissistic patients and how he can work optimally with them. He can also remember that the theoreticians described in this paper have treated narcissistic personality disorder patients and are optimistic about the outcome, although they have emphasized the difficulty of the task.

COUNTERTRANSFERENCE

Both Kernberg and Kohut have described the boredom experienced by the therapist in treating the narcissistic personality disorder patient who is functioning as if he were self-sufficient (Kernberg) or in a merger self-object transference (Kohut). This boredom can help the therapist in understanding the transference and exploring it. The therapist's countertransference responses to boredom that can cause difficulties in the work include withdrawal, indifference, and sadistic confrontations. The latter can occur because the patient's withdrawal defends against his envy and anger. The therapist's sadistic response can be a manifestation of countertransference projective identification.

Projective identification is a useful concept that helps us to understand much of the countertransference experience and difficulty in working with patients who have a primitive personality organization, including patients with narcissistic personality disorder. In projective identification the patient symbolically places a part of himself onto the therapist and then acts toward the therapist in a way that provokes a response consistent with the projected part (Ogden 1979). This can result in the therapist's either acting out the patient's projected difficulties or tolerating them while attempting to help the patient understand them. The therapist thus reprocesses the projection so that the patient can reinternalize another version of the projection (the "identification" aspect of projective identification).

Another difficulty with the narcissistic personality disorder patient (as well as with the borderline patient) is his tendency to devalue the therapist (Adler 1970), which Kernberg ascribes to his need to keep his envy under control. The countertransference problem this experience provokes is related to the normal need of all therapists to feel adequately valued and validated in their work (Adler 1984); the patient who consistently devalues his therapist does not offer such a validation. When coupled with projective identification, which places a devalued part of the patient onto the therapist and provokes a devaluing countertransference response, the therapist's feeling of self-worth may be seriously diminished, and guilt may be aroused in him because of the angry, sadistic fantasies that can accompany these countertransference experiences. The burden of tolerating such countertransference feelings in part explains why therapists limit the number of such patients they treat at any one time.

An area of countertransference controversy involves the therapist's response to the patient's idealization. Since Kernberg is concerned about the narcissistic personality disorder patient's defensive use of idealization, he emphasizes that the therapist may help the patient avoid his anger by accepting the idealization at face value. Kohut, who viewed the idealization as a reactivation of failures in idealization of parental figures in the patient's past, described the countertransference problem of therapists who are uncomfortable with being idealized. He related these difficulties to unresolved issues in the therapist, which can lead to failure of the idealizing self-object transference to develop optimally. The clinician who is faced with these opposing views can wonder whether both theoretical positions are valid at different times in treatment and with different patients who have a narcissistic personality disorder.

When the many complex issues outlined in this paper are evaluated, the clinician can understand why these patients may be so difficult to treat and why a respected colleague can be useful for consultation, either at crisis points or on an ongoing basis. Although Kernberg and Kohut have elaborated the treatability of patients with narcissistic personality disorder, they have emphasized the many problems, both clinical and theoretical, and the long journey for both patient and therapist. Further work by many clinicians is required to answer the questions raised in this chapter and to add further clarity to a complex clinical and theoretical dilemma and debate.

REFERENCES

Adler, G. (1970). Valuing and devaluing in the psychotherapeutic process. *Archives of General Psychiatry* 22:454–461.

———— (1981). The borderline-narcissistic personality disorder continuum. *American Journal of Psychiatry* 138:46–50.

———— (1984). Issues in the treatment of the borderline patient. In *Kohut's Legacy: Contributions to Self Psychology,* ed. P. E. Stepansky and A. Goldberg, pp. 117–134. Hillsdale, NJ: Analytic Press.

Brandchaft, B., and Stolorow, R. D. (1984). The borderline concept: pathological character or iatrogenic myth? In *Empathy II,* ed. J. Lichtenberg, M. Bornstein, and D. Silver, pp. 333–357. Hillsdale, NJ: Analytic Press.

Jacobson, E. *The Self and the Object World.* New York: International Universities Press.

Kernberg, O. (1975). *Borderline Conditions and Pathological Narcissism.* New York: Jason Aronson.

———— (1980). *Internal World and External Reality.* New York: Jason Aronson.

Kohut, H. (1971). *The Analysis of the Self.* New York: International Universities Press.

———— (1972). Thoughts on narcissism and narcissistic rage. *Psychoanalytic Study of the Child* 27:360–400. New Haven: Yale University Press.

———— (1977). *The Restoration of the Self.* New York: International Universities Press.

Masterson, J. F. (1981). *The Narcissistic and Borderline Disorders.* New York: Brunner/Mazel.

Modell, A. (1963). Primitive object relationships and the predisposition to schizophrenia. *International Journal of Psycho-Analysis* 44:282–292.

———— (1976). "The holding environment" and the therapeutic action of psychoanalysis. *Journal of the American Psychoanalytic Association* 24:285–307.

Ogden, T. H. (1979). On projective identification. *International Journal of Psycho-Analysis* 60:357–373.

Ornstein, P. H. (1974). A discussion of the paper by Otto F. Kernberg on "further contributions to the treatment of narcissistic personalities." *International Journal of Psycho-Analysis* 55:241–247.

Rinsley, D. B. (1982). *Borderline and Other Self Disorders.* New York: Jason Aronson.

Spruiell, V. (1974). Theories of the treatment of narcissistic personalities. *Journal of the American Psychoanalytic Association* 22:268–278.

III

BACK TO THE SOURCE

The inner source of object relations theory is individual psycho-analytic work with narcissistic, borderline, and psychotic patients. Advances are still being made in that area. The following four chapters demonstrate recent advances in work with difficult patients.

11

On "Doing Nothing" in the Psychoanalytic Treatment of the Refractory Borderline Patient

Glen O. Gabbard

Glen Gabbard has played an important role in applying object relations theory to new areas of study—general psychiatry, hospital treatment, the psychology of physicians, and drama. In this chapter, he returns to the source, creatively extending our understanding of and ability to treat patients with refractory borderline disorders in intensive psychotherapy.

Gabbard illustrates that the source of insight is not in the subject matter alone, the patient to be observed, but also within the psychotherapist who observes himself in relation to the patient. As one aspect of this process, he reminds us, the therapist "must monitor what one projects into the patient" (p. 218).

Gabbard's clear writing and mastery of the concepts make his exposition of paradox seem straightforward, almost simple. For example, he demonstrates how actively "doing nothing" can be a central intervention when the patient needs the therapist to exist for him without doing anything to him. The focus of the work is on a way of being with the patient. Perhaps the way we are with patients is also at the center of

*psychotherapy with healthier individuals, with whom it is not
so apparent, as well as with more disturbed individuals.*

*Gabbard's understanding of object relations theory's place
in general psychiatry and its relationship to ego psychology
and self psychology is discussed in his fine text, Psychodynamic Psychiatry in Clinical Practice (Gabbard 1990).*

"There is room for the idea that significant relating and
communicating is silent." D. W. Winnicott (1963)

It is the psychoanalyst's lot in life to endure prolonged silences in
the course of his practice. Much has been written about the
optimal technical approach to periods of silence in the resistant
neurotic patient. As these patients are generally amenable to
verbal interventions, a variety of interpretations, confrontations,
and inquiries have been advocated and used with varying degrees
of success. Since the neurotic patient is ordinarily capable of
forming a therapeutic alliance with the analyst in pursuit of a
common goal, i.e., analyzing the resistance, such silences are often
relatively short lived.

Much less has been written about the analytic management of
silence with regressed borderline patients. In the long-term psychoanalytic hospital, one not uncommonly encounters personality-
disordered patients who systematically defeat all treatment efforts. While some employ splitting maneuvers for this purpose
(Gabbard 1986), others use passive, silent resistance. These latter
patients do not sign themselves out of the hospital, yet they seem
incapable of developing an alliance with those who seek to help
them. In the most refractory cases, the analyst may feel like he is
"doing nothing" for protracted periods of time while the patient
refuses to collaborate in the analytic task. Verbal interventions
may simply intensify the patient's commitment to thwart the
analyst and result in more intense passivity.

The analyst who is confronted with these circumstances must
devise strategies to persevere in the face of the slings and arrows of
outrageous resistance. How does one endure the monotony? The
assault on one's therapeutic effectiveness? The helplessness? The
frustration? The hatred of one's tormentor? The wish to give up?

It has been said that nothing is more practical than a good

theory. The analyst's application of theoretical understanding to the here-and-now transference–countertransference situation may enable him to survive such adverse developments. In the most optimistic scenario, it may even lead to a breakthrough of the stalemate. In actual fact, of course, the analyst is not "doing nothing," as it might appear to the naive observer. On the contrary, with the help of his own associative train of thought and his knowledge of theory, he actively seeks to understand the patient's silence and the vicissitudes of the internal object relations that lie behind it.

THEORETICAL AND TECHNICAL CONSIDERATIONS

All considerations of theory and technique with the silently resistant borderline patient must follow from one basic assumption: a relationship is always present, even in the absence of verbalization. Moreover, the presence of a relationship between patient and analyst implies that there are transference and countertransference elements to be understood and analysed. As Rangell (1982) has observed, Freud's assertion that patients suffering from "narcissistic neuroses" do not form transferences is one of his few clinical observations that has not been validated by subsequent analytic experience. The apparent absence of transference *is* the transference (Brenner 1982). One component of "doing nothing," then, is the analyst's systematic examination of the vicissitudes of transference and countertransference, even if conducted in total silence. As the analyst sits in the stillness of the consulting room, he ponders the question, "What object relationship paradigms from the past are being repeated in the present?"

With the primitively organized, regressed patient, transference and countertransference are best understood as externalizations of internal object relations (Ogden 1983). Via projective identification, the analyst is the recipient of both the patient's internal object-representations and his internal self-representations. A number of authors (Bion 1967, Grotstein 1981, Heimann 1950, Malin and Grotstein 1966, Ogden 1982) have written about the therapeutic processing of these projective identifications. One of the principal functions of the analyst is to serve as a container for the self- and object-representations, as well as the affects connected with them, that are projected into the analyst by the patient. Bion (1967) linked his model of the "container-contained" to his understanding of the developmental process of the infant, who projects the unwanted aspects of his internal world (the contained) into the breast-mother, who serves as a container. The mother holds and processes the projected elements and returns them in modified and detoxified form to the infant. In a similar manner the analyst contains and modifies the patient's projections before the patient reintrojects them. In both the original developmental situation and the later therapeutic one, the result is growth and integration of one's internal self- and object-representations.

As Langs (1976) contends, however, the analyst is not simply a blank screen or a container without contents of its own. The projective identification process works both ways. Especially in cases of refractory silent patients, the patient becomes a container for the projections of the analyst. This aspect of treatment is stunningly portrayed in Bergman's *Persona,* where a nurse is given responsibility for a patient who has become completely mute. The absence of verbal information from the patient makes her an ideal repository for the projections of the nurse-therapist, who becomes increasingly out of control as she treats her patient as if she were an embodiment of her own (the nurse's) internal objects. Searles (1975) similarly notes that the patient attempts to treat the analyst by becoming what the analyst wants him to be, and he links these efforts to the infant's need to "cure" the mother.

The form of silent mental processing that is being advocated here requires an openness or receptivity to the patient's projections without getting carried away to the point of countertransference acting out (Ogden 1982). The analyst must retain enough objectivity to observe what is happening to him while he is experiencing the powerful affects associated with the projected contents. In a similar vein, one must monitor what one projects into the patient. The analyst may not be able to process and understand the projective identifications until after he has been "coerced" by the patient into playing a role in the patient's internal drama. The analyst's task is to keep this role-playing in the realm of a feeling state rather than an action. The feeling of wanting to strike the patient, for example, may lead to a recognition of projective identification, which in turn leads to a processing of the interaction that heads off an actual striking out at the patient.

After the analyst has recognized his collusion in the object world of the patient, he may wish to return the projection to the patient via interpretation. More often, however, with the regressed and recalcitrant borderline patient, who has sworn an oath of silence, the interpretation will only heighten the resistance. Hence, the analyst must silently note his observation, formulate the interaction in his own mind, and allow the understanding to inform his subsequent interaction with the patient. The analyst's task is succinctly summed up by Ogden (1982):

> The perspective of projective identification neither requires nor excludes the use of verbal interpretations; the therapist attempts to find a way of talking with and being with the patient that will constitute a medium through which the therapist may accept unintegratable aspects of the patient's internal object world and return them to the patient in a form that the patient can accept and learn from. [p. 42]

Quite apart from any interpretive efforts, then, the analyst's response to the projections provides a new object and affect for internalization by the patient. In this regard he breaks the repetitive cycle of pathological object relations that has characterized the patient's life. These patterns originated in early relationships with parental figures—what Epstein (1979) refers to as primary maturational failure. The patient evokes similar reactions in his adult life, and these can be labeled *secondary* maturational failures. The reactions of others to the patient so consistently fit this pattern that he rarely experiences a maturationally corrective response. Epstein suggests that the analyst's strategy is to figure out a way to be with the patient that *is* maturationally corrective. In other words, the analyst attempts to provide a relationship in which he does *not* respond to the patient's projections like everyone else and therefore avoids another *secondary* maturational failure.

One final theoretical point comes from Winnicott's (1963) observations regarding the need not to communicate: "There is an intermediate stage in healthy development in which the patient's most important experience in relation to the good or potentially satisfying object is the refusal of it" (p. 182). He asserts that at the core of the true self in all of us is a segment that must remain incommunicado. This isolation preserves an authenticity that is sacred to the evolving self. Winnicott insists that our technique must accommodate the patient who is communicating to us that he is not communicating. Being "alone," yet in the presence of the analyst, may fulfill an important developmental need that the analyst should not violate by bombarding the patient with interpretations. Winnicott notes that a lengthy period of silence may be the most therapeutic experience for certain patients, and the analyst who patiently waits may be more helpful than one who insists on verbal communication.

Winnicott's technical recommendations grow out of his theoretical understanding of an important transition in the infant's internal object world. The maternal object is originally perceived by the infant as a *subjective* phenomenon, an extension of the infant. As a result of development, the subjective object is transformed into an *objective* object, one that is partly created by the infant and partly the by-product of the infant's increasing attunement with external reality. Explicit communication is a requirement for the objective object, but is entirely unnecessary when relating to the subjective object. In Winnicott's view, overt communication always runs the risk of creating a false self that merely complies with the demands of the object. When this lack of authenticity begins to disturb the developing child, he retreats into silent communication with the subjective object as a way of restoring a sense of a true and real self. Hence Winnicott postulates that there is a fundamental split in the self: One part communicates explicitly with objective objects, while another communicates silently with subjective objects. The latter aspect of the self must be respected and validated for healthy development to proceed.

CLINICAL EXAMPLE: DISENGAGING FROM THE PATIENT'S PROJECTIVE IDENTIFICATION

A fragment of an actual analysis may be helpful in illustrating these theoretical and technical points as they apply to prolonged periods where the analyst is apparently doing nothing.

John was an 18-year-old young man who came to the Menninger Hospital after defeating all previous treatment experiences. He had failed to graduate from high school despite above average intelligence and numerous tutorial sessions, and he had been fired from several part-time jobs. His academic and vocational endeavors were torpedoed largely because of his refusal to get out of bed. On the numerous mornings in which John stayed in bed, his father would typically return home from work and scream at him to get up and get dressed. These coercive efforts culminated in his father's attempts to physically lift John out of bed and dress him. As John tipped the scales at around 240 pounds, all such heroic efforts were doomed to failure.

On a typical day, John would rise late in the afternoon and go to the tennis courts, where he apparently distinguished himself, having won several tournaments. Other areas of poor impulse control, however, caused the family a good deal of distress. On two occasions, John had disappeared for days with the family station wagon; and on another, he had impulsively stolen a car. Outpatient psychotherapy had been unsuccessful since John had refused to attend the sessions. After a girlfriend jilted him, he made an impulsive suicide attempt and ended up in a hospital near his home. There he stayed in bed until 5 P.M. every day and refused to participate in any of the treatment activities. His psychiatrist finally referred him to the Menninger Hospital, and he indicated in his referral that all his efforts to force John to talk during therapy sessions had been for naught.

When he arrived at the Menninger Hospital, John signed himself into the institution on a voluntary basis and seemed motivated to overcome his inability to "follow through on commitments." A thorough diagnostic evaluation revealed no signs of psychosis or major depression. The social worker assigned to the case described John's mother as intrusive and overinvolved. His father came across as demanding and authoritarian. Psychological testing revealed borderline ego functioning and paranoid-schizoid tendencies. He seemed incapable of conceptualizing his internal experience, so he resorted to communication through action. Specifically, the testing suggested that when he felt forced to submit to what he perceived as unrealistic expectations, he became resentful and enraged. He responded to these unacceptable feelings by retreating into a passive, withdrawn state of silence.

During the first few preparatory sessions of his analytic work with me, he talked openly in our face-to-face meetings about his history and his wish to turn his life around. He failed to show up for his fourth session, and the unit staff called to inform me that he would not get out of bed. When he did not attend the next session, I went to his hospital room, as was the common practice at that time. John was lying in bed, clearly awake, but with his eyes closed, feigning sleep. In a rather calm tone of voice, I asked him to get out of bed and come to my office. I informed him that I could not help him accomplish his goal of turning his life around if he would not come to my office and talk with me. My statements were met, of course, with stony silence. I advised him that he was repeating his pattern here and asked him if that were really what he wanted to do. More silence. I felt myself becoming increasingly irritated at John, and as I stood at his bedside, I had a conscious fantasy of pulling him out of bed and forcing him to sit up and talk to me. I sat down in his desk chair and joined him in silence. I reflected on how surprised I was by the intensity of my anger. Since patients typically repeat their family situations in the hospital, I should have taken this repetition as a matter of course.

I continued to sit in John's room for a few more sessions. As my anger subsided, I realized how utterly powerless and helpless I felt in my attempts to get through to John and to forge some semblance of a therapeutic alliance with him. Although it was premature to offer interpretations, I nevertheless asked periodic questions regarding the function of his silence, all of which were met with unwavering quiet. When I heard from a nurse that he arose in the evening and played cards with his peers, I was again irritated. I asked him why he could get up to play cards, but could not get up for our sessions. No response. As I left his room at the end of one session, a nurse informed me that he had hung up on his parents the night before when they asked him why he would not get out of bed.

As I sat with John the following day, I reflected further on the internal object relations that were being played out in the stark silence of John's hospital room. I had responded to John's passive resistance much as his father had. I unconsciously identified with the projected internal object characterized by an angry, demanding expectation that he should do what I wanted him to do. My reaction occurred in muted form as compared to the father's, but I could certainly empathize with the father's more extreme reaction. My anger regarding his selective interest in getting up to play cards undoubtedly paralleled his father's anger that he could get up for tennis but not for school. The information from the nurse about the phone call helped me understand that the more I expected him to conform to my expectations, the more he would withdraw.

I spent several more sessions silently associating and interpreting to myself the various meanings of the interaction between John and me. I continued to experience alternating feelings of anger and helplessness.

It was extraordinarily useful for me to contain and process these feelings for a number of sessions without attempting to force the projections back into John. Such interventions would have been experienced as an intrusion or violation of John's privacy and his right not to communicate in a verbal mode. Moreover, containing the feelings allowed me to make further connections to John's own internal object relations. For example, when I felt strongly that I wanted to "unload" some of the feelings back on to the patient with a verbal barrage, I sensed that I was very likely identifying with the same projected internal object that the intrusive and overinvolved mother aligned herself with. On the other hand, in those moments where I felt most helpless and powerless, it became clear to me that I was identifying with an aspect of John's self-experience. Through this projective identification process, John *was* communicating to me. He was letting me know how it felt to be powerless and helpless, as he so often did.

As my attention ebbed and flowed during those many hours of silence, I noted how strongly invested I was, at least at times, in making John talk. Although at some level I was undoubtedly identifying with the demanding father, I associated to my own need to change John as a representation of an object in my own intrapsychic world. This object-representation of mine, which was undoubtedly influenced by parental figures in my childhood, had been externalized in this analytic process because it paralleled in many ways the interaction between John and his father. My own tendency to expect John to conform to my wishes provided a kernel of reality (Ogden 1982) onto which John could conveniently project his demanding internal object associated with his father.

I realized that as long as I conformed to the demanding father, I would not be providing a maturationally corrective experience for John, and we would be at a stalemate. Even as I sat silently, I was nevertheless expecting something from John. I was clearly not content for him to be silent. To disengage from the expectation that he should talk would also be to disengage from a pathological and repetitive projective identification process involving a demanding object-representation and a recalcitrant and oppositional self-representation. Following Searles's (1965) recommendation regarding periods of silence in the treatment of the schizophrenic patient, I began bringing reading material to the sessions. At the beginning of each hour, I explained to John that I was going to read during our time together. I further conveyed to him that I would be happy to put down my reading at any time, if he wished to discuss anything with me, but that I would be equally content to pass the time in silence with him.

I began this practice after approximately one month of silence. I continued to read and pass the sessions in silence for nearly three more months. As I became absorbed in my reading matter over a period of time, I realized that I had successfully disengaged from my wish to make John talk. I was content to allow him his private, quiet space while I occupied myself with my own interests. In the third month of this arrangement, an evening nurse informed me that John was getting quite angry at me because he felt I was "treating him like a baby" by sitting in his room every day with him. The astute nurse replied that if he truly disliked what was going on, all he had to do was get up and come to my office every morning for our sessions. Shortly thereafter, I was shocked to leave my office one morning on the way to the hospital unit only to find John sitting in the waiting room outside my office. I shall never forget the gleeful, triumphant look on his face when he saw my surprise. I invited him into my office, where we continued the analysis from that point on. Although he was not sure why he had decided to get up and come to my office, it was clear to me that my disengagement from the projective identification process had allowed John to take back his anger and his demandingness and begin to own them as aspects of himself. He was then able to use them constructively to motivate himself for treatment. Throughout the rest of his hospital stay, he continued to get up at eight o'clock every morning and participate in all the treatment activities and in his analysis.

Discussion

Psychoanalysis may be characterized as much by what the analyst does not do as by what he does. His decision not to make any verbal interventions may be the most therapeutically effective strategy with which to approach the refractory silent borderline patient. The case of John illustrates Ogden's (1982) point that psychoanalytic work does not need to be interpretive to be considered psychoanalytic. A systematic examination of the months of silence described above allows us to enumerate a number of significant intrapsychic and interpersonal phenomena that transpired during a period where the analyst to all outward appearance seemed to be doing nothing:

(1) Diagnosis of the patient's internal object relations. By serving as a container for the patient's projective identifications, I

was able to formulate a tentative diagnostic understanding of the patient's internal world. At varying times, I identified with a demanding, coercive object-representation (most often associated with father); a violating, intrusive object-representation (most often associated with mother); and a helpless and powerless self-representation. Obviously, an intimate knowledge of the patient's internal object relations helps the analyst gain a greater understanding of the patient's pathological interpersonal relations as well.

(2) Self-analysis. As I contained various projections from the patient, I also made associative linkages to my own internal object- and self-representations. This form of self-analysis enabled me to clarify certain aspects of the analytic interaction in which I was using the patient as a container for my own projections and thus enacting repetitive interactions from my own life.

(3) Disengagement from the projective identification process. My processing of the patient's projected contents enabled me to avoid behaving like a projected aspect of the patient's internal world. Instead of responding in a manner that Grinberg (1979) refers to as projective counteridentification, i.e., as a demanding internal object to the patient's passive resistant self, I was able to provide a maturationally corrective experience. In Epstein's (1979) terms, I was able to figure out a way to be with the patient that *corrected* rather than *perpetuated* the secondary maturational failures to which the patient had become accustomed.

(4) Disengagement from expectations. Bion (1970) repeatedly advised the analyst to approach the patient without expectations, desire, or memory. As I became aware that even my silent and patient waiting for John to talk was perceived by John as a pathological repetition of the demands and expectations of his parents, I was gradually able to divorce myself from my own need to engage in a verbal and mutual understanding of the analytic interaction. I am convinced that my own contentment with my role of quietly reading in John's presence was crucial to John's eventual emergence from his withdrawal. At some point he undoubtedly sensed that his passivity was no longer thwarting my efforts to make him talk, thus losing its psychological importance.

Another way of understanding the change in the patient's ego functioning as a result of the period of silence is that I had passed an unconscious "test" constructed by the patient. Through extensive study of actual transcripts of analyses with neurotics, Weiss and colleagues (1986) have evolved a hypothesis that suggests such tests may be of paramount importance in a successful analysis. A patient develops pathological beliefs based on early interactions with parental figures, according to this hypothesis, and seeks unconsciously to disconfirm these beliefs in analysis so that development can proceed. The analyst is treated in the same way as the patient treated his parents to see if the analyst will respond similarly to them. In other words, when I failed to respond with demands and expectations to the patient's silence and passivity, I disconfirmed his belief that all parental figures would violate his privacy and force him to conform to their expectations. Relief and an increase in generalized ego functioning often result from such disconfirmations. Although the work of Weiss and his colleagues was based on neurotic patients in classical analyses, one can assume that a similar mechanism may operate in more disturbed patients such as John.

(5) Modification of projections for reintrojection. The processing of the self- and object-representations deposited in me by the patient allowed John to take them back in a modified and more tolerable form. John's conversation with the evening nurse suggests that the intense rage of the demanding and overbearing internal object associated with father was modified to a more constructive form of anger. He was able to verbalize his feelings of anger at me for what he experienced as an infantilization of him, and he was able to use it to mobilize his ego resources to break the cycle of self-destructive passivity. Similarly, the persecutory and coercive quality of the internal object was "detoxified" into a more reasonable internal demand to change.

(6) Legitimization of the private, noncommunicative core of the self. In disengaging myself from pressuring John to speak, I also communicated to him that I respected his need for silence. In speaking of the adolescent's need to isolate himself, Winnicott (1963) notes: "This preservation of personal isolation is part of the search for identity, and for the establishment of a personal technique for communicating which does not lead to violation of the central self" (p. 190). Winnicott observes that many adoles-

cents experience psychoanalysis as a kind of spiritual rape because their evolving identity is repeatedly intruded upon by the curious analyst. The formation of a therapeutic alliance is generally considered to be critically important in the treatment of the borderline patient (Gabbard et al. 1988). In patients such as John, silent respect for the patient's central self may be the only viable technical approach to fostering the therapeutic alliance.

As the analyst legitimizes the patient's choice not to communicate through words, he also allows for the transition from being perceived as a subjective object to one that is predominantly perceived as an objective object. Winnicott warns of the danger inherent in verbally intruding on the patient before this important transition has been completed. A premature violation of this "subjective object" period may overwhelm the patient and lead to psychotic disorganization. Searles (1986) seems to grasp Winnicott's point in his observation that

> Winnicott's concept of the good enough holding environment implies that the analyst be not merely relatively stably there, for the patient, but also relatively destructible (psychologically) by the patient, time and again, as the patient's persistent needs for autistic (omnipotent) functioning still require. Hence the analyst needs intuitively to provide his own absence, perhaps as often as his own presence, to the patient at timely moments. [p. 351]

In the course of analytic work with refractory borderline patients, the analyst will experience protracted periods of silence. The analyst's verbal interventions are likely to fall on deaf ears and produce little change in the stalemate. The analyst may then need to resort to silent processing of the projective identification process transpiring between patient and analyst and use it to inform the manner in which he functions with the patient. In this chapter I have dissected out six active components of these phases of analysis where the analyst may appear to be doing nothing.

REFERENCES

Bion, W. R. (1967). *Second Thoughts*. New York: Jason Aronson.
———— (1970). *Attention and Interpretation*. London: Tavistock.

Brenner, C. (1982). *The Mind in Conflict*. New York: International Universities Press.

Epstein, L. (1979). Countertransference with borderline patients. In *Countertransference,* ed. L. Epstein and A. Feiner. New York: Jason Aronson.

Gabbard, G. O. (1986). The treatment of the "special" patient in a psychoanalytic hospital. *International Review of Psycho-Analysis* 13:333–347.

Gabbard, G. O., Horwitz, L., Frieswyck, S., et al. (1988). The effect of therapist interventions on the therapeutic alliance with borderline patients. *Journal of the American Psychoanalytic Association* 36:697–727.

Grinberg, L. (1979). Projective counteridentification. In *Countertransference,* ed. L. Epstein and A. Feiner, pp. 169–191. New York: Jason Aronson.

Grotstein, J. S. (1981). *Splitting and Projective Identification*. New York: Jason Aronson.

Heimann, P. (1950). On counter-transference. *International Journal of Psycho-Analysis* 31:81–84.

Langs, R. (1976). *The Bipersonal Field*. New York: Jason Aronson.

Malin, A., and Grotstein, J. S. (1966). Projective identification in the therapeutic process. *International Journal of Psycho-Analysis* 47:26–31.

Ogden, T. (1982). *Projective Identification and Psychotherapeutic Technique*. New York: Jason Aronson.

——— (1983). The concept of internal object relations. *International Journal of Psycho-Analysis* 64:181–198.

Rangell, L. (1982). The self in psychoanalytic theory. *Journal of the American Psychoanalytic Association* 30:863–891.

Searles, H. F. (1965). *Collected Papers on Schizophrenia and Related Subjects*. New York: International Universities Press.

——— (1975). The patient as therapist to his analyst. In *Tactics and Techniques in Psychoanalytic Psychotherapy,* vol. 2, *Countertransference,* ed. P. Giovacchini, pp. 95–151. New York: Jason Aronson.

——— (1986). *My Work with Borderline Patients*. Northvale, NJ: Jason Aronson.

Weiss, J., Sampson, H., and The Mount Zion Psychotherapy Research Group. (1986). *The Psychoanalytic Process: Theory, Clinical Observation and Empirical Research*. New York: Guilford.

Winnicott, D. W. (1963). Communicating and not communicating leading to a study of certain opposites. In *The Maturational Processes and the Facilitating Environment,* pp. 179–192. New York: International Universities Press.

Misrecognitions and the Fear of Not Knowing

Thomas H. Ogden

*T*homas Ogden's key work clarifying interpersonal aspects
of projective identification established for him a place in
North American object relations theory. Subsequently, he
built on these ideas, discussing how the human mind emerges
from a matrix of self and other relationships and develops
into a different kind of matrix, comprised of transformed
self and other elements, eventually coalescing into a coherent, overarching sense of self. In The Matrix of the Mind
(Ogden 1986), he describes this growth process.

   The following chapter reports Ogden's work with a patient
whose life was based on a series of misrecognitions between
self and object. Here, Ogden uses an awareness of his own
feelings of detachment within the therapy and the concept of
projective identification to understand how not being known
for himself formed the foundation of his patient's internal
world. Facing the anxiety of not being known, the patient
and analyst can find the kernel of a solid and honest
relationship. How interesting that this patient discovers a
genuine relationship for the first time only when his analyst
recognizes his profound lack of relatedness to the patient,
tolerating it without having to change it.

Similar to Gabbard's preceding chapter, the key to this difficult therapy is based on the understanding of paradox using the concepts of projective identification and counter-transference. Perhaps a study of projective identification helps unravel therapeutic paradoxes because it removes the immutability of the self-object dichotomy, while acknowledging that self and other are distinguishable.

The work of a group of British and French psychoanalytic thinkers, including Bion, Lacan, McDougall, Tustin, and Winnicott, has led me to understand certain psychological difficulties in terms of an unconscious fear of not knowing. What the individual is not able to know is what he feels, and therefore who, if anyone, he is. The patient regularly creates the illusion for himself (and secondarily for others) that he is able to generate thoughts and feelings, wishes and fears, that feel like his own. Although this illusion constitutes an effective defense against the terror of not knowing what one feels or who one is, it further alienates the individual from himself. The illusion of knowing is achieved through the creation of a wide range of substitute formations that fill the "potential space" (Winnicott 1971) in which desire and fear, appetite and fullness, love and hate, might otherwise come into being.

The "misrecognitions" that are used as defenses against the fear of not knowing represent a less extreme form of alienation from affective experience than "alexithymia" (Nemiah 1977), states of "non-experience" (Ogden 1980, 1982), and "disaffected" states (McDougall, Chapter 13, this volume) wherein potential feelings and fantasies are foreclosed from the psychological sphere. It is also a less extreme psychological catastrophe than schizophrenic fragmentation wherein there is very little of a self capable of creating, shaping, and organizing the internal and external stimuli that ordinarily constitute experience. The patients I will be focusing upon have the capacity to generate a sense of self sufficiently integrated and sufficiently bounded to be able to know that they do not know. That is, they are able to experience the beginnings of feelings of confusion, emptiness, despair, and panic as well as being able to mobilize defenses against these incipient feelings.

As will be discussed, in the course of development a sense of self evolves in the context of the management of need by the mother–infant pair. When the mother can satisfactorily tolerate the recognition of her own desires and fears, she is less afraid of states of tension generated by her infant that are in the process of becoming feelings. When the mother is capable of tolerating the infant's tension over time, it is possible for her to respond to a given tension state as a quality of the infant's being alive.

A THEORETICAL BACKGROUND

The development of the idea of misrecognitions of one's internal state is in a sense synonymous with the development of psychoanalytic theory. One of the cornerstones upon which Freud constructed his theory of psychological meanings is the idea that one knows more than he thinks he knows. The creation of psychological defenses can be understood as the organization of systematic misrecognitions (e.g., it is not my anger that I fear, it is yours). Freud (1911), in his discussion of the Schreber case, explored the idea that psychosis involves the misrecognition of one's internal state through its attribution to external objects.

It is beyond the scope of this paper to review, or even list, the multitude of contributions to the question of psychological misrecognition and the defenses associated with it. I will, however, briefly discuss a group of concepts developed by French and British psychoanalytic thinkers that have particular relevance to the ideas being developed in the present paper.

Lacan (1948) believed that Freud in his later work "seems suddenly to fail to recognize the existence of everything that the ego neglects, scotomizes, misconstrues in the sensations" (p. 22). Lacan's (1953) understanding of the ego as the psychic agency of *méconnaissance* (misrecognition) derives from his conception of the place of the ego in relation to language and to the imaginary and symbolic orders of experience. The realm of the imaginary is that of vital, unmediated, lived experience. In this realm, there is no space between oneself and one's experience. The acquisition of language provides the individual a means by which to mediate between the self as interpreting subject and one's lived experience. Since language and the chain of signifiers that constitute language predate each of us as individuals, the register of symbols that is made available to us through language has nothing to do with us as individuals. We do not create the symbols we use; we inherit them. As a result, language misrepresents the uniqueness of our own lived experience: "It [language] is susceptible to every alienation or lie, wilful or not, susceptible to all the distortions inscribed in the very principles of the 'symbolic,' conventional dimension of group life" (Lemaire 1977, p. 57).

In becoming a subject capable of using symbols to interpret our experience rather than simply being trapped in our own lived sensory experience, we exchange one form of imprisonment for another. We acquire human subjectivity at the cost of becoming profoundly alienated from our immediate sensory experience (which is now distorted and misrepresented by the symbols we use to name it). In this way, we unwittingly engage in a form of self-deception, creating for ourselves the illusion that we express our experience in language, while according to Lacan, we are in fact misnaming and becoming alienated from our experience.

Joyce McDougall, an important contributor to the French psychoanalytic dialogue, has discussed her work with patients who seemed "totally unaware (and thus kept the analyst unaware) of the nature of their affective reactions" (Chapter 13, this volume, p. 254). She understands this phenomenon as a dispersal of potential affect into a variety of addictive actions, including drug abuse, compulsive sexuality, bulimia, "accidental" injuries, and interpersonal crises. Such addictive activities are understood as compulsive ways of defending against psychotic-level anxieties. When the defensive use of the affect-dispersing action becomes overtaxed, the individual regresses to psychosomatic foreclosure of the psychological sphere. Under such circumstances, what might have become psychological strain is relegated to the domain of the physiologic and becomes utterly disconnected from the realm of conscious and unconscious meaning.

Such a conception of the destruction not only of psychological meaning, but of the apparatuses generating psychological meaning, represents an elaboration of the work of Wilfred Bion. Bion (1962) suggests that in schizophrenia (and to lesser degrees in all personality organizations), there is a defensive attack on the psychological processes by which meaning is attached to experience. This represents a superordinate defense in which psychological pain is warded off, not simply through defensive rearrangements of meaning (e.g., projection and displacement) and interpersonal evacuation of endangered and endangering internal objects (projective identification); in addition, there is an attack on the psychological processes by which meaning itself is created. The outcome is a state of "nonexperience" (Ogden 1980, 1982) in which the individual lives in part in a state of psychological deadness, i.e., there are sectors of the personality in which even unconscious meanings and affects cease to be elaborated.

In the course of his writing, Winnicott developed the concept of a "potential space" in which self-experience is created and recognized (Winnicott 1971; see also Ogden 1985, 1986). Potential space is the space in which the object is simultaneously created and discovered. That is, in this space, the object is simultaneously a subjective object (an object omnipotently created) and an object objectively perceived (an object experienced as lying outside of the realm of one's omnipotence). The question of which is the case — is the object created or discovered? — never arises (Winnicott 1953). This question is simply not a part of the emotional vocabulary of this area of experience. We do not move through, or grow out of, this state of mind. It is not a developmental phase; rather, it is a psychological space between reality and fantasy that is maintained throughout one's life. It is the space in which playing occurs; it is the space in which we are creative in the most ordinary sense of the word; it is the space in which we experience ourselves as alive and as the authors of our bodily sensations, thoughts, feelings, and perceptions. In the absence of the capacity to generate potential space, one relies on defensive substitutes for the experience of being alive (e.g., the development of a "false self" personality organization [Winnicott 1960]).

The "fear of breakdown" described by Winnicott (1974) represents a form of failure to generate experience, in which the patient is terrified of experiencing for the first time a catastrophe that has already occurred. The very early environmental failure that constituted the catastrophe could not be experienced at the time that it occurred because there was not yet a self capable of experiencing it, i.e., capable of elaborating the event psychologically and integrating it. As a result, the patient forever fearfully awaits his own psychological breakdown.

In the present paper, I shall be addressing a specific facet of the phenomenon of the alienation from, and destruction of, experience. My focus will be on the anxiety associated with the dim awareness that one does not know what one feels and therefore one does not know who one is. In this psychological state, the individual has not foreclosed experience psychosomatically or failed to psychologically elaborate early experience, nor has he entered into a state of "nonexperience." The patients to be discussed have often attempted, but have not entirely succeeded in, warding off the anxiety of not knowing by means of addictive actions. The form of experience that I am interested in here is one in which the individual is sufficiently capable of generating a space in which to live such that he is capable of knowing that he does not know; he never entirely frees himself of this terror, much as he unconsciously attempts to lure himself and the analyst into mistaking his systematic misrecognitions for genuine self-experience. Such experience is universal and is manifested in a wide variety of forms that reflect the individual's personality organization.

A DEVELOPMENTAL PERSPECTIVE

At the outset, it is the infant's relationship with his mother that is the matrix within which psychological tension is sustained over time sufficiently for meanings to be created and desire and fear to be generated. For example, what will become hunger is initially only a physiologic event (a certain blood sugar level registered by groups of neurons in the brain). This biological event becomes the experience of hunger and desire (appetite) in the context of the mother's conscious and unconscious response to the infant: her holding, touching, nursing, rocking, and engaging in other activities that reflect her understanding of (her conscious and unconscious resonance with) the infant (Winnicott 1967). Such understandings and attendant activities are the outcome of a crucial psychological function provided by the mother: the psychological process by which the mother attempts to respond to her infant in a way that "correctly names" (or gives shape to) the infant's internal state.

The work of Bick (1968), Meltzer (1975), and Tustin (1981, 1986) has afforded analytic theory a way of conceptualizing the earliest organization of experience into sensation-dominated forms, including autistic shapes ("felt shapes" [Tustin 1984]) and autistic objects (Tustin 1980). In the development of "normal autism" (what I have termed the elaboration of the *autistic-contiguous position* [Ogden 1988, 1989]), the infant in the context of the mother-infant relationship achieves the earliest sense of boundedness, the sense of having (being) a place (more specifically, a surface) where one's experience occurs and where a sense of order and containment is generated.

In the earliest mother–infant relationship, the mother must be capable of immersing herself in the infant's sensory world as she allows herself to deintegrate into relative shapelessness. This represents the sensory level of primitive empathy. The mother allows her identity as a person and as a mother to "become liquid" (Seale 1987) in a way that parallels the internal state of the infant. This "deintegration" (Fordham 1976) is not experienced by the mother as disintegration when she is able to create for herself a generative dialectical tension between the shapeless and formed, the primitive and mature, the mysterious and the familiar, the act of becoming a mother for the first time and the experience of having "been here before" (in her identification with facets of her experience with her own mother). In this way, the mother helps the infant give shape, boundedness, rhythm, edgedness, hardness, softness, etc., to his experience.

The mother and infant must attempt to sustain the strain of the very inexact, trial-and-error means by which each attempts to "get to know" the other. The mother's efforts at reading, comforting, and in other ways providing for and interacting with her infant are inevitably narcissistically wounding to the mother, since she will often feel at a loss to know what it is her baby needs and whether it is within the power of her personality to provide it even if she somehow could discover what he "wants." Winnicott's (1974) use of the word *agonies* for infantile anxieties applies equally to the pain of the mother's experience of not knowing.

THE STRUCTURALIZATION OF MISRECOGNITION

The early relationship that is of central interest in the analytic setting is not that of mother and infant, but that of the internal-object-mother and the internal-object-infant. This internal object relationship is manifested in the transference–countertransference phenomena that constitute the analytic drama. A mother–infant relationship is never directly observable in the analytic setting even when the patient is a mother describing current experience with her child. Instead, what we observe, and in part experience, in analysis is a reflection of internal object relations (our own and the patient's, and the interplay between the two). Therefore, when I speak of the internal relationship between mother and infant, it must be borne in mind that the patient is both mother and infant. This is so because an internal object relationship consists of a relationship between two unconscious aspects of the patient, one identified with the self and the other identified with the object in the original relationship (Ogden 1983). Regardless of how fully autonomous an internal object may seem to the patient, the internal object can have no life of its own aside from that deriving from the aspect of the self involved in this identification. In what follows, I will describe a set of pathological internal mother-infant relationships in which the patient is both mother and infant, both the misnamer and the misnamed, both the confused and the confusing.

The (internal object) mother may defend against the feeling of not knowing by utilizing obsessive-compulsive defenses, for example by relying on rigidly scheduled (symbolic) feedings of the (internal object) infant. In this way, the mother (in this internal object relationship) invokes an impersonal external order (the clock) to misname hunger. The infant is responded to as if he were sated every four hours and as if he were not hungry between the scheduled feeds. Such misnaming generates confusion in the infant as well as a sense that hunger is an externally generated event. In the extreme, this mode of defense against not knowing becomes a persecutory authoritarian substitution of the mother's absolute knowledge for the infant's potential to generate his own thoughts, feelings, and sensations.

Mothers enacting this sort of internal object relationship in their actual relationships to their own children are often "psychologically minded" and offer verbal interpretations of their children's unconscious feeling states. For example, a mother being seen in analysis informed her 7-year-old child that even though he claimed to be doing the best job that he could in learning to read, the truth of the matter was that he was angry at her and was doing a poor job of it because he knew precisely how to drive her crazy. Such "interpretations" may be partially accurate (due to the universality of such unconscious feelings as anger, jealousy, and envy in a mother–child relationship), but such comments predominantly have the effect of misnaming the child's internal state. The effect of such interpretation is the creation in the child of a feeling that he has no idea how he "really feels" and that only his mother has the capacity to know this. This patient's behavior in relation to her child represented an enactment of an internal object relationship derived from her own experience with a mother who used fundamentalist religious dogma in the misrecognition of the patient's childhood feeling states. When such a relationship becomes established in the patient's internal object world, the role of this type of internal-object-mother is then projected onto the analyst. As a result, the patient comes to experience the analytic setting as an extremely dangerous, authoritarian one wherein the analyst will certainly tear apart the patient's character structure (including his conscious experience of himself) and "interpret" the shameful truth regarding the patient's unconscious thoughts and feelings.

The analyst may unwittingly be induced (as an unconscious participant in the patient's projective identification) to enact the role of such an authoritarian internal-object-mother (cf. Ogden 1982). Under such circumstances the analyst may find himself interpreting more "actively" and "deeply" than is his usual practice. He may come to view the analysis as bogged down and feel despairing that the patient will ever arrive at meaningful insight. The analyst may rationalize that the patient needs a more didactic approach in order to demonstrate to him what it means "to think reflectively and in depth." Alternatively, the analyst may feel moved to pursue a line of analytic thinking espoused by his "school of psychoanalysis" or an idea about which he has recently read. Reliance upon analytic ideology represents a common method of warding off the analyst's anxiety of not knowing.

Balint (1968) has suggested that the Kleinian technique of "consistent interpretation" represents a countertransference acting out of the role of an omniscient internal object. From the perspective of the ideas being explored in the present paper, the analyst's unconscious identification with the omniscient internal-object-mother represents a form of defense against the anxiety of not knowing what it is the patient is experiencing. (Obviously, this is so whether or not the analyst is a Kleinian.) The patient's internal version of an early object relationship is in this way being replicated in the analytic setting and, unless analyzed in the countertransference and in the transference, will reinforce the patient's unconscious conviction that it is necessary to utilize omnipotent substitute formations in the face of confusion about what he is experiencing and who he is.

Analytic candidates and other trainees frequently utilize this type of unconscious identification with an omnipotent internal object (e.g., an idealized version of one's own analyst). This identification serves as a defense against the anxiety that the candidate does not feel like an analyst when with his patients. Searles (1987) has described his own experience during psychiatric residency when he would "prop himself up" while talking with his patients by authoritatively offering them interpretations given to him only hours earlier by his analyst. Decades later, he became aware that he had experienced his own analyst (more accurately, his own internal-object-analyst) as similarly propped up and filled with self-doubt. This deeper level of insight reflects the way in which the omniscient internal object serves as a substitute formation obscuring an underlying confusion about who one is and who the object is.

Patients may also enact the role of the omniscient internal-object-mother, for example, by controllingly interpreting the analyst's shifting in his chair as a reflection of his anxiety, sexual excitement, anger, etc. When consistently subjected to this form of "interpretation" (that is indistinguishable from accusation), the analyst may unconsciously identify with the internal-object-infant (within the patient) who is exposed to continual misnaming of his

internal state. Anxiety arising in the analyst under such circumstances may lead him into a form of countertransference acting
out in which he attempts to "assist the patient in reality testing" by
denying to the patient that he (the analyst) is feeling or acting in
accord with the patient's interpretations.

A second form of defense against the fear of not knowing how
to make sense of the feeling state of the internal-object-infant is
the unconscious effort on the part of the patient to act as if he
knows what the internal-object-infant is experiencing. In this way
he creates a substitute formation for the feeling of being at a
complete loss to make use of his capacities for understanding and
responding to the internal-object-infant. Reliance on such a set of
defenses may result in a rather stereotypic form of self-knowledge.
A mother while in analysis described her attempts at being a
mother by imitating the mothers portrayed in books and on
television, by imitating her friends who had children, and by
imitating the analyst's treatment of her. She later attended every
PTA and cub scout function, arranged for swimming, tennis and
music lessons, painstakingly prepared home-made pumpkin pies
at Thanksgiving and mince pies at Christmas, etc. The schizophrenic child of another such mother told his mother, "You've
been just like a mother to me." Such mothers are "just like"
mothers, but do not experience themselves (nor are they experienced by their children) as being mothers. The self-esteem of such
mothers is brittle, and these women often collapse into depression
or schizoid withdrawal as they become emotionally exhausted in
their efforts at imitating a psychological state from which they feel
utterly alienated.

A 30-year-old psychologist, Dr. M., in the course of his analysis
generated a transference–countertransference externalization of
the form of internal object relationship just described. During the
first two years of work, I frequently questioned the value of the
analysis despite the fact that all seemed to be proceeding well. In
the third year, the patient began to wryly refer to me as "the
perfect analyst." He described how he was the envy of all his
colleagues for his unusual good fortune in having the opportunity
to work with me. Only recently had he begun to become aware of
his strong belief that he and I were colluding in an effort to hide
our awareness of my shallowness and extreme emotional detach-

ment. Dr. M. presented a dream in which he had graduated from college but was completely illiterate. In the dream, the patient was unable to work because he could not read and was unable to go back to school for fear of shaming his teachers.

This dream represented Dr. M.'s emerging feeling (that had been the unconscious context for the entire analysis) that he and I were going through the motions of analysis. Eventually he would have to pretend to be "cured," which would mean that he would live in absolute isolation without hope of ever genuinely feeling a connection with anyone. In this case, the internal object relationship that was recreated in the transference–countertransference involved the defensive use of an illusion of perfection (the reliance on form as a replacement for content) as a substitute for the real work of analyst and patient awkwardly and imprecisely attempting to talk to one another.

A third form of defense against the pain of feeling utterly confused about that which the internal-object-infant is experiencing is pathological projective identification. In this process one "knows" the other by (in fantasy) occupying the other with one's own thoughts, feelings, and sensations and in this way short-circuiting the problem of the externality (and unpredictability) of the other. Under such circumstances, a mother (enacting an internal drama in relation to her own infant) may decide to allow her infant to cry for hours on end because she "knows" that the infant has such tyrannical strivings (the mother's own projected feelings about herself) that it is essential that she not be bullied by this baby Hitler. The mother under such circumstances is not only defending herself against the destructive power of her own tyrannical internal-object-infant by locating these feelings in the actual infant (and at the same time maintaining an unconscious connection with this part of her internal object world); in addition, she is allaying the anxiety of not knowing by experiencing the actual infant as the fully known and predictable internal object for which she has a long-standing, clearly defined plan of defensive action.

In a sense, transference in general can be viewed as serving the function of making known the unknown object. Transference is a name we give to the illusion that the unknown object is already known: each new object relationship is cast in the image of past object relations with which one is already familiar. As a result, no encounter is experienced as entirely new. Transference provides the illusion that one has already been there before. Without this illusion, we would feel intolerably naked and unprepared in the face of experience with a new person.

CLINICAL EXAMPLE: MISRECOGNITION OF AFFECT

Mrs. R., a 42-year-old woman who had been seen in analysis for almost three years, punctuated each meeting with efforts to cajole, trick, plead, and in other ways coerce me into "giving [her] something specific" in the form of advice or insight. She hoped that she would be able to take with her what I gave her during the meeting and apply it to her life outside the analysis. When I was silent for an entire session, the meeting was considered wasted since "nothing had happened." Mrs. R. responded with an intense display of emotion to any disruption of analytic routine. If I were a few minutes late in beginning the hour, she would either quietly cry or remain angrily silent for the first ten to fifteen minutes of the hour. She would then tell me that my being late could only mean that I did not give a damn about her. Consistent efforts at analyzing the content and intensity of Mrs. R.'s reactions were made. She related the current set of feelings to her childhood experience of waiting for what seemed like hours for her mother (a college professor) while her mother spoke with students after class. However, there reached a point when the material did not become any richer as the patient repeatedly returned to the image of angrily waiting for her mother. I found myself becoming increasingly annoyed and was aware of fantasies of making sadistic comments as the patient cried in response to my informing her of a vacation break or a rare change of the time of a given appointment.

In a session at the end of the third year of analysis I was three or four minutes late in beginning the session. Mrs. R. was visibly upset when I met her in the waiting room. In what had become her customary pattern, the patient lay down on the couch, folded her arms across her chest, and was silent for about ten minutes. She finally said that she did not know why she continued in analysis with me. I must hate her; otherwise I would not treat her in such a callous manner. I asked her if she were really feeling at that moment that my lateness had reflected the fact that I hated her. She reflexively said, "Yes," but it was apparent that the question had taken her by surprise. After a few minutes, she said that in fact my lateness had not bothered her, even though she had behaved as if it had. She said that in retrospect her recent reactions to me seemed to her to have been a little like play-acting, although she had not had that sense of things until I asked the question that I did today. I suggested that by acting as if she had felt crushed by my lateness, she obscured for herself the feeling that she did not know how she felt about it.

Over the succeeding year, as the analysis took on an increasing feeling of authenticity, it was possible to identify a plethora of forms of defense against the anxiety connected with the feeling of not knowing. The patient recognized that she had been unable to progress in her efforts to become an opera singer because she had from the beginning of her training bypassed various fundamentals of technique. She could create an initial impression of being a very accomplished singer, but this could not be sustained. The inability to "begin at the beginning" and to tolerate the tension of not knowing had severely interfered with Mrs. R.'s ability to learn. She felt it necessary to create the illusion of being very advanced from the outset. Mrs. R. also became aware that it was extremely difficult for her to accurately identify her sensory experience — for example, whether she was anxious or in physical pain, in what part of her body the pain was arising, whether a given sensation reflected sexual excitement or a need to urinate, whether she was hungry or lonely, etc.

The analysis then centered on Mrs. R.'s fear of the "spaces" in the analytic hour which had formerly been filled by what she referred to as "play-acting" or by pleading with me to give her something that she could take with her from the session. In the period of work during which these matters were being discussed, Mrs. R. began a session by saying that since she did not want to overdramatize, nor did she want to throw a temper tantrum, she was having trouble knowing what to say. Later in the same meeting the patient reported the following dream: she was in the office of a dentist who removed two of her molar teeth. She had not known he was going to do this, but had the feeling that she had somehow agreed to have it done. When he showed her the teeth, they looked perfect — they were perfectly shaped and had gleaming white enamel "like something you'd see in a story book." She thought that it was strange that they did not have roots. The extraction had not been painful, and afterwards, instead of pain, there was simply a strange feeling of an empty space in the back of her mouth. The hole that was left in the gums rapidly closed over itself and did not require stitches. In her associations, Mrs. R. was able to understand that the two teeth had represented two ways of behaving that she felt she was giving up in the analysis: the overdramatization and the temper tantrums. She said that like the teeth, these ways of being seemed to be losses that left a weird space. Moreover, this loss was a loss of something that did not seem to be quite real—like "storybook teeth without roots." This dream represented the beginnings of a phase of the analysis in which the patient was able to become gradually less reliant on misrecognition as a defense against the experience of not knowing.[1] These misrecognitions had filled the potential space in which inchoate desires and fears might have evolved into feelings that could be felt and named.[2]

MISRECOGNITION AS A DIMENSION OF EATING DISORDERS

Patients with a wide range of eating disorders, including anorexia nervosa and bulimia, regularly report that their overeating or refusal to eat has nothing whatever to do with the experience of appetite. These patients are rarely able to generate an emotional/physiologic state that they can correctly recognize as an appetite for food. The psychological difficulty underlying the inability of these patients to generate appetite affects their capacity to generate almost every form of desire, including sexual desire, desire to learn, desire to work, desire to be with other people, desire to be alone, etc.

In the course of my work with patients suffering from eating disorders, it has made increasing sense to me to think of many of these patients as suffering from a disorder of recognition of desire. An important aspect of the experience of these patients is an

---

[1]There are, of course, conflicted sexual and aggressive meanings suggested by the manifest content of this dream. However, it was necessary to analyze the patient's experience of not knowing what she was experiencing before it became possible to analyze the conflictual content of that experience.

[2]It is characteristic of the analytic process that each insight (recognition) immediately becomes the next resistance (misrecognition). The patient's awareness of and understanding of the experience of not knowing is no exception to this principle. Invariably, as the analysand recognizes his or her warded off state of not knowing, the feeling of confusion itself is utilized in the service of defending against that which the patient consciously and unconsciously knows, but does not wish to know.

unconscious fear that the patient does not know what he desires. This leads him to ward off the panic associated with such awareness by behaving as if it is food that is desired. The patient may then obsessionally (usually ritualistically) eat and yet never feel full, since what has been taken in is not a response to a desire for food. Rather, the eating represents an attempt to use food *as if* that is what had been desired when in fact the individual does not know what it is to feel desire. In one such case, an adolescent girl, in a state of extreme anxiety bordering on panic, consumed several loaves of bread and two cooked chickens which resulted in gangrenous changes in her stomach secondary to the compromise of blood supply caused by the overdistention of the gastric walls. Surgical removal of two-thirds of her stomach was required. This adolescent had told her mother over the course of the preceding week that everything appeared colorless. The patient's mother had told her that it was natural to feel gray in the autumn; everybody does.

This adolescent, in her frantic eating, was not attempting to meet a need or to fulfill a desire; the problem was that she could not create a psychological space in which either need or desire could be generated. The patient therefore felt, to a large degree, as if she already were psychologically dead, and it was this feeling that had led to her state of panic. Paradoxically, the patient was desperately eating in an attempt to create the feeling of hunger. More accurately, she was eating in order to create the illusion that she could feel hunger which would serve as evidence that she was alive.

The early relationship between this patient and her mother seems to have been characterized by the same fear of recognition of the internal state of the patient that was reflected in the mother's comment about the universality of feelings of melancholy and grayness in the autumn. The bits of meaning that the patient had managed to attach to her own experience (in this case, the experience of colorless, lifeless depression) were stripped of meaning in the interaction with her mother (cf. Bion 1962). The beginnings of meaning, generated in an internal psychological space, were transformed into a universal and therefore impersonal truth. This had had the effect of obliterating not only the bits of meaning that had been created, but more importantly, the internal psychological space that the patient had tenuously achieved.

PSYCHOLOGICAL CHANGE IN THE AREA OF RECOGNITION AND MISRECOGNITION

The following is an excerpt from the analysis of a 46-year-old computer scientist who began treatment not knowing why he had come for therapy (but at the same time did not seem aware of his not knowing).

During the initial face-to-face interviews prior to his beginning to use the couch, Dr. L. described situations in which he felt anxious, such as while waiting to be assigned a table in a restaurant and before making business phone calls. The explanations the patient offered for his anxiety in these situations were almost verbatim formulae extracted from his extensive reading of popular self-help books.

Dr. L., by the time he turned 40, was internationally known and had amassed a large fortune as a result of his innovations in the area of computer technology. Even though the vast bulk of his money was now invested very conservatively, he experienced both his financial situation and his status in his field as extremely precarious. These fears led him to devote himself with ever-increasing intensity to his work. Only after several months of analysis did he say that he awoke every night in a state of extreme anxiety. He supposed he was anxious about his work, but he was not sure since he was unable to remember his dreams.

It is beyond the scope of this paper to describe the analytic work underlying the psychological changes that ensued. My intention here is simply to illustrate the nature of psychological change in the area of the creation and recognition of desire. I shall use as an illustration of such change a dream presented by Dr. L. at the beginning of the third year of analysis.

I was standing in front of a large house and could see through the windows that the paint on the ceiling was cracking as a result of water that had leaked in from the roof. To my surprise, the old man who owned the house came out and asked me to come in and talk. He asked me if I knew who he was. I didn't, and I told him that. The

old man thanked me for being truthful. He told me who he was. . . .
I can't remember what his name was. He told me he was going to die
in two weeks and would like to give all of his money to me. I said
that I didn't want the money. He took me into the next room which
was lined with fine old books and very beautiful antique furniture.
He offered me the house and everything in it. I again said that I
didn't want it. I told him that I could get the water damage fixed.
The old man said that the peeling paint was part of the house as he
knew it, and he didn't want it changed. I told him it could damage
the house. The old man was very calm and explained that he had
lived a happy life and that he would be dead in two weeks and so it
didn't matter.

Dr. L. said that he woke up from this dream feeling a profound
sense of contentment that he associated with memories of his
maternal grandfather. Dr. L. recalled how his grandfather, at the
age of 85, had loved his garden, planting seeds for flowers one day,
seeds for lettuce the next, seeds for other flowers the next, and so
on. One day, when the patient was about 6 years old, he said to his
grandfather as his grandfather was planting flower seeds,
"Grandpa, you planted that same row with carrot seeds yesterday."
The patient's grandfather laughed and said, "Bobby, you don't
understand. The point is the planting, not the growing."

This dream and the associations to it represented a layering of
alteration of what had previously been misrecognitions of affect.
Dr. L. said that it had been "cleansing" to experience himself in the
dream as a person who talked in language that "cut to the bone," in
contrast to the "bullshit" with which he felt he usually filled his life.
"I didn't know who the old man was and I simply said so. I felt a
glimmer of temptation to accept his money and all of his stuff, but
I really didn't want his money. Ordinarily, I would have thought
that what I wanted was his money. I can see myself acting in a way
that would have made him think that that's what I was after.[3]
Actually, I just liked being with him. The old man and I offered
one another things the other didn't want or have any use for. What
meant so much to me was the way we explained ourselves to each

---

[3]It had taken me most of the first year of the analysis to become aware of the
way Dr. L. unconsciously attempted to lure me into misrecognitions of his
internal state by repeatedly mislabeling them, giving me misleading pictures of
himself and of his relationships, leaving out important details, leading me to
believe that he understood what was going on in an interpersonal situation when
he did not, etc.

other. I could feel all the tension in me subside when the old man said that he lived in the house as it was and didn't want it changed."

Over the course of the meeting, the dream was understood to be a representation of the way Dr. L. wished that he and I could talk together. In the dream, the patient felt momentarily freed from his usual isolation that resulted from layer upon layer of misnamings and misrecognitions of his own internal state and that of the other.[4] The defensive internal misrecognitions had made it impossible for him to feel that he understood anything of what he felt toward other people and what they felt toward him. These misrecognitions had left the patient feeling alone and disconnected from a self (and the other) that he only dimly knew.

In the course of the succeeding months of analysis, Dr. L. became increasingly able to understand why he had come to see me in the first place and why he was continuing in analysis. Although he had been unaware of it at the time, the anxiety that he had experienced in going into restaurants and before making business phone calls had, in part, reflected an anticipation of the painful confusion and loneliness that he would feel in talking to people. He unconsciously expected that once again there would be only the illusion of two people talking to one another.

Dr. L. gradually related the set of feelings just discussed to a persistent childhood feeling of isolation. He had felt that his parents operated according to a logic that he could not fathom. In the course of analysis, Dr. L. was able to reexperience and articulate this powerful, but heretofore wholly unrecognized set of background childhood feelings. The patient, in discussing the events of his current life, would return again and again to such statements as, "What kind of sense does that make?" "That doesn't add up. Why can't anyone see that?" "What kind of bullshit is this?" "Doesn't anyone have any common sense?" Such feelings were increasingly experienced in the transference, for example in relation to my policy of billing the patient for missed appointments. These feelings of outrage served an important defensive

---

[4]If the individual is unable to know what he feels, he is equally at a loss to know what it is that the other is experiencing. This is simply another way of stating that in the internal object relationship under discussion, the individual is both internal-object-mother and internal-object-infant, both misrecognized and misrecognizing. The outcome is a feeling of alienation from the other experienced by both the self and the object component of the internal object relationship.

function: it was necessary for the patient to feel that he knew better than anyone else "what the story was." This served to obscure the patient's feeling of being utterly confused and disconnected from a firmly grounded sense of what he was feeling, what he wanted or why he wanted it, and most basically, what it meant in a visceral sense to experience (and name) desires and fears that felt like his own.

As the analysis went on, the patient increasingly came to experience me as disturbingly insubstantial and infinitely malleable. Dr. L. felt quite alone during the sessions and said that attempting to have a relationship with me was like "trying to build a house on a foundation of Jello." He became preoccupied with the feeling that he had no idea who I was. The patient engendered in me (by means of what I eventually understood as a projective identification) a sense of detachment that I have rarely experienced with a patient. The couch concretely felt as if it were located at a very great distance from my chair. At these times I found it extremely difficult to focus on what Dr. L. was saying. This sense of isolation in the relationship with me was gradually understood in terms of the patient's internal relationship with a schizoid mother who "gave the appearance of being there until you realized that she was unable to think."

In this chapter, I have discussed a set of unconscious, pathological internal object relations in which misrecognitions of affect play a central role. These internal object relations timelessly perpetuate the infant's subjective experience of the mother's difficulty in recognizing and responding to the infant's internal state. Internal object relationships are understood to involve a relationship between two unconscious aspects of the ego, one identified with the self and the other identified with the object of the original object relationship. Accordingly, in the kind of internal object relationship under discussion, the patient is both mother and infant, both misrecognized and misrecognizing. In the context of this internal relationship, the patient experiences anxiety, alienation, and despair in connection with the feeling of not knowing what it is that he feels or who, if anyone, he is.

Substitute formations are utilized to create the illusion that the individual knows what he feels. Examples of such substitute formations include obsessional, authoritarian, as-if, false self, and projective identificatory forms of control over one's internal and external objects. While these substitute formations help to ward off the feeling of not knowing, they also have the effect of filling the potential space in which feeling states (that are experienced as one's own) might arise.

In the analytic setting, internal object relations are externalized and, through the medium of the transference–countertransference, are given intersubjective life. I have presented clinical illustrations of analytic work addressing the anxiety of not knowing one's internal state and the defenses serving to ward off this anxiety.

REFERENCES

Balint, M. (1968). *The Basic Fault: Therapeutic Aspects of Regression.* London: Tavistock.

Bick, E. (1968). The experience of the skin in early object-relations. *International Journal of Psycho-Analysis* 49:484–486.

Bion, W. R. (1962). *Learning from Experience.* New York: Basic Books.

Fordham, M. (1976). *The Self and Autism.* London: Heinemann.

Freud, S. (1911). Psycho-analytic notes on an autobiographical account of a case of paranoia (dementia paranoides). *Standard Edition* 12:3–82.

Lacan, J. (1948). Aggressivity in psychoanalysis. In *Ecrits: A Selection,* pp. 8–29. New York: Norton, 1977.

_____ (1953). The function and field of speech and language in psychoanalysis. In *Ecrits: A Selection,* pp. 30–113. New York: Norton, 1977.

Lemaire, A. (1977). *Jacques Lacan.* Boston: Routledge & Kegan Paul.

Meltzer, D. (1975). Adhesive identification. *Contemporary Psychoanalysis* 11:289–310.

Nemiah, J. C. (1977). Alexithymia: a theoretical statement. *Psychotherapy and Psychosomatics* 28:199–206.

Ogden, T. H. (1980). On the nature of schizophrenic conflict. *International Journal of Psycho-Analysis* 61:513–533.

_____ (1982). *Projective Identification and Psychotherapeutic Technique.* New York: Jason Aronson.

_____ (1983). The concept of internal object relations. *International Journal of Psycho-Analysis* 64:227–241.

_____ (1985). On potential space. *International Journal of Psycho-Analysis* 66:129–141.

_____ (1986). *The Matrix of the Mind: Object Relations and the Psychoanalytic Dialogue.* Northvale, NJ: Jason Aronson.

_____ (1989). On the concept of the autistic-contiguous position. *International Journal of Psycho-Analysis* 70:127–140.

_____ (1988). On the dialectical structure of experience: some clinical and theoretical implications. *Contemporary Psychoanalysis* 24:17–45.

Seale, A. (1987). Personal communication.

Searles, H. F. (1987). *Concerning unconscious identifications.* Presented at the Boyer House Foundation Conference: The Regressed Patient. San Francisco, March 21.

Tustin, F. (1980). Autistic objects. *International Review of Psycho-Analysis* 7:27–40.

_____ (1981). *Autistic States in Children.* Boston: Routledge & Kegan Paul.

_____ (1984). Autistic shapes. *International Review of Psycho-Analysis* 11:279–290.

_____ (1986). *Autistic Barriers in Neurotic Patients.* New Haven: Yale University Press, 1987.

Winnicott, D. W. (1953). Transitional objects and transitional phenomena. A study of the first not-me possession. In *Playing and Reality,* pp. 1–25. New York: Basic Books, 1971.

_____ (1960). Ego distortion in terms of true and false self. In *The Maturational Processes and the Facilitating Environment: Studies in the Theory of Emotional Development,* pp. 140–152. New York: International Universities Press, 1965.

_____ (1967). Mirror-role of mother and family in child development. In *Playing and Reality,* pp. 111–118. New York: Basic Books.

_____ (1971). The place where we live. In *Playing and Reality,* pp. 104–110. New York: Basic Books.

_____ (1974). Fear of breakdown. *International Review of Psycho-Analysis* 1:103–107.

The "Dis-affected" Patient: Reflections on Affect Pathology

Joyce McDougall

*J*oyce McDougall, even though living in Paris, writes in English and has had a wide and beneficial effect on North American psychotherapy. She has advanced in the tradition of using object relations theory to analyze the unanalyzable.

In this chapter, McDougall discusses her work with disaffected patients, those who have broken the affective link between themselves and others. The patients she describes are perhaps a bit more inaccessible than those Gabbard and Ogden discuss, but they are similar in that they seem to get worse with increasing treatment efforts. McDougall indicates that one key to staying with these patients is in exploring the therapist's own feelings, both those arising from the patient's projective identifications and those from the therapist's own experiences and backgrounds. Therapists must explore within themselves how these patients attack their inner vitality, while sustaining a belief that some courage for change will arise within the patient. McDougall's idea of maintaining such a belief may be related to the concept of the analyst's projective identification within the containing function or to Kohut's concept of providing a sustaining selfobject function.

McDougall suggests that therapists must find their own courage to ask themselves why they would continue to take patients into analysis whose primary aim is to show them they cannot help them, or perhaps their aim is to destroy the therapists' capacity for concern. Why would therapists undertake such a task? Asking this question helps therapists understand such patients better.

Looking within themselves as a way of understanding severely disturbed individuals, finding a way to be with the patient as a primary agent of change, these are new directions in object relations theory and object relations-influenced psychotherapies. They arise from the deepest inner sources— within patients and within therapists.

Theaters of the Mind (McDougall 1986) is a book-length account of McDougall's work.

This chapter might well have been entitled "The *Analyst*'s Affective Reactions to Affectless or 'Dis-Affected' Patients." I should perhaps explain my reasons for the use of the term "disaffected," which, I am well aware, is a neologism. I am hoping to convey a double meaning here. The use of the Latin prefix "dis-," which indicates "separation" or "loss," may suggest, metaphorically, that some people are psychologically separated from their emotions and may indeed have "lost" the capacity to be in touch with their own psychic reality. But I should also like to include in this neologism the significance of the Greek prefix "dys-" with its implications in regard to illness. However, I have avoided spelling the word in this way because I would then have invented a malady. Although a brief might be held, in severe cases of affect pathology, for considering a total incapacity to be in touch with one's affective experience to be a grave psychological illness, such terms in the long run tend to concretize our thinking and leave it less open to further elaboration. (The word "alexithymia," to which I shall refer later, has already been exposed to this inconvenience. Certain colleagues say, "This person is suffering from alexithymia," as though it were a definable illness rather than simply an observable but little understood phenomenon.)

LIFELESSNESS OF EMOTIONAL EXPERIENCE

I first became interested in the psychic economy of affect and the dynamic reasons for which certain patients appear to have rendered much, if not all, of their emotional experience totally lifeless as I tried to come to terms with my countertransference reactions to these analysands. In many cases the analytic process seemed to stagnate for long periods of time, or it failed even to have begun. The analysands themselves frequently complained that "nothing was happening" in their analytic experience, yet each one clung to his analysis like a drowning man to a life vest. Although these patients had sought analytic help for a wide variety of reasons, they had one personality feature in common: they appeared pragmatic and factual, unimaginative and unemotional, in the face of important events, as well as in relationships with important people in their lives. As time went on, these analysands made me feel paralyzed in my analytical functioning. I could neither help them to become more alive nor lead them to leave analysis. Their affectless type of analytic discourse made me feel tired and bored, and their spectacular lack of analytic progress made me feel guilty. In my first attempt to conceptualize the mental functioning of these patients, I called them "anti-analysands in analysis" (McDougall 1972, 1978), since they seemed to me to be in fierce opposition to analyzing anything to do with their inner psychic reality. Later, in view of their conspicuous lack of neurotic symptoms, I referred to them as "normopaths"; while clearly disturbed, they seemed to shelter themselves behind or, indeed, to suffer from a form of "pseudonormality." However, I was unable to see further into this curious condition, except to conjecture that it was probably rather widespread among the population at large.

Today I have some hypotheses to propose regarding the mental functioning that contributes to the creation of the dis-affected state. These hypotheses deal, on the one hand, with the dynamic reasons that may be considered to underlie the maintenance of a psychic gap between emotions and their mental representations and, on the other, with the economic means by which this affectless way of experiencing events and people functions. It is difficult to avoid the conclusion that such an ironclad structure must be serving important defensive purposes and that its continued maintenance must involve vigorous psychic activity, even if the patients concerned have no conscious knowledge of this and the analyst has little observable material upon which to found such an opinion.

THE PROBLEM OF AFFECT PATHOLOGY

I shall summarize briefly the different stages in my theoretical exploration and elaboration of the problems of affect pathology before going on to present two clinical vignettes that illustrate the proposed theoretical conceptualizations.

One of my first research interests, again stimulated by uncomfortable transference feelings, was directed to grasping the nature of all that *eludes* the psychoanalytic process and, in so doing, contributes to the interminability of some of our analytic cases. Certain of my patients, while diligent in the pursuit of their analytic goals and reasonably in touch with their mental pain and psychic conflicts, would for long periods of time appear to stagnate in their analytic process. Insights gained one day were lost the next, and there was little psychic change. These patients resembled my "normopaths," in that in certain areas of their lives they remained totally unaware (and thus kept the analyst unaware) of the nature of their affective reactions. I came to discover that this was due in large part to the fact that any *emotional arousal was immediately dispersed in action.* In other words, these patients, instead of capturing and reflecting upon the emotional crises that arose in their daily lives or in the analytic relationship, would tend to act out their affective experiences, discharging them through inappropriate action rather than "feeling" them and talking about them in the sessions. For example, some would attempt to drown strong emotional or mental conflict through the use of alcohol, bouts of bulimia, or drug abuse. Some would engage in frenetic sexual exploits of a perverse or compulsive nature as though making an addictive use of sexuality. Others would suffer a series of minor or major physical accidents that were not entirely "accidental." Others would create havoc in their lives by unconsciously manipulating those closest to them to live out their unacknowledged crises with them, thereby making addictive use of other people. From the point of view of the mental economy, *these all represent compulsive ways of avoiding affective flooding*. I came to realize that these analysands, due to unsuspected psychotic anxieties or extreme narcissistic fragility, were unable to contain or cope with phases of highly charged affectivity (precipitated as often as not by external events). They saw no choice but to plunge into some form of action to dispel the threatened upsurge of emotion. It might be emphasized that this could apply to exciting and agreeable affects as well as to painful ones.

Like the "normopaths," the addictively structured patients either made no mention of their acting out experiences or recounted them in a flat and affectless manner, although, on occasion, they would complain of the compulsive nature of the action symptoms. Of course, it is in no way difficult for us to identify ourselves with these action patterns. To seek to dispel painful or disappointing experiences through some form of compensatory action is typically human. However, this is a serious problem when it is the dominant or, indeed, the only method of dealing with internal and external stress.

In my attempt to better conceptualize the mental processes involved in the radical dispersal or compulsive discharge of affective experience, I was considerably helped by research workers in other fields, in particular by the published papers and ongoing research of psychoanalysts who were also psychosomaticists. Curiously enough, the latter were the first people to observe and carefully document the phenomenon of affectless ways of experiencing and communicating; they were led to delineate a so-called "psychosomatic personality." The concept of *operational thinking* (i.e., of a delibidinized way of relating to people and of being in contact with oneself) was developed by the Paris school of psychosomatic research. The concept of *alexithymia* (i.e., an incapacity to be aware of emotions, or if aware, the inability to distinguish one emotion from another, as, for example, to distinguish among hunger, anger, fatigue, or despair) was developed by the Boston school of psychosomatic research. I have found the latter psychological phenomena to be equally characteristic of addictive personalities, many of whom did not

suffer from psychosomatic manifestations. An alcoholic patient
of mine would make such statements as: "I frequently don't know
whether I'm hungry or anxious or whether I want to have sex — and
that's when I start to drink." In my experience, the incapacity to
discriminate among different somatic and affective sensations,
allied with the tendency to plunge into familiar action symptoms,
is equally characteristic of people with organized sexual perver-
sions, drug abuse patients, and character disordered patients who
tend to seek out senseless quarrels or to engage in meaningless
erotic adventures during states of conflict.

Although I remained dubious about the validity of the psychosomaticists' theoretical conceptions (insofar as my own patients
were concerned), their work helped me to become aware of the
fact that my two groups of "dis-affected" analysands, the addictive personalities and the normopaths, would frequently tend to
somatize when under the pressure of increased external or internal
stress. Events such as the birth of a baby, the death of a parent,
the loss of an important professional promotion or of a love
object, as well as other libidinal and narcissistic wounds, when
they were not worked through emotionally or otherwise effectively
dealt with, would cause a sudden disturbance in the analysand's
narcissistic equilibrium. This was due to a breakdown in the
habitual ways of dispersing affect in addictive behavior or to an
overcharge of the alexithymic devices, with their defensive function of warding off deep-seated anxieties, thus opening the way to
psychosomatic dysfunctioning. In fact, it has often occurred to me
that narcissistic defenses and relationships and addictive action
patterns, while they may cause psychological suffering to the
individuals concerned, might, at the same time, for as long as they
continue to function, serve as a protection against psychosomatic
regression.

The extreme fragility in the narcissistic economy and the
incapacity to contain and elaborate affective experience pose
questions about the possible etiology of this kind of personality
structure. A study of predisposing factors goes beyond the scope
of this paper, centered as it is on the *hic et nunc* of the analytic
relationship and process. Briefly, it might be mentioned that the
family discourse has often promulgated an ideal of inaffectivity,
as well as condemning imaginative experience. Over and beyond

these factors of conscious recall, I have also frequently been able to reconstruct with these patients a paradoxical mother–child relationship in which the mother seems to have been out of touch with the infant's emotional needs, yet at the same time has controlled her baby's thoughts, feelings, and spontaneous gestures in a sort of archaic "double-bind" situation. One might wonder whether such mothers felt compelled to stifle every spontaneous affective movement of their babies because of their own unconscious problems. What in the intimate bodily and psychological transactions between the mother and the nursling may have rendered affective experience unacceptable or lifeless can sometimes be deduced in the analytic experience of dis-affected patients. Pulverized affect comes to light as part of the discovery of a lost continent of feeling. First, the conspicuous lack of dream and fantasy material is frequently replaced by somatic reactions and sensations; then, affects, in coming back to consciousness, may express themselves in the form of transitory pseudoperceptions. These "dream equivalents" that often follow primary process thinking may also be regarded as "affect equivalents." Thus, we might deduce that dis-affected patients, unable to use normal repression, must instead have recourse to the mechanisms of splitting and projective identification to protect themselves from being overwhelmed by mental pain. This aspect of their analysands' analytic discourse often alerts the analyst — through the confused, irritated, anxious, or bored affects that are aroused in the analyst — and enables him or her to feel, sometimes poignantly, the double-bind messages and the forgotten pain and distress of the small infant who had to learn to render inner liveliness inert in order to survive.

I hope that the following clinical examples will make clearer the theoretical notions here advanced.

When searching for suitable clinical examples among the many at my disposition, I noticed, somewhat tardily, that the patients I thought of frequently had had a previous analysis or had been in analysis with me for a number of years. In other words, I realized that this kind of affect problem *may have passed unnoticed* in analytic work for many years. The patients themselves, of course, were unaware that they suffered from an inability to recognize their emotional experiences since these were either entirely split off from consciousness or, if briefly conscious, were immediately dispelled in some form of action. One dominant feature was a conscious sense of failure, of missing the essence of human living, or of wondering why life seemed empty and boring. With my dis-affected analysands, I often discovered that the initial years of analysis had been useful in overcoming a number of neurotic problems and inhibitions, but once these were out of the way, what was laid bare was a strong but undifferentiated impression of dissatisfaction with life, of which the analysands had hitherto been unaware, much as though the neurotic structures had served, among other functions, to camouflage underlying states of depression and emptiness or of unspecified anxiety. The fact that these patients had little affect tolerance was a further discovery that the ongoing analytic process brought in its wake.

CLINICAL EXAMPLES: HANDLING THE
AFFECTLESS STATE

Here is a brief clinical excerpt from the analysis of a 40-year-old man. I shall call him TIM, short for The Invisible Man.

TIM had undergone five years of analysis before coming to see me, three years later. Although his previous analysis had made him feel less isolated from other people and his relationship with his wife had slightly improved (that is, *she* complained less about his distance and inaccessibility), he felt that none of his basic problems had been resolved. I asked what these were. TIM: "I never feel quite real, as though I were out of touch with the others. I suppose you'd call me a schizoid kind of person. I can't enjoy things. My work bores me. . . ." And he went on to give details of the two occasions on which he had changed career directions. Now it was too late to contemplate further changes. My asking him to tell me something of his private family life led to one additional observation: although TIM did not suffer from any sexual problems in the ordinary sense of the word, he mentioned that his sexual relations and the ejaculation itself were totally devoid of any sensation of pleasure. He wondered what people meant when they talked so eagerly of sexual "excitement." He seemed to me to experience sexuality as a need, but he appeared never to have known sexual desire.

Usually, his sessions resembled each other, with little change, day after day, week after week, so that the small harvest of disturbing childhood memories had become especially precious. One involved the death of his father when TIM was seven to eight years old. He recounted that he had been on holiday at the time with relatives and had had an unaccountable bowel accident one night. The following day, his aunt told the sad news of his father's sudden death. The little boy was worried for some time by the thought that his bowel accident, in some mysterious manner, had been the cause of his father's death. In adolescence, he had suffered for long periods from insomnia and, at such times, he would tiptoe around the house, seriously concerned because of the fantasy that his state of tension and restlessness might shake the walls of the house and waken or even kill his mother and older sisters if the house were to fall down! I was touched by these memories. They showed me a little boy profoundly convinced of, and terrified by, his hidden power to mete out death and destruction to those nearest and dearest to him. TIM, on the other hand, felt completely devoid of feeling about these childhood recollections. He remained literally "un-affected" by either the memories or my interpretation of them. He, in fact, denied that he had ever really felt sad or anxious as a child. The recovered memories were an object of intellectual, rather than emotional, interest, and as such, they brought no psychic change in their wake.

It was not in any way surprising that TIM complained of an utter lack of transference feeling toward either his analysis or his analyst. Explaining carefully that he neither wished nor expected to experience any emotional attachment to his analytical enterprise, he nevertheless complained of the lack, because friends and colleagues in analysis talked with such enthusiasm about their transference affects that he began to wonder if there were something wrong with him.

TIM frequently arrived twenty minutes late, and often he missed sessions altogether. He gave no specific reason, except that he just hadn't felt like coming or that some minor complication had made it easier not to come. He agreed intellectually that his absenteeism could be regarded as the expression of a need to keep a certain distance between us and that this might be due to anxious or hostile feelings, but he was unaware of having captured any affects of this nature, even briefly. A further complication, equally typical of dis-affected patients, was that TIM consistently failed to remember what had arisen in the previous sessions. As with most of my analysands who suffer from an inability to become aware of their affective experience, to the point of believing that they had none, I intuitively felt that the

expectant silence, which is both containing and reassuring to the
"normal-neurotic," was in some way dangerous for TIM. It had
nothing to do with a countertransference difficulty in supporting
silence; on the contrary, it was as though one had to fight the
temptation to give in to deathlike forces. Often such patients drive the
analyst into a countertransference corner where it is easier to sit back
in bored silence, etc. Therefore, with TIM, after more than a year's
analytic work, I began to make longer and more complicated interventions, often involving my own feelings and puzzlement, in the hope
of rendering him more emotionally alive (although I must admit that
my countertransference wish to just daydream or think of other things
had many a time to be forcibly overcome!).

On one such occasion I told TIM that everything he had recounted
in the two years we had spent together made me keenly aware of the
existence of a sad and embittered little boy inside him who doubted
whether he really existed or whether his existence was meaningful for
other people. His mother, his wife and children, and his analyst were
felt to be indifferent to the psychic survival of this unhappy child.
After a short silence he replied: "This idea that maybe I don't really
exist for other people affects me so strongly that I am almost unable
to breathe." I had the feeling that he was choking back sobs.

I eagerly awaited the next day's session. After a customary ten
minutes silence, TIM began: "I'm tired of this analysis and your
eternal silence. Nothing ever happens, since you never say a word. I
should have gone to a Kleinian!"

Later I was able to understand that at the very moment TIM had
begun to have difficulty in breathing, he was already engaged in
eliminating all trace of my words and of their profound affective
impact. Perhaps even before the session had ended, there had been
no feelings left to color his thoughts. This kind of psychic
repudiation or foreclosure is of a quite different order from that
of either repression or denial of affectively toned ideas and
experiences. In other words, although my Invisible Man took in
my interventions and presence during the sessions, once he crossed
the threshold on his way out, my image and my interpretations
were simply evacuated from his inner world, like so many
valueless fecal objects.

I do not use the anal metaphor lightly insofar as TIM is
concerned since most of his fears and fantasies, when he was able
to capture them long enough to communicate them, invariably

revealed a consistent preoccupation with anal-type dramas and relationships. The fantasy of having killed his father through fecal expulsion was but one outstanding example. Sometimes he was convinced that he had brought mud into my building and at other times he could not free his mind of the obligation to tell me that he had once again squashed out his cigarette butt on the carpeted stairway leading to my apartment. Later he wondered if he had left dirt in my entrance hall, and on one occasion he was hampered by the obsessive thought that my consulting room smelled of feces and that he had caused it by bringing dog droppings in on his shoes. "I hope I'm not polluting the air you breathe," he mumbled. I pointed out at various times that all this fantasied shit seemed to be working its way farther and farther into my living quarters, as symbolic representations of my body and myself: into the building, my entrance, my office, and, finally, my lungs. On each occasion, TIM thought these interpretations might be intellectually valid, but he felt nothing, invariably went on to forget that they had ever been formulated, and had difficulty recalling the material on which they had been based. He nevertheless conceded that perhaps forbidden fantasies of exciting or dangerous fecal exchanges were responsible for the fact that, since starting his analysis with me, he dressed better and had even taken to shining his shoes. I suggested that this gift could also be a clean "cover-up," so that he might continue with impunity to find pleasure in the fantasy of filling me up with his anal products. He burst into laughter, a rare occurrence for TIM, and said: "I'm sure that's right. While you were talking of the possible significance of all this, I thought to myself 'Too bad for her!' "

It is no doubt evident from these few examples that TIM scarcely fits into the conception of a patient with an obsessional neurotic structure, in spite of certain similarities. While it was true that he had many unresolved oedipal problems, his deepest anxiety was less related to conflicts about his adult right to enjoy sexual and professional pleasures than it was to conflicts about his right to exist without being threatened by implosion or explosion in his contact with others.

In the course of TIM's attempts to overcome his narcissistic and psychotic-like anxieties, we were able to discover, albeit very slowly, that his anxiety had been dealt with by rendering himself feelingless and to a certain extent lifeless (which gave him the impression that he was a "schizoid" personality). In the place of obsessional defenses and object relations, TIM displayed a more primitive mode of mental functioning that depended less on repression than on foreclosure from psychic awareness of all that was conflictual or was in other ways a source of mental pain. Processes of splitting and projective identification had to do duty in place of repression. Repressive mechanisms, of course, were present, but they were difficult to uncover because of TIM's terror of his own psychic reality, which had finally put him out of contact with it.

I could only guess, during the early stage of our work, that this ironclad system of eliminating from memory all of my interpretations and other interventions, as part of his dis-affected way of experiencing himself and others, must have been constructed to keep unbearable mental pain at bay, in all probability archaic anxieties concerned with feelings of rage and terror. It seemed to me that what had amounted to a struggle against any transference affect whatsoever, as well as his continual fight against the analytic process and against the libidinal temptation to let himself enjoy giving himself up to the luxury of free association, had enclosed him in an anal fortress of almost impregnable strength that might well continue to prevail for years to come.

Instead of fighting with constipated silence or with rapid elimination of any affective arousal, other patients with affect disturbance similar to that of my Invisible Man would have recourse to more "oral" means of attack and defense. Far from remaining silent, they would throw out words and imprecations, like so many concrete weapons. In spite of this apparently lively form of communication, I came to discover that these analysands were also severely dis-affected.

Here is a brief excerpt from the analysis of Little Jack Horner. In nine years of analysis, although Jack often arrived, as he put it, "deliberately fifteen minutes late because the analysis is of no value," he never once missed a session. He had had twelve years of analysis with two male therapists before coming to see me. From the first week of our work together, he expressed the conviction that I was unable to understand him and was incompetent to help him. "I cannot imagine where you get your good reputation from," he would proclaim. After a couple of years, this plaint changed slightly: "Maybe you are able to do things for the others, but I can tell you right now, *it's never going to work with me!*" When I asked him how he felt about such a situation, he remembered something he had heard about Doberman guard-dogs. He said that these animals apparently suffer from character problems. They become passionately attached to their first master and are even capable of transferring this affection to a second, but should they be unfortunate enough to find themselves with a third master, they might just tear him to pieces. I said, "And I am your third analyst." There followed a moment of heavy silence before Jack Horner could gather his plums together again: "Really! You and your little analytic interpretations!" As can be imagined, the analysis of transference affect was no simple matter. Indeed, he often cut me off in the middle of a sentence, just as though I had not been speaking at all. When I once pointed this out to him, he said that I was there to listen to him and there was nothing he wished to hear from me.

I noted some years ago with my dis-affected anti-analysands that if one does not remain vigilant to the countertransference affects in the analytic relationship, one runs the risk of simply remaining silent or even of disinvesting the work with them. Instead of being pleased by analytic discoveries, patients like Jack Horner tend to be narcissistically wounded by them. Sadly enough, they sometimes finish by paralyzing our analytic functioning and rendering us, like themselves, alexithymic and lifeless. The point I am trying to make here is that *this is the essential message.* It is a primitive communication that is intended, in a deeply unconscious fashion, to make the analyst *experience* what the distressed and misunderstood infant had once felt: that communication is useless and that the desire for a live affective relationship is hopeless.

To return to Jack, it can be said that I was not a fecal lump destined to be evacuated in the ways practiced by TIM; metaphorically, I was more a defective "breast" that, in consequence, needed to be demolished. The fact that one is constantly denigrated or eliminated as imaginary feces or breasts, without embodying any of the potentially valuable aspects of these part objects, is not the problem. On the contrary, these unconscious projections are a sign that something is happening in the analytic relationship. In spite of their continuing negativism, I was rather fond of the two patients in question, even though I frequently felt fed up with both of them. My discouragement with them arose from the fact that, in spite of vivid signs of suppressed affect, the analyses stagnated. It is the quasi-total lack of any psychic change in such analysands that evokes, as far as I am concerned, the more painful countertransference feelings. The constant attack upon the analytic setting or upon the relationship and the process itself, is profoundly significant and can potentially give valuable insight into the patient's underlying personality structure, but its meaning holds no interest whatever for the patients involved. It is actively either forgotten or denied.

Although many features of the psychic structure of patients like TIM and Jack Horner might be taken into consideration, I wish here to emphasize mainly the profound affective disturbance. Such analysands are out of touch with their psychic reality, insofar as emotional experience is concerned. In their dis-affected way, they also have as much difficulty in understanding other peoples' psychic realities, including the analyst's. The upshot is that *the others* become strongly "affected" instead!

The fundamental problem is of a preneurotic nature. It is as though such individuals had been crushed by an inexorable maternal law that questioned their right to exist in a lively and independent way. My clinical experience leads me to the conviction that this deeply incarnated "law" was one of the first elements to develop in their sense of self and that it was transmitted, in the beginning, by the mother's gestures, voice, and ways of responding to her baby's states of excitement and affect storms. She alone had decided whether to encourage or restrain her infant's spontaneity. However, it is not my intention to explore, in this presentation, the personal past or the phallic and archaic oedipal organizations of the patients in question. I wish to limit my research to the present-day factors in the analytic experience, from the point of view of the psychic economy.

In stating that the problems are preneurotic, I am not suggesting that neurotic manifestations are lacking. They are clearly evident, but their existence either is not recognized by the analysands or fails to elicit any interest on their part. When neurotic features are accessible to analysis, we frequently come to find that they have served as an alibi for the more profound psychic disturbances I have described. Jack Horner, for example, brought to his first interview with me, like a present, a couple of classical, "good neurotic symptoms." He had managed to maintain, throughout forty years of life, including the twelve previous years of analysis, a certain form of sexual impotence and a recalcitrant insomnia that had dogged him since his adolescence. Both these symptoms disappeared after three years of analysis, but Jack was in no way happy about these changes. If anything, he resented this passage in his analytic adventure. "No doubt, you congratulate yourself on the disappearance of my two problems. But nothing's really changed. It's perfectly normal to sleep at nights, and as for making love, you might as well know that, as far as I'm concerned, it's something like cleaning my teeth. I feel it's necessary, and sometimes I feel better afterwards. But as for *me,* I'm more unhappy than ever before. My symptom, my real symptom, is that *I don't know how to live!*" Behind the evident pathos of such a statement, we might also wonder who "me" is for Jack Horner. Is it the person who sleeps soundly? Or is it the one who makes love without difficulty? In a sense this is not "him." His true "me," as he understands it, suffers from an inner deadness for which he feels there is no cure, as though a part of him had never come alive. *Moreover, should it threaten to come to life, it must immediately be rendered lifeless, feelingless, and therefore mean-ingless.*

Our analytic work up to this point would seem to have shown that his former neurotic symptoms were a mere alibi that served to camouflage the background scene; once gone, they left behind a dis-affected, empty depression that laid its imprint on his sleep, devoid of dreams, and on his sexual life, devoid of love. His sense of identity seemed rather like a faded photograph, to which he nevertheless clung as a sign of psychic survival. Have I become the frame in which the sepia-tinted portrait can be guaranteed a place? Jack Horner says that he cannot leave me in spite of his conviction that I can do nothing to bring him to life. How are we to understand his impression of inner death that paralyzes each vital impulse? It is as though it were forbidden to Jack, for impalpable reasons, to enjoy life, to delight in his own experience of being alive in each important facet of his existence.

TIM, although a very different kind of personality, functions with the same narcissistic affective economy. He, too, constantly attacks each affective link that might bring him into closer contact either with others or with his own inner psychic reality. It seems clear that such continual psychic activity must be imbued with important defensive value. TIM and I needed five years to be able to put his symptom into words. (As already mentioned, he did not denigrate and destroy the meaning of interpretations as did Jack Horner, but simply evacuated them from his memory.) For years, I had the feeling that I had expended considerable effort to render TIM more sensitive to his lack of contact with his affective life, yet there was little change in his detached way of feeling and being. One day, he said: "I simply don't know what an emotion really is. Wait a minute, I recognize one—those moments when I have cried here. As you well know, I would do anything in the world to avoid such a feeling, and yet sometimes it makes me feel more real. I wish I could read a book about emotion; maybe Descartes would help me. I know. There are two emotions: sadness and joy. I guess that's the lot." I wonder to myself how TIM managed to remain unaware of his rage, anger, guilt, anxiety, terrors, and feeling of love, to mention only a few common human emotions. I limited myself to the remark that sadness and joy were valuable psychic possessions.

In the following session, to my delight, TIM had not gotten rid of his discovery. He said that he had felt deeply moved after the session and, once in his car, had found tears in his eyes. He had said to himself that he must at all costs try to formulate the emotion that flooded him and that it had taken this form: "Incredible! My analyst is concerned about me. She worries about my lack of emotion." On the way home, the tears again had come to the surface. This time he had said: "But why is it she and not my mother who taught me this?"

In the following months we became able to understand that expressions of emotion had been felt to be despicable in his family milieu and that behind this pathological ego ideal had lain other anxieties, in particular, the fear of going crazy, of exploding, of losing one's grasp of external reality if one should let oneself be invaded by emotion. Later on, TIM gained insight into his need to maintain a desert-like solitude around him for fear of melting into others and becoming confused with *their* psychic realities, as well as the recognition that he feared that were he to be invaded with emotion he would no longer be able to cope with catastrophic events (such as car accidents) with his habitual alexithymic or, as he would say, his "schizoid calm," a character trait of which he was proud. In other words, his Cartesian motto might have been: "I am not really there; therefore I am," or it might have been "I am unmoved; therefore I can function." I regard this kind of mental functioning, which manages to pulverize all trace of affective arousal, as an attempt at psychic survival in the face of near-psychotic anxieties of disintegration and loss of identity.

What happens to inaccessible affect in this case? Clearly, it does not follow the economic and dynamic paths described by Freud in hysteria, obsessional neurosis, and the so-called actual neuroses. With the analysands mentioned in this presentation, there is, on the contrary, a serious deficiency of protective defenses and of effective action in the face of mental pain, whether this is connected with narcissistic- or object-libidinal sources. The fear of being overwhelmed, or of implosion or explosion in relationships with others, often obliges the individual to attack not only his perception of his affects but also any external perceptions that run the risk of arousing emotion. In the course of analysis, we are sometimes the privileged observers of this kind of attack upon emotionally charged perceptions and can discover what actually happens to the stifled affect. This may take the form of fleeting moments of distorted external perception. These might be regarded as affect equivalents.

To illustrate this, here is a further fragment from the analysis of Jack Horner. For years, he had arrived ten to fifteen minutes late, proclaiming that, in any case, he was better off in the waiting room than on the couch. As a result of my prodding, he eventually became curious about the meaning of his unpunctuality and told me that he would come right on time for the following session. In fact, he came ten minutes early. Due to unforeseen and unavoidable circumstances, however, I myself was ten minutes late. Given the context, I found this most unfortunate, and I told him so. As he lay down on the couch, he said: "Good God, I couldn't care less! I was very happy there alone. The time passed quickly because I was reading an interesting article. In fact, when you came to the door, I didn't even see you—that is, I got a vague impression that you were unusually small. Actually, I was aware that you aren't dressed with your usual elegance. Seems to me you are wearing a sort of dirty grey thing. [My dress was in fact of apricot-colored suede.] Oh yes, and you didn't have any head. That's it—you looked shrunken and colorless."

In trying to examine the significance of these perceptions, he deduced, in what sounded like an exercise in logic, that perhaps he could have been a little hostile toward me because of the long wait—but he felt absolutely nothing of the kind and doubted that he could be capable of such emotion. From here, he went on to a chain of associations that included screen memories from the past, some key matters we had discussed in the course of his long analysis (recent "screen memories," so to speak, that belonged to our analytic work together), and certain constructions we had made.

Jack took up a fantasy (that had become a certitude for him over the years) that something disastrous and irrevocable had happened between him and his mother when he was four months old. He then thought of a photograph of himself as a little boy of about fifteen months, which he called the photograph of "the baby sitting alone in the snow." In reality, the snapshot, which he had once brought to show me, showed him sitting in sunshine on white sand. (My own free-floating thoughts in response to his associations went as follows: "There's Jack Horner, 'baby-alone-in-the-snow,' sitting in my waiting room, determined to know nothing of his feelings in this situation.") Without making any link, Jack went on to remember a moment, in the second year of treatment, in which he had expressed the wish to break off the analysis. Since he had often described the tempestuous manner in which he had broken off his first two analyses, I had suggested that, this time, we should make space to examine his wish to leave analysis instead of repeating an old pattern. From that time on, Jack consistently reproached me for not understanding the supreme importance of his spontaneous wish to leave me and claimed that I have permanently destroyed his chances of experiencing a true desire: "You know I would never have left in any case. But you spoiled everything. It's ruined forever."

Here, then, was little Jack Horner, picturing himself, four to fifteen months old, full of life, making spontaneous and meaningful gestures toward me, but perceiving me as an implacable mother who forcefully communicates to him with my lateness that he cannot aspire to personal freedom, vitality, excitement, and desire, except at the price of losing his mother's love. His reaction was to attack his perception of the mother he perceived as rejecting and hurting him: his mother had no head; she becomes small and colorless, a desiccated, devitalized image from which he pulls away as he internalizes her in order to become his own mother.

For the infant he feels himself to be cannot give up his mother; he would rather give up his own internal vitality than lose her. He would rather freeze himself forever into the "baby-sitting-in-the-snow," playing the simultaneous, dual roles of the rambunctious child vigorously restrained by the disapproving, unresponsive, uncomprehending mother.

In his book, *Le Discours Vivant,* André Green (1973), speaking of psychotic modes of experiencing affect, writes: "Paradoxical affectivity expresses itself in action and in impulsive behavior of an explosive and unexpected kind. The link between affect and representation can be glimpsed in the relationship between acts and hallucinatory activity. The affect is acted out and its representation no longer obeys reality." Green then goes on to quote Bion's view that, for certain psychotic patients, reality as such is hated, with resulting inhibition of affective experience by the ego. At the same time, there are destructive attacks on all psychic processes. There are attacks upon the object, upon the subject's own body, and above all, upon his own thought processes. Affects not only are infiltrated with hatred, but are hated as such.

The patients of whom I am speaking do indeed use psychotic defense mechanisms, but they do not suffer from psychotic thought processes. TIM referred to himself as "schizoid," and Little Jack Horner said on a couple of occasions that he regards himself as an "autistic child"; but, in either case, it is the adult part of the personality that is observing and commenting on the distressed and traumatized child within. The countertransference difficulties with such analysands do not reside in inability to identify with the nursling hidden in their inner psychic worlds. They derive instead from their utter inability to cope with the distress they feel or even to listen to it in a meaningful way. In other words, such patients lack identification with an inner, "caretaking," maternal figure. This is painfully evident in the analytic relationship, where the analyst is thrust into the role of the inadequate, incompetent, or even totally absent mother, with whom the analysand has to settle accounts from the past. Over and beyond this complicated projection, the analyst also has to accept being made into the father who has failed in his task. Not only is this father felt to forbid any attachment to the "breast-mother," but in addition he is thought to offer no compensation for the renunciations involved. Sometimes this may be expressed in the use of an addictive substance; with the patients who concern us here, the analyst and the analysis itself can become an addictive substance, that is, a substitute mother, felt, as with a drug, *not to be an object of desire but of need*. The archaic father becomes a figure who refuses the nursling the right to live, in an archaic oedipal organization in which sexuality is interwoven with oral and anal fusion wishes. Thus, it is Narcissus rather than Oedipus who implores us to rescue him. This means that the analyst is asked to support the blows of an enraged child who is struggling, with whatever means he has at his disposal, for the right to exist.

COUNTERTRANSFERENCE PITFALLS

From the standpoint of the countertransference, our own "Narcissus" is sorely tried. We are tempted to ask ourselves: "Why should this child need so much more understanding, care, nourishment, than the others?" A great deal of patience, of "holding," is required. We ourselves must manage to restrain and elaborate our affective reactions while we wait for the birth of a true desire in the other. This is more difficult than it might sound, because much of the time we are faced with a death-seeking factor that tends to paralyze our own inner vitality as well as that of the analysand. The phrase that somebody "just bores us to death" is a telling one in this connection. The analysand's dis-investment of inner vitality, which is undoubtedly on the side of death, runs the risk of becoming installed within the analyst as well. The latter needs to believe that some psychic change is possible, as well as to believe that the analysand, one day, will have the courage to give up his survival techniques and begin truly to live.

One final question, also concerning our countertransference reactions, needs to be raised. Why do we accept patients into analysis who resist the analytic process as though their lives were in danger — patients whose personalities are characterized by continual acting out, continual attacks upon the analytic setting or the analytic relationship, and continual elimination from memory of every insight that comes to the surface? Why do we accept patients with an incapacity to cope with the feelings, thoughts, and fantasies that, for the first time, they are able to put into words? Why do we choose to work with people who refuse to interest themselves in the painful past and present experiences that might enlighten the mysteries of their infantile past, who intuitively and methodically destroy each potentially valuable acquisition? Why do we take into analysis analysands whose primary aim is to show us that we can do nothing for them? "Please help me, but you will see that I am stronger than you" is the credo of these patients.

Although we are frequently unaware of the difficult analytic path ahead of us when we engage ourselves in such analyses, we are also conscious, looking back on the first interviews, that we might well have forecast some of the difficulties. We have a tendency to project onto each future analysand considerable potential to undertake an analytic adventure. We tend to believe that he will be capable of making good use of us and to convince ourselves that, even in our preliminary meetings, we are able to perceive positive dimensions of his psychic being of which he is unconscious, so that we think we can be optimistic about uncovering a latent workable discourse beyond the conscious unworkable one he proffers. This is, of course, a problem of countertransference and unrealistic, hopeful expectation. There is a Dr. Knock hidden inside each one of us, who wishes to believe that anyone who asks for analysis is potentially analyzable and that every analytic adventure is worth undertaking. I know that, as far as I am concerned, when I listen to patients who wish to undertake analysis, so long as they seem to be in contact with their psychic suffering and show themselves willing to search further for the causes of their psychic distress, I should like to take them all! To the extent to which they demonstrate a wish to make discoveries about their inner world, they evoke in me a similar desire. Even those who have already spent long years in analysis yet wish to continue their quest evoke in us the desire to know more about their analytic adventure and to discover what remains to be brought out from inside them, as though it were a challenge to us and our capacity for analytic understanding.

Can the countertransference pitfall perhaps be our desire to know *too much?* Bion once remarked that an analyst is someone who prefers to read a person rather than a book.

But suppose we are fooling ourselves? What if there is no readable story in this book or all the chapters are repetitive and identical? Perhaps the end of the story may even be merely the beginning, with little hope that we can do more than go around in circles. Once we start, we must assume responsibility for the mutual enterprise. Admittedly, we do this at a certain price. The analysands who are the most difficult, who cannot allow us to read their history because they have never dared to turn the first page themselves, paralyze our "reader-analyst" functioning and arouse in us terrible feelings of malaise, anxiety, frustration, guilt, and, even worse, boredom and fatigue. How can we give life to these patients who ask us only to keep their prison walls intact and to keep our affect reactions to ourselves? How are we to deal with the feeling of total impotence, of inability to help them become less dis-affected and more alive, so that they can truly develop the desire to leave us and to live? Above all, what are we to do with our own feelings of disaffection and despair?

It is said that if one looks at anything for a long enough time, it becomes interesting. Although we are always alone with our difficult dis-affected patients, and although we well know that nobody is going to come and help us, we at least have the possibility of sharing our disquiet, our incomprehension, and our sense of incompleteness. This is one of the reasons we gather together to share our clinical experiences and our theoretical conceptualizations with one another. If we have the impression that these difficult analysands have led us into an interminable analytic experience, at least they have opened a field of research before us.

Little Jack Horner once said to me, after some eight years of analysis: "I have neutralized you completely. It doesn't matter what you do or what you say; you will never get anywhere with me. This analysis is utterly useless, but no doubt you will manage to make an article out of it!"

REFERENCES

Green, A. (1973). *Le Discours Vivant.* Paris: Presses Universitaire de France.

McDougall, J. (1972). The anti-analysand in analysis. In *Psychoanalysis in France,* ed. S. Lebovici and D. Widlöcher, pp. 333–354. New York: International Universities Press, 1980.

———— (1978). *Plea for a Measure of Abnormality.* New York: International Universities Press, 1980.

———— (1986). *Theaters of the Mind.* New York: Basic Books.

14

Identification and Its Vicissitudes as Observed in Psychosis

Otto F. Kernberg

*T*his chapter by Otto Kernberg takes us beyond his work with borderline patients to the sources of self identity in individuals suffering from psychosis.

As he did in the first chapter of this collection, Kernberg takes care to clarify concepts and differentiate among normal, borderline, and psychotic thought processes. It is important that he is able to distinguish psychotic introjection from normal, infantile symbiosis, something that Melanie Klein failed to do.

As Kernberg points out, however, there came a time in the therapy described here when not only was the patient unable to distinguish her thinking from the therapist's, but he could not distinguish his thinking from hers. Here we see Kernberg at his most insightful. We see him willing to engage with his patient at the symbiotic level and to contain that experience within his understanding. It is this willingness to let go of the differentiating faculty and to experience with the patient that is required of anyone who works meaningfully with patients who have major psychotic elements to their thinking and relating. Equally important is the ability to regain that differentiating faculty at will.

*All therapists need theory, sometimes elaborate theories,
not only as a system to organize data, but also as a sort of
"mental skin," something to pull them back from and
differentiate them from their experience with patients—and
with one another, for that matter. Perhaps when therapists
develop competing theories and argue with colleagues about
schools of thought, they are not only disputing the organization of data, but like Kernberg's Miss A. and her accusations, they are using their arguments to "establish a boundary
between us, a 'mental skin' so to speak" (p. 191). And why
shouldn't therapists do that? Everyone needs a skin, as long
as it has a certain permeability to it.*

My principal aim in this chapter is to illustrate, by describing
the treatment of a schizophrenic patient, the vicissitudes of
psychotic identification as observed in the transference, and the
development of a sense of identity. In order to facilitate an
understanding of my technical approach, let me briefly summarize
the concepts underlying that approach, concepts I have described
in detail elsewhere (Kernberg 1984a,b).

CONCEPTS UNDERLYING THE APPROACH

I am using Edith Jacobson's ideas (1964, 1971) and my own earlier
development of these (1976, 1984b) as the theoretical frame within
which I propose the following terminology.

I use *internalization* as an umbrella concept to refer to the
building up of intrapsychic structures that reflect both actual and
fantasied interactions with significant objects under the impact of
drive derivatives represented by specific affect states. The basic
unit of internalization, as I see it, is a dyadic one, that is, it
consists of a self and object representation in the context of a
specific affect representing libidinal and/or aggressive drives.
Introjection, identification, and *identity formation* are conceived
as a series of progressive levels of internalization.

Introjection, the most primitive of these, occurs during the
symbiotic stage of development (Mahler and Furer 1968, Mahler
et al. 1975), when self and object representations are not yet

differentiated from each other; *identification* takes place when self and object representations have been differentiated from each other, that is, in the stage of separation-individuation.

Identity formation refers to the more general intrapsychic process of integration of libidinally and aggressively invested self representations into a cohesive self, in parallel to the simultaneous integration of libidinally and aggressively invested object representations into broader representations of significant objects. Ego identity is the result of this process. It includes both a longitudinal and a cross-sectional integration of the self.

Identifications occur in a sequence of what might be called steps. First is the more or less realistic perception of an external object and of the relation of one's self to that object under the impact of a determined affect. (Degrees of distortion always exist of the perception of any relation under the impact of drive derivatives.) The second step consolidates an internal representation of the object linked by a specific affect to a corresponding self representation; the third, a modification of the self representation under the influence of the object representation; and the fourth, a modification of the general concept of the self under the impact of this particular self representation. The entire process eventually leads to an expression of this intrapsychic transformation in the actual or fantasied relation of the individual with the original and/or other objects.

Normal identifications are partial or selective: they imply the modification of the self concept under the influence of the object, but, at the same time, an increase in the differentiation between the self and object is implied in the very discrimination of which aspects of the object are incorporated and which are not. They thus have progressive or growth-promoting functions.

I shall now contrast identification that normally takes place during development with *psychotic identification,* a pathological process that may take place at any time. Psychotic identifications reflect a defensive regression to the symbiotic stage of development. They are characterized by the internalization of an object relation that is defensively re-fused, including the refusion of "all good" self and object representations under the dominance of real or fantasied gratification as a defense against the dread of annihilation resulting from the parallel re-fusion of "all bad" self and object representations that reflect internalized object relations dominated by aggression.

It is important to distinguish what takes place during normal symbiosis from the phenomena characteristic of the psychotic process. Normally during symbiosis, the "all good" fused self-object representations result from gratifying relations with the object. Normal introjections build up fused, or undifferentiated self-object representations separately under libidinally invested and aggressively invested relations with the object. In contrast, the defensive destruction of or escape from object relations characteristic of psychosis and the defensive blurring of the boundary between self and non-self with a consequent loss of reality testing is characteristic of psychosis and not of normal symbiosis. In essence, psychotic identification is a defense against a dread of annihilation.

In my view, psychotic identifications include two mechanisms: (1) *psychotic introjections* characterized by a defensive re-fusion of "all good" self and object representations that threatens the destruction of the self as a consequence of defensive blurring between these self and object representations (Jacobson 1964), and (2) *projective identification,* representing an effort to escape from an intolerable world of aggression within which self and object can no longer be differentiated. I have suggested in earlier work (1984b) that projective identification may constitute the means whereby the infant tries to differentiate itself from the object under conditions of peak negative affects. Normal introjection, in contrast, facilitates the infant's gradual, cognitive differentiation of self from object. Extreme pleasure states establish an "all good" undifferentiated self-object representation within which self and object components will then be gradually differentiated as heightened attention is drawn to these experiences, while extreme unpleasure states motivate efforts to escape from and eliminate this unpleasure by placing its source "out there," creating an "all bad" fused self-object representation in the process. Here again, self and object are thus gradually differentiated.

The effort during normal symbiosis to eliminate an "all bad" relationship implies both an effort at differentiation, but also the creation of a potentially dangerous external reality that, in consequence, needs to be controlled to avoid "persecution." There is a potential distortion of external reality involved here that relates primitive projection to the regressive projective processes in psychosis. In contrast, more adaptive projective mechanisms, encountered in neurotic structures, do not aim at controlling the object of projection.

Therefore, I have proposed to designate the earliest or primitive form of projection *projective identification,* and to reserve the term *projection* for more adaptive, later forms of this defensive operation. The reasons for this decision are that the term projective identification, as utilized in the literature on psychosis, is more current and has been better defined in clinical terms than the term *psychotic projection;* the normal early projective mechanism and those observed in both psychotic and borderline psychopathology are practically identical, justifying one term for both normal and pathological early projection; and the term projection is most frequently described with characteristics that correspond to later, more adaptive forms of the mechanism observed in neurotic disorders. In contrast, normal introjection and psychotic introjection are not only clinically different from each other, but psychotic introjection is, in fact, only observable in psychosis. Therefore, I refer to introjection as the normal process, and psychotic introjection as its psychotic counterpart.

In my view, projective identification may be defined as a primitive defense mechanism consisting of (1) projecting intolerable aspects of intrapsychic experience on to an object, (2) maintaining empathy with what is projected, (3) attempting to control the object as a continuation of the defensive efforts against the intolerable intrapsychic experience, and (4) unconsciously inducing in the object what is projected in the actual interaction with the object. The more mature defense of projection, in contrast, consists of (1) repression of an unacceptable intrapsychic experience, (2) projection proper of that experience on to an object, (3) lack of empathy with what is projected, and (4) distancing or estrangement from the object as an effective completion of the defensive effort.

I believe that projective identification is not necessarily a "psychotic" mechanism, unless the term *psychotic* is used as a synonym for *primitive,* an idea I would reject. Projective identification may occur with patients presenting a psychotic structure. When it does, it represents a last-ditch effort to differentiate self from object, to establish a boundary between the self and the object by means of omnipotent control of the latter. Projective identification is the patient's way of trying to avoid a complete loss of self in psychosis. Without recourse to projective identification the patient would lapse into a confusional state in which he or she would no longer be able to know whether aggression came from the inside or the outside.

In patients with borderline personality organization, whose boundaries between self and object representations, and between self and external objects are well differentiated, projective identification has different functions. Here it is the primitive dissociation or splitting of "all good" from "all bad" ego states that the patient attempts to maintain. In patients with borderline personality organization, projective identification weakens the differentiation between self and external objects by producing an "interchange of character" with the object, so that something internally intolerable now appears to be coming from the outside. That exchange between internal and external experience tends to diminish reality testing in the area of the exchange, but the patient maintains a boundary of a sort between the projected aspects and his or her self-experience.

The clinical observation that the interpretation of the unconscious meanings in the "here and now" of projective identification in psychotic patients may temporarily increase a patient's confusion and *reduce* his reality testing, whereas such interpretation of projective identification in borderline conditions temporarily *increases* the patient's reality testing and ego strength are empirical observations that support, in my view, the theoretical conclusions suggested.

In psychosis, psychotic identifications, including psychotic introjections and projective identification, predominate. These processes lead to delusional distortions or re-creation of external objects and pathological efforts to control them within an overall context of loss of reality testing derived from the loss of ego boundaries that results from self-object blurring. Psychotic identifications, in short, signify regression to an abnormal symbiotic phase. They bring about an obliteration of the self under the influence of psychotic introjection, and destruction of the object world under the influence of projective identification (Jacobson 1964, Kernberg 1984b). The ultimate cause of the activation of psychotic identifications is the prevalence of severe aggression, which triggers a defensive refusion of "all good" self and object representations and activates projective identification to deal with the threatening infiltration of aggression into all internalized object relations.

As an important consequence of all these developments, there is a profound sense of loss or dispersal of identity in psychosis, a phenomenon usually obscured when the psychotic transferences are active (true merger experiences in the transference), which reflects the patient's inability to differentiate between self and object representations. It is only when psychotic transferences are being resolved that the problem of loss of and struggle for the recovery of a sense of identity in the psychotic patient becomes apparent. The case description that follows illustrates some of these aspects of identification processes in psychosis, including the emergence of struggles around a sense of personal identity at a point of resolution of the psychotic transference.

The patient I am about to describe fulfilled what Michael Stone (1983) has considered positive criteria for intensive psychotherapy with psychotic patients, namely, (1) a capacity for relatedness, (2) a character structure free of all but the slightest measure of antisocial features, (3) psychological mindedness, and (4) average to better-than-average intelligence. In addition, the fact that my initial contacts with the patient took place before her psychotic break may have been a beneficial factor in her treatment.

CLINICAL EXAMPLE: THE IDENTIFICATION PROCESS IN PSYCHOSIS

Miss A., an attractive young woman in her late twenties, was referred by an internist she had consulted for a variety of somatic complaints, for which no organic basis could be found, and because she complained about a growing sense of confusion and lack of purpose in her life. Her history disclosed no major psychopathology—her parents were caring and accepting, the mother on the controlling side (occasionally very domineering), the father more passive. She had been a good student, bright, sociable, if a bit willful. After graduating from college she had performed effectively in a position that called for considerable responsibility and for working with other people. She had three younger brothers, and it was shortly after the marriage of one of her brothers that the first signs of trouble became manifest.

Because of the diagnostic implications, I shall describe her recent history as she gave it to me over a series of interviews.

About two years before our initial interview, Miss A., for reasons she did not make clear to me, left her job and undertook psychotherapy with a Dr. B., who, Miss A. emphasized, "rescued" her from what had become a boring and unsatisfactory profession by encouraging her to shift to painting and the decorative arts and to increase her body awareness by creative dancing.

Miss A. referred to a number of relations with men, an area of her life she portrayed so confusingly that it was impossible for me to gain any understanding of it. She said, in response to my questions, that she had always felt very erotic, yet sexually unresponsive to men. She was interested in men but did not feel committed to them. She described them all as interesting and valuable but, for reasons mysterious to her, they had all left her. Miss A. described having had intense erotic feelings for Dr. B., but said she had never been able to discuss these or any of her sexual difficulties with him. In fact, she stated that these feelings were the reason she stopped the treatment with him and, against his advice, decided to enter a workshop on 'bodily awareness' in a distant city.

This four-month workshop, which ended a few months before her first consultation with me, created in Miss A. an increasing sense of confusion. She felt that the woman in charge of the workshop was trying to break down her free will and her mind, "grind me down to self-oblivion" so that she could "reconstruct myself again." She implied somewhat confusedly that the workshop leader represented an unimaginably awful invasion of her mind, repeating what she described as her mother's dominant, controlling, infantilizing behavior. She had never been able to tell "who was crazy" between herself and her mother. The picture I got of the patient's father and of her three brothers was extremely vague, but the picture of her mother as controlling was clear enough.

In ensuing interviews, she impressed me as losing her contact with reality. She had lost all her money, the savings of four years, when she left her job, and she now had trouble differentiating the loss of money from the loss of her capacity to think about what was going on in her life. She felt she had difficulties in communicating her feelings to others without being able to clarify to herself what the problems in communication were. She felt she could not relate to others anymore because of that confusion.

She showed some anxiety and, at times, anger when talking about the manipulative behavior of other people, particularly her mother. When I shared with her my observations about her confusing way of talking, she became more disorganized, thus demonstrating a definite absence of the capacity for understanding ordinary social criteria of reality, and loss of reality testing in our interaction.

Further exploration of her sexual life led to vague comments about being sexually excited with women as well as with men, occasionally with her mother, but an affirmation of her basically heterosexual nature. She said that she liked men, but they seemed totally interchangeable to her. My efforts to explore with her the nature of this feeling again led to great confusion. Miss A. denied having hallucinations or delusions, but said she had a heightened sensitivity to the environment: she could anticipate when her telephone would ring and she was now aware of people's sex, age, and occupation even if they approached her from behind. She had no explanation for this heightened capacity, was puzzled and both frightened and excited by it. She felt that it implied a change in her body and mental functioning that she could not account for. This change in her mental functioning was, at the same time, a major source of anxiety.

Throughout the diagnostic interviews with me Miss A. became increasingly restless and suspicious. She saw me as a "traditional psychiatrist," not like the free, open, and "nonestablishment" Dr. B. She was afraid I would force her into verbal communication when, in fact, what she felt she needed was to increase her body communication because only thus, through the arts and workshops, lay the road to psychological liberation. Before I had a chance to start treatment, Miss A. decided to stop her sessions, although I had formulated to myself the diagnosis of a schizophrenic illness and stressed to her the need for further evaluation and treatment.

A few weeks later, her anxious parents called and asked me to see her because her condition had worsened alarmingly. When I saw her again her anxiety level was very high and her speech pressured. She described what seemed to me delusional thinking and hallucinatory experiences. She felt that her physical energy was blocked and at the same time expanding from her body through her neck into her head and external environment, so that she had an increased sensitivity to all stimuli to an extent she found very confusing. Her detailed description of the flow of energy in her body had a clearly delusional quality, and she presented auditory hallucinations on several occasions. While she was very anxious, there were no marked mood fluctuations, and her sensory and cognitive disturbances clearly predominated over any affective ones.

Miss A. accepted my recommendation that she be hospitalized. Over the next few days her anxiety and agitation increased, she became more overtly delusional, gave evidence of having auditory and visual hallucinations, and was verbally violent with the nursing staff.

Once the diagnostic conclusion of schizophrenic illness, undifferentiated type, had been reconfirmed, the staff decided to treat the patient with the combination of neuroleptic medication, Thiothixene, up to 40 milligrams daily, hospital milieu therapy, and psychoanalytic psychotherapy that I would carry out. Dr. C., a staff psychiatrist, would continue to control her medication once the patient was able to move out into the Day Hospital and would also take care of practical decisions affecting her daily life, her relations with her parents, and any other decision-making that might be indicated in support of her psychotherapeutic treatment with me. After about six weeks, the patient was discharged into the Day Hospital and into a halfway house, where she continued for about six months before moving on to an outpatient status, and continued only in her psychotherapy with me and weekly controls with Dr. C.

Because of the development of extrapyramidal symptoms, Thiothixene was first reduced and then changed to Thioridazine at a daily dose of 300 milligrams, which was gradually reduced over the next six months to 150 milligrams and in the following five months to 50 milligrams daily. All medication was discontinued after approximately one year of treatment. Miss A. responded to initial reductions of Thioridazine with increased agitation and anxiety, but later reductions did not increase anxiety or restlessness. To the contrary, the patient was pleased because she no longer had a feeling of muscular rigidity or mental "dullness," which she attributed to the medication. I shall now describe the developments in our psychotherapeutic relationship.

The First Year of Psychoanalytic Psychotherapy

The first month of treatment occurred while Miss A. was hospitalized in one of our acute treatment units. The content of our sessions was filled with her references to the energy flow from her body through her spine into her head and out into space, "blockings" of these energy transfers, and various somatic symptoms she attributed to these blockings. I considered these statements to represent her sense of loss of boundaries between her self and external reality. There was an atmosphere of intense erotization of these references to energy floating throughout her body, expressed in a seductive attitude and exhibitionistic display of her body, while she simultaneously also manifested intense anxiety and agitation. Any questions I raised about what was so frightening about these experiences immediately shifted Miss A.'s attention to the female nursing staff, whom she accused of being sadistic and controlling. Miss A. bitterly complained that I had betrayed her trust in me by hospitalizing her in this prison run by women torturers.

My initial efforts to clarify her fears that her body energy might dissipate and get out of control intensified her agitation. She implied that, by trying to induce her to tolerate her energy flow and energy loss, I was attempting a sexual seduction that would deliver her into the hands of the nursing staff as a punishment for illicit sexual relations with me. She denied having sexual feelings toward me, and clearly implied that any question about her sexual feelings reflected simply a sexually seductive assault from me. I thought that I represented a sexually seductive father, who was attempting to disguise his wish to rape his daughter by accusing her of a sexual assault on him to an enraged and punishing mother. But when I tried to share this idea with her (the nurses representing the punishing mother), Miss A.'s agitation, denial, and terror increased. I was trying to drive her crazy and deliver her to the nurses by talking about sex. I think this episode illustrates the activation of projective identification and the temporarily disorganizing effects of an interpretive approach to it.

At the same time, any efforts to question whether her concerns about energy transfer in her body might be imaginary also led to increased anxiety, agitation, and rage. In other words, the patient could not tolerate either any pointing to the differences between her and my views, that is, any threat to the re-fusion between her "good" images of herself and me in her remaining area of trust and reliance on me. And so I decided to sit back and listen, adopting the stance of a "neutral" and friendly observer. Now Miss A. would occasionally produce a warm smile and express her appreciation of my presence. Such fragmentary moments, however, were quickly followed by a resumption of pressured speech and the description of energy flows. Miss A. also presented auditory hallucinations, macropsia, and micropsia.

The effect of neuroleptic medication was dramatic. In six weeks, Miss A.'s anxiety and agitation decreased enormously. During the final week of her hospital stay, she was no longer agitated, only moderately anxious, and while she experienced energy flows and blockings, these thoughts had a less compelling quality, and there was a marked reduction of her experience of sensorial overstimulation and physical symptoms. Both the intensity of her erotic behavior and her rage and suspicion decreased, and Miss A. became verbally more coherent.

She now entered the Day Hospital, moved into a halfway house, and was able to come to my office for her sessions. She spent much time vigorously complaining about the mistreatment she had suffered from the nurses and Dr. C., her hospital physician. These complaints gradually crystallized into a description of the hospital as a sadistic but mindless, mechanical institution for control and repression. She said she was deeply disappointed in me for having delivered her into the hands of that mindless team of nurses and doctors.

I thought she was now expressing her fears and rage towards a combined, sadistic father–mother image in more reality-couched terms, and referring more directly to realistic aspects of her parents as she had perceived them. At the same time, she was attempting to preserve her relation with me by portraying me as the relatively innocent, misguided victim of the parental ideology that was replicated by my medical background and training. When I attempted to express these thoughts to her, telling her that she was trying to maintain a good relationship with me by dissociating me from the rest of the staff of the hospital, thus avoiding a frightening perception of me as the combination of the features of both her parents, Miss A. became more anxious but did not seem to become more confused in the hours. For the first time, she showed that she could tolerate an interpretive approach without immediate regression into confused thinking. In fact, there were moments when she smiled as if acknowledging that my not dissociating myself from the rest of the hospital team implied an act of honesty on my part.

Miss A. now started to talk about her previous therapist, Dr. B., describing how he had stimulated her to move into the world of art, to express herself physically, how free and open he was regarding sexual matters, encouraging her to have affairs with men without being so bound by traditional moral constraints. When I tried to make a connection between what she was saying and her fear that I would seduce her and deliver her to the nursing staff, and when I reminded her that she had previously said she had never discussed sexual problems with Dr. B., Miss A. grew agitated, disorganized, and angrily accused me of trying to smear Dr. B. She indicated, in short, that she had to deny this aspect of her relationship with Dr. B. and had to maintain the split between her paranoid reaction to me and her idealization of him in order to avoid a psychotic sense of confusion. She was afraid of losing control over her dangerous sexual impulses towards both of us as father images.

A curiously confusing and confused series of sessions evolved over a period of two months. The patient focused endlessly on how she was dealing with her daily life, and denied any aspect of her internal life of fantasy. She accused me of trying to "rehabilitate," "reeducate," "resocialize" her. At the same time she was actually making what seemed to me intelligent use of the efforts on the part of the Day Hospital and Dr. C., her hospital psychiatrist, to help her adapt to the life of the local community. In other words, it was true that Dr. C. was trying to help her adjust to life outside the hospital, discussing her living arrangements, work, professional orientations, study, and the relationship with her parents, and that, insofar as we all explicitly constituted a treatment team I was implicitly in agreement with these arrangements.

I tried to clarify that, while I was in agreement with these immediate arrangements, this did not imply that I had any long-range master plan for her and for what she wanted to do with her life. But Miss A. angrily accused me of being dishonest. Why, she asked me suspiciously, could I not acknowledge openly that these were my own ideals?

I eventually decided that the real issue was tangential to this manifest theme: it was the patient's concern that she had no way of protecting herself against *any* plan about her life arrived at by either Dr. C., the Day Hospital Staff, or myself, because we controlled her thinking completely. It became evident that Miss A. could not separate her own thinking from mine. Thus, she felt that if I appeared to be arguing with her in the session, my anger would contaminate her mind with anger, and we would both be in an enraged battle in which she would no longer be able to differentiate herself from me. The patient was now able to verbalize her sense that any sexual feelings toward me would immediately activate similar feelings in me, and lead to a destructive orgy.

Miss A.'s fear of confusing herself with me first became apparent to me when, provoked by Miss A. in one session into a minor argument about the philosophy of her daily life, I found myself in such confusion about who was saying what that I was unable to clarify even to myself, after the session, what we had been talking about. One might say that, in response to the patient's psychotic identification with me, and to the related blurring of the boundaries between her self representation and her representation of me, a concordant identification with her in my countertransference induced in me a corresponding temporary loss of differentiation between her and myself. Any effort to maintain empathy with the subjective experiences she was conveying to me, led me immediately into a sense of confusion and paralysis of my own thinking.

I now discovered that Miss A. felt compelled to follow to the letter whatever "instructions for healthy living" Dr. C. (in reality) or I (in her fantasy) might give her. Such instructions confused her and made her feel as if she had no identity of her own. She experienced herself as an automaton, a behavior machine controlled by Dr. C.'s and my will, so that she was projecting her decision-making process on to us, while, at the same time, she experienced Dr. C., me, and herself as a single psychic unit. I believe these developments illustrate the mechanism of psychotic introjection that, together with projective identification, characterizes psychotic identifications.

Once I became aware that, as a central fear in the sessions, the patient was afraid of invasion of her mind by my thoughts and wishes, I was able to spell out these fears. Miss A. immediately acknowledged that that was exactly what she was afraid of. She also made it clear that she found it reassuring when I pointed to differences between how she perceived me in the hours and how I perceived myself. The issue was not to convince each other, but to acknowledge our differences in perceiving reality. Further exploration of these issues led to dramatic moments, in several sessions, when indeed Miss A. repeated something I had said in a previous session as if she herself had said it and she also attributed to me statements that she had made. The confusion between herself and me as a consequence of pervasive introjective and projective processes was dramatically evident in the hours. It was as if her major task had become to disentangle her thinking from that of Dr. C. and myself.

At the same time, there was a marked diminution in the erotic atmosphere in the hours, a dramatic suppression of all sexual behavior and fantasies. Miss A. now came dressed in an inappropriate, childlike fashion, giving an impression of asexuality in stark contrast to the earlier atmosphere in the sessions. She also seemed to have adopted a sense of indifference towards herself, as if she were drifting, and merely going through the motions of "adjusting" to external life. There were only occasional moments in the hours when she would suddenly fix me with an intense gaze that I experienced as sexually seductive, but in a fashion so dissociated from the rest of our interactions that it was gone before I had a chance to clearly think about it.

After about six months, Miss A. left the Day Hospital and the halfway house and moved into an apartment, and her life in the outer world assumed aspects of normalcy. She found herself a position suitable to her capacities, but in her hours with me a marked change occurred. I can best describe what took place as a process of emptying out. She spoke monotonously, without convictions or depth, about the superficial relations she was establishing at work and in her social life. It was as if all intensely aggressive, sexual, or dependent feelings had become unavailable. She not only looked sleepy but sometimes seemed almost to fall asleep during the sessions. Yet, from the information provided by Dr. C., and from what Miss A. said about herself, she seemed perfectly awake in her ordinary interactions with others.

And I, too, found myself sleepy in the hours, to a degree I had never before experienced. What was taking place was a reactive withdrawal on my part. Because these sessions were punctured by brief moments when Miss A. looked at me intensely in an erotized fashion, I commented that she was withdrawing from any contact with me to avoid the emergence of sexual feelings that would create the danger of sexual response from me and a frightening emergence of her fears of being sexually attacked by a father figure. I considered my own sleepiness to be partly a defense against intense oedipal feelings in the countertransference, and a reflection, by concordant identification, of the patient's defensive withdrawal from sexual impulses crystallized in a stereotyped oedipal form.

She immediately talked about her fear that, had she experienced and expressed sexual feelings towards Dr. B., her former psychotherapist, he would have responded sexually and created the experience in her of having sex with her father! This surprisingly open response to my interpretations, however, was immediately submerged in what might be called a sea of sleepy meaninglessness, and left no traces in the sessions of the following days and weeks. I therefore focused on the emptiness itself. When Miss A. once asked me if I was falling asleep, I told her I had to struggle to keep awake, and I wondered if this could be related to her own experience of having to struggle against falling asleep in the hour. She readily acknowledged her struggle to keep awake, and said it was easier to fall asleep than to face the sense of complete emptiness in our encounter. I agreed with her that the hours felt empty, and I wondered whether it came from her trying to tell me that she felt totally lost and abandoned in a confusing landscape of infinite and veiled spaces. In fact, while I spoke, I had a very concrete image of an endless surface of ice and a pervasive fogginess. Miss A. not only accepted that image as corresponding to her own experience, but both of us became wide awake as we spoke.

This incident initiated a period of exploring her sense of living from one emotional reaction to another without any sense of continuity, any sense that she was really a person living these experiences. I believe her sense of having no wishes, no initiative, illustrates the loss of a sense of self, of ego identity. She could look at herself and describe what she was experiencing at any particular moment, but she felt that there was no central person in her putting all of this together. I acknowledged my understanding of what she was saying, and added that it was as if, inside of her, there was nobody taking care of her, concerned for her, so that she was living, as it were, in an artificial state of calm that was hiding the fact that the natural caretaker had abandoned the field of her inner life. And she could not even feel anxious about that. Miss A. said that she felt I understood. Both of us were now able to tolerate that experience without having to escape into sleepy withdrawal.

I think this stage of her treatment illustrates what might be considered the loss of identity in psychosis, a condition usually masked by the dominance of primitive, part object relations in the transference. The empty space of identity diffusion is populated, so to speak, with psychotic fusion experiences. In other words, psychotic identifications mask the painful absence of an integrated self experience. Miss A. could now spell out very fully her sense that she was no longer worried about herself, that she did not know what she wanted, that she had no wishes, no initiative, and that she was not even able to worry about the absence of these functions that she remembered having experienced in the past. When I commented that it was as if she had been left alone by herself and by me, during these times when I seemed to become sleepy, Miss A. said she was no longer worried over the similarity between her and my experience, implying that she was less afraid of confusion between herself and me. I acknowledged that, and said that her no longer being afraid of confusion between the two of us also meant that she was beginning to be able to tolerate her own internal confusion. At the same time, I added, in experiencing herself as safely different from me, she was also feeling very much alone.

Following that session the patient brought in a newspaper article about "the laying on of hands," adding something about the influences of radiations that originated in the body. I suggested that she was testing to see whether I could accept her own past experiences of energy flowing from her body, thus indicating that I could tolerate her "crazy" experiences. Miss A. laughingly acknowledged that it would please her if I also became confused about what was scientific reality and what was "crazy."

A repetitive sequence of events now followed, which eventually became predictable. Sessions in which Miss A. felt I understood her sense of isolation and drifting were followed by sessions in which she would dare to talk briefly about her fears of discussing sexual matters, fears that would rapidly escalate into fantasies about seducing me sexually and the conviction that I would respond to such seductiveness with a sexual attack. This set of experiences was then followed by intense anxiety and a sense of confusion on Miss A.'s part, about the extent to which these were her or my fantasies. These sessions, in turn, were followed by "empty" sessions in which she again appeared aloof and distant, emotionally unavailable, and I sensed the lack of any meaningful material emerging. The cycle repeated itself over three months, with the patient becoming increasingly aware of the cyclical nature of the process.

And then she returned to an earlier theme, accusing me of being too square and conventional, disapproving of her wishes and fantasies of a free and promiscuous sexual life, and so forth. It was as if a replay of her earliest relationship to me was taking place at a more reality oriented, less disorganized level. But now I could interpret these wishes to escape and her image of me as a defense against her frightening fantasies of sexual involvement with me as her father. Such interpretations were no longer followed by severe disorganization in the hours.

I understood Miss A.'s accusations as serving to establish a boundary between us, a "mental skin," so to speak. They were also a residue of her confusion of herself with me, a working through, one might say, of her psychotic identifications.

DUAL NATURE OF THE SELF

In the course of psychoanalytic treatment, when the analyst communicates to the patient his observations not only about the patient's behavior but also regarding the patient's self-awareness, the boundaries of that self-awareness expand, incorporating the perceptions communicated by the analyst. The patient's self representations also become more sophisticated, absorbing into the self concept the self-reflecting aspects that were the analyst's focus of attention and were incorporated by the patient in identification with him.

I propose that the self always includes two layers, or rather, what might be visualized as a central sphere of self representations and a surrounding sphere of self-reflectiveness derived from identification with the observing and concerned mother in the original dyadic relationship at a level of development when self and object representations are differentiated from each other. One might also describe this dual nature of the self as a grouping of functions of self-representations, one group centering on self-differentiation, another on retaining the observing functions of the parental images internalized into the self.

What is missing in psychosis as a consequence of lack of differentiation between self and object representations is not only reality testing but also the capacity for self-awareness normally derived from the early identification with the differentiated object. My patient illustrated this state of affairs dramatically when, in spite of the fading away of her primitive, affectively charged internalized object relations in the transference, her lack of differentiation of self and object representations was so clearly shown by her confusion between her own and my thinking. At the same time, she had a sense of being completely alone and abandoned with no concern for herself or any central, integrated awareness of herself as a person.

Ordinarily, the intense activation of primitive object relations in psychotic transferences totally occupies the field of analytic exploration. The lack of an integrated concept of the self remains in the background under such circumstances. But when there is a relative lull in the activation of intense primitive affect states, the underlying structural characteristics of the failure to differentiate self and object and the painful loss of a sense of identity represented by the absence of the "surrounding sphere" of self-reflectiveness may become dramatically apparent.

In this connection, I wish to stress that the medication during the early stage of Miss A.'s treatment markedly decreased her affective responses. The diminution of anxiety, rage, and sensory input decreased the intensity of activation of primitive internalized object relations in the transference, and, by the same token, highlighted the structure of her psychotic personality organization, the identity issues under examination.

I would now add that her struggle with her painful sense of confusion and of being controlled by sadistic parental authorities, and her seduction fantasies regarding the paternal image left her with two alternatives. She could either increase her sense of confusion by a total fragmentation of all intrapsychic experiences, or else, by withdrawing from the emotional situation into a total psychological isolation, be condemned to face her sense of loss of an integrated view of herself, of what might be called the "self-holding" function of ego identity: the normal identification with a parental or maternal attitude towards one's own self which is part of the double-layered self structure I have described.

Patients with borderline personality organization also present a lack of integration of the self concept, the syndrome of identity diffusion. With them, however, the lack of integration of the self concept serves the defensive function of avoiding that aggressively invested internalized object relations destroy the libidinally invested ones. By the same token, the self-reflective function of ego identity is also missing with borderline patients, not because they do not have the capacity for self-reflection but because of the defensive splitting of contradictory aspects of self-reflectiveness as well as contradictory aspects of self representations in a narrow sense. In each of the mutually dissociated ego states of borderline patients there exists a capacity for some self-reflectiveness. The interpretation of splitting mechanisms in borderline patients permits an integration of self-reflectiveness as the first phase of an integration of the self concept.

The borderline patient, as a consequence of interpretation, may become aware of the contradictory aspects of his experience, behavior, or thinking, and painfully face his conflicts around ambivalence. The psychotic patient, in contrast, does not have the capacity for self-reflection. The confusion between self and object representations masks the lack of a self-reflective function. If and when the patient begins to tolerate the notion of differentiation between himself and the therapist, the sense of aloneness and the absence of a sense of concern for himself may emerge. This loneliness differs from the loneliness that reflects the depressive experience of abandonment or a guilt-determined sense of loss of the relation with good internal and external objects. Depressive loneliness only emerges with further integration of part-object into total-object relations, a later phase in the psychoanalytic therapy of psychotic patients, characterized by integration of "all good" and "all bad" internalized object relations.

The first psychotherapeutic task with severely regressed psychotic patients, particularly schizophrenic patients who have lost the capacity for ordinary verbal communication, who require protective treatment in a hospital setting, and have only the most tenuous grip on reality, is that of establishing a significant contact. In Searles's (1961) terms, the therapist facilitates the transformation of "out of contact" states into primitive transferences at whatever level of regression, within which primitive defensive operations, particularly projective identification, psychotic introjection, omnipotent control, extreme forms of splitting or fragmentation, and denial are predominant. These primitive transferences at a symbiotic level involve a full display of the patient's psychotic identifications.

The patient's capacity gradually to experience intense all aggressive, all sexualized, or all ecstatic emotional states may signal the development of the capacity for symbiotic transferences within which self and object representations cannot be differentiated, but which are differentiated from each other in terms of their dominant affect. Splitting now permits the dissociation of mutually opposite affect states and their corresponding undifferentiated object relations. Under these conditions, the capacity for self-reflectiveness is still absent, the "surrounding sphere" of the self structure is totally unavailable, and the "central sphere" of fragmented self representations are not yet differentiated from their corresponding object representations. Here, in short, problems of identity are still irrelevant.

At a second stage of treatment of psychotic patients, or with psychotic patients who come into treatment with the predominance of intense primitive transferences under the influence of mutually dissociated aggressive and primitively idealized object relations, the main task is gradually to increase the patient's tolerance of fusion and confusion, and then to contribute to differentiating thd patient's self-experience from that of the analyst.

In other words, the patient gradually has to become aware that, in contrast to his confusion of the experience of what comes from him and what comes from the therapist, he and the therapist have different experiences, so that they may live in incompatible realities. The patient has to learn to be able to tolerate exploring this incompatibility without having to resolve it. This tolerance leads to the acceptance of separateness from the therapist and facilitates the development of self-reflectiveness.

Later on, defensive withdrawal protects the patient from dangerous fusion experiences but, at the same time, also from full awareness of the absence of an integrated sense of being a person in his own right. Now the interpretive work may proceed simultaneously to increasing the patient's tolerance of fusion experiences, analyzing the nature of these fusion experiences, and, at moments of beginning consolidation, analyzing the patient's fear and avoidance of the sense of disintegrated aloneness. This is the stage of the treatment that prevailed with Miss A.

In advanced stages of the treatment of psychotic patients, once reality testing has been restored, a beginning internalization of the concern and the observing function of the therapist consolidates nuclei of self-reflectiveness, and thus creates the possibility of eventually interpreting the functions of defensive splitting of self-awareness against the tolerance of ambivalence. This technical approach is related to Winnicott's (1960) conception of "holding" in the transference, although Winnicott did not differentiate the psychopathology of psychosis from that of borderline conditions.

Now the analyst carries out a "holding" function, not only in the sense of resisting the patient's aggression without being destroyed, in assuring the patient of his continuing existence and availability, and in being available as a potential good object on whom the patient can depend. He also becomes an interpretive agent whose interpretations link the islands of self-reflectiveness in the patient's mind and permit the consolidation, through identification with the analyst in this function, of the patient's self-awareness simultaneously with an integration of the dissociated self representations under contradictory affective experiences.

This stage frequently brings about intense experiences of depressive loneliness.

The integration of all self representations throughout time and cross-sectionally into a central, comprehensive concept of the self is matched by a parallel integration of a surrounding sphere of self-reflectiveness that provides a background of ongoing self-evaluation. This surrounding sphere of self-reflectiveness merges temporarily with the central self in the case of conscious action in concrete areas; it submerges itself, one might say, under conditions of non-self-reflective consciousness, but remains as a potential "split in the ego" in a descriptive sense. In other words, self-evaluation may become a preconscious structure of the ego that carries out a supraordinate ego function, the self-observing function of the ego (Freud 1933, Sterba 1934).

In conclusion, unconscious roots in the dynamically repressed id as well as in the dynamically repressed aspects of the superego codetermine the functions of the double sphere of the self at all times. Self-observation may be taken for granted in the neurotic personality organization; self-reflectiveness, thus considered, is a precondition for, but not equivalent to emotional introspection or insight. Powerful neurotic defensive operations (such as rationalization, intellectualization, and negation) may reduce emotional introspection even in patients with solid ego identity and excellent reality testing. Self-observation is always a crucial focus of the interpretive work in the case of borderline personality organization, where defensive dissociation of the self represents a major, ongoing resistance. Finally, the absence of self-reflectiveness and of the corresponding internalization of a self-concerned agency derived from the originally symbiotic, dyadic relationship, may become a basic concern in some stage of the psychoanalytic psychotherapy of psychotic patients, as illustrated in the case reported in this paper.

I have described the mechanisms that operate in psychotic identification. One mechanism is psychotic introjection, characterized by a re-fusion of "all good" self and object representations. This re-fusion threatens the destruction of the self as a consequence of the defensive blurring of these self and object representations. The second operative mechanism is projective identification, which I have defined in comparison with and in contrast to projection. Projective identification threatens the destruction of the relation with the object.

The case I have described in detail illustrates these psychotic identifications, the development of psychotic transferences wherein the patient cannot differentiate herself and her thinking from the therapist and his thinking, and the struggle around a sense of personal identity at a point of resolution of the psychotic transference.

This case also illustrates that an integrated self includes two types of self-representations: those centered on self differentiation and those which reflect the observing functions of the parental images internalized into the self.

REFERENCES

Freud, S. (1933). New introductory lectures on psycho-analysis. *Standard Edition* 22:3–182.

Jacobson, E. (1964). *The Self and the Object World*. New York: International Universities Press.

———— (1971). *Depression*. New York: International Universities Press.

Kernberg, O. (1976). *Object Relations Theory and Clinical Psychoanalysis*. New York: Jason Aronson.

———— (1984a). *Severe Personality Disorders: Psychotherapeutic Strategies*. New Haven: Yale University Press.

———— (1984b). *Projection and projective identification: developmental and clinical aspects*. Presented at the First Conference of the Sigmund Freud Center of the Hebrew University of Jerusalem, May 28, 1984.

Mahler, M., and Furer, M. (1968). *On Human Symbiosis and the Vicissitudes of Individuation*. New York: International Universities Press.

Mahler, M., Pine, F., and Bergman, A. (1975). *The Psychological Birth of the Human Infant*. New York: Basic Books.

Searles, H. (1961). Phases of patient–therapist interaction in the psychotherapy of chronic schizophrenia. *British Journal of Medical Psychology* 34:169–193.

Sterba, R. (1934). The fate of the ego in analytic therapy. *International Journal of Psycho-Analysis* 15:117–126.

Stone, M. H. (1983). The criteria of suitability for intensive psychotherapy. In *Treating Schizophrenia Patients: A Clinical-Analytical Approach,* ed. M. H. Stone et al., pp. 119–138. New York: McGraw-
Hill.
Winnicott, D. W. (1960). The theory of the parent–infant relationship.
In *The Maturational Processes and the Facilitating Environment,* pp.
37–55. New York: International Universities Press, 1965.

Afterword

The foregoing chapters represent some directions object relations psychotherapies have been taking in the recent past and indicate some paths toward the future. Applications to broader patient populations have evolved, though this movement is more prominent in clinical work than in the formal literature. This deficit in formal discussion, which probably arises from loyalties to schools of thought, is beginning to be corrected.

Throughout these chapters, clinical theory is seen as more than an organization of data. It is also a way therapists define themselves in relation to patients and colleagues. Clinical theory, like psychotherapy itself, springs from the inner source, which is not only within the patient's internal world, but also within the clinician's. The foregoing chapters seem to share this common viewpoint.

Since people grow and change and retain diversity—diversity among people and within the person—an increased tolerance for variation in how to understand people is evolving in this field of psychotherapy. Yet, there is a certain unity within individuals, as they grow and change, something called identity or self-cohesion or simply the self. There are commonalities among people, too. As these chapters indicate, clinical theory, which arises from within people and between people, will increasingly take into account both the unity and the diversity of patients and therapists. How that will happen remains uncertain. It is too late to return to the search for a unitary psychology of psychotherapy. That much seems certain.

Acknowledgments

Chapter 1: "A Critical Review of Object Relations Theory," by N. G. Hamilton. Copyright © 1989 by *American Journal of Psychiatry,* vol. 146, pp. 1552–1560. Reprinted by permission of *American Journal of Psychiatry* and the author.

Chapter 2: "An Ego Psychology-Object Relations Theory Approach to the Transference," by O. F. Kernberg. Copyright © 1987 by *Psychoanalytic Quarterly,* vol. 56, pp. 197–221. Reprinted by permission of *Psychoanalytic Quarterly* and the author.

Chapter 3: "The Interpretive Moment: Variations on Classical Themes," by F. Pine. Copyright © 1984 by *Bulletin of the Menninger Clinic,* vol. 48, pp. 54–71. Reprinted by permission of *Bulletin of the Menninger Clinic.* This chapter also appeared in *Developmental Theory and Clinical Process* by F. Pine. Reprinted by permission of Yale University Press and the author.

Chapter 4: "Formulation of States of Mind in Psychotherapy," by M. J. Horowitz. Copyright © 1988 by *American Journal of*

Psychotherapy, vol. 42, pp. 514–520. Reprinted by permission of *American Journal of Psychotherapy* and the author.

Chapter 5: "Splitting and Projective Identification among Healthier Individuals," by N. G. Hamilton. Copyright © 1990 by *American Journal of Psychotherapy,* vol. 44, pp. 414–423. Reprinted by permission of *American Journal of Psychotherapy* and the author.

Chapter 6: "Projective Identification and Couple Therapy," by D. E. and J. S. Scharff originally appeared as "Object Relations Theory and Projective Identification in Marriage" and "The Management of Impasse: Midphase Therapy with an Apparently Impossible Couple," pp. 43–60 and 147–160 in *Object Relations Couple Therapy* by D. E. Scharff and J. S. Scharff. Copyright © 1991 by David E. Scharff and Jill S. Scharff. Reprinted by permission of the authors.

Chapter 7: "The Selfobject Function of Projective Identification," by G. Adler and M. W. Rhine. Copyright © 1988 by *Bulletin of the Menninger Clinic,* vol. 52, pp. 473–491. Reprinted by permission of *Bulletin of the Menninger Clinic* and the authors.

Chapter 8: "The Containing Function and the Analyst's Projective Identification," by N. G. Hamilton. Copyright © 1990 by Institute of Psycho-Analysis. *International Journal of Psycho-Analysis,* vol. 71, pp. 445–453. Reprinted by permission of the Institute of Psycho-Analysis and the author.

Chapter 9: "Intersubjectivity in Psychoanalytic Treatment: with Special Reference to Archaic States," by R. D. Stolorow, B. Brandchaft, and G. E. Atwood. Copyright © 1983 by *Bulletin of the Menninger Clinic,* vol. 47, pp. 117–128. Reprinted by permission of *Bulletin of the Menninger Clinic* and the authors.

Chapter 10: "Psychotherapy of the Narcissistic Personality Disordered Patient: Two Contrasting Approaches," by G. Adler. Copyright © 1986 by *American Journal of Psychiatry,* vol. 143, pp. 430–436. Reprinted by permission of *American Journal of Psychiatry* and the author.

Chapter 11: "On 'Doing Nothing' in the Psychoanalytic Treatment of the Refractory Borderline Patient," by G. O. Gabbard. Copyright © 1989 by the Institute of Psycho-Analysis. *International Journal of Psycho-Analysis,* vol. 70, pp. 527–534. Reprinted by permission of the Institute of Psycho-Analysis and the author.

Chapter 12: "Misrecognitions and the Fear of Not Knowing," by T. H. Ogden. Copyright © 1988 by *Psychoanalytic Quarterly,* vol. 57, pp. 643–666. Reprinted by permission of *Psychoanalytic Quarterly* and the author.

Chapter 13: "The 'Dis-affected' Patient: Reflections on Affect Pathology," by J. McDougall. Copyright © 1984 by *Psychoanalytic Quarterly,* vol. 53, pp. 386–409. Reprinted by permission of *Psychoanalytic Quarterly* and the author.

Chapter 14: "Identification and Its Vicissitudes as Observed in Psychosis," by O. F. Kernberg. Copyright © 1986 by the Institute of Psycho-Analysis. *International Journal of Psycho-Analysis,* vol. 67, pp. 147–159. Reprinted by permission of the Institute of Psycho-Analysis and the author.

Index

Abraham, K., 185
Addictive personalities, 255, 256.
    See also Affect pathology;
    Misrecognition of affect
Adler, G., 4, 6, 7, 11, 12, 14, 16,
    18, 19, 150, 151, 157, 159,
    165, 166
  on Kernberg/Kohut
    approaches, 196–211
  on selfobject function of pro-
    jective identification,
    140–160
Affect pathology. *See also*
    Misrecognition of affect
  addictive personalities, 255, 256
  alexithymia, 255–256
  clinical examples, 258–264,
    265–269
  compulsive discharge of affect,
    254–256
  countertransference pitfalls,
    269–273
  emotional lifelessness, 253

etiology, 256–257
  "normopaths," 253, 254, 256
  preneurotic nature of, 264–265
Aggression
  in countertransference, 47
  in narcissistic personality disor-
    ders, 204–205, 207
  psychotic identifications and,
    281
Alexander, F., 16, 175
Alexithymia, 230, 252, 255–256
Allsbrook, L., 11, 12, 13
Ambivalence, borderline disorders
    and, 199
Analyst. *See* Therapist
Andrulonis, P. A., 13
Atwood, G. E., 182–192
Autistic-contiguous position, 235
Autistic phase, 8

Balint, M., 100, 238
Beahrs, J. O., 10, 11

Behrends, R. S., 174
Bertalanffy, L., 10, 11
Bibring, E., 174
Bick, E., 235
Bion, W. R., 15, 17, 18, 48, 94,
    100, 101–102, 109, 110,
    113–114, 152, 153, 163, 164,
    165, 166, 174, 217, 218, 225,
    230, 232, 244
  container concept of, 7, 8
Blanck, G., 12, 14, 69
Blanck, R., 12, 14, 69
Blatt, S. J., 174
Bogart, L., 17
Bollas, C., 101, 114–115, 117
Borderline disorders. See also
    Refractory borderline patient
  ambivalence and, 199
  diagnosis and, 12
  effect of interpretation of, 280
  integration of self-concept in,
    293
  interpretation of splitting mech-
    anisms in, 293
  intersubjectivity and, 186–187
  narcissistic personality disorder/
    psychosis and, 205
  projective identification in, 280
  self-reflective function in, 293
  structural organization of,
    31–32
Bowen, M., 17
Bowlby, J., 1
Brandchaft, B., 207
  on intersubjectivity in psychoan-
    alytic treatment, 182–192
Brende, J. O., 13, 94
Brenner, C., 217
Brown, S. L., 17
Buchele, B. J., 17
Buie, D. H., 11, 156
Burnham, D. L., 4, 19

Cobliner, W. G., 9
Colson, D. B., 19
Communication, refractory bor-
    derline patient and, 216–227
Complementary identification
  in countertransference, 45–46
  in marriage, 117
Concordant identification
  in countertransference, 45
  in marriage, 117
Container–contained concept
  containing function, 7, 8,
    152–153, 164, 218
  clinical example, 167–171
  projective identification and,
    164–166
Countertransference, 16, 94, 95
  affect pathology and, 269–273
  aggression in, 47
  boredom and, 209
  devaluation of therapist and,
    210
  ego psychology-object relations
    theory and, 44–49
  of impasse, 134
  intersubjectivity and, 183–184
  patient idealization and, 210
Couple therapy. See also Projec-
    tive identification
  concordant/complementary
    identification and, 114
  extractive introjection and,
    114–115
  family therapy contributions
    to, 110–113
  management of impasse, 118
    clinical example, 118–134
  object relations theories and,
    100–104
    Bion, 101–103
    Dicks, 103–104
    Fairbairn, 100–101

sex therapy contributions to, 113
   valency and, 113–114
Crafoord, C., 18

Devaluation of therapist, narcissistic personality disorder
   and, 210
Diagnosis, object relations theory
   and, 11–12
Dicks, H. V., 100, 103–104, 110,
   111, 115
Dis-affected patients. See Affect
   pathology
Double-bind situation, affect pathology and, 257

Eating disorders, misrecognition
   of affect in, 243–245
Ego psychology-object relations
   theory, transference and,
   30–49
   clinical examples, 35–36, 37–39,
      40–41
   countertransference, 44–49
   technique, 41–44
   theoretical background, 30–35
Eissler, K. R., 16
Empathy
   concordant/complementary
      identifications and, 45, 48
Epstein, L., 219, 225
Erikson, E. H., 30
Etiology, object relations theories
   and, 12–13
Extractive introjection, 114–115

Fairbairn, W. R. D., 7, 30, 99,
   100, 101, 103
Family therapy
   contributions to couple ther-
      apy, 110–113
   object relations theory and, 17

Fear of not knowing. See Misrec-
   ognition of affect
Fordham, M., 235
Fragile patients, interpretation
   and, 53–72
Fraiberg, S. R., 9
Freud, A., 2, 95, 175
Freud, S., 4, 11, 33, 54, 55, 94,
   101, 107, 174, 185, 190, 231,
   296
   drive theory of, 2
   object relations theory of, 3
Frick, R., 17
Friedman, H. J., 18
Fromm-Reichmann, F., 16
Frosch, J., 157
Furer, M., 30, 276

Gabbard, G. O., 4, 7, 18, 19, 87,
   95, 165, 216, 227
   on treatment of refractory bor-
      derline patient, 216–227
Ganzarain, R. C., 17
Gill, M. M., 43, 54
Giovacchini, P. L., 14, 16
Glover, E., 33, 55, 174
Grandiose self, 200–201, 206
Green, A., 269
Greenberg, J. R., 11
Grinberg, L., 166, 225
Grosskurth, P., 95
Grotstein, J. S., 4, 6, 86, 106,
   108, 152, 154, 165, 166, 217
Group therapy, object relations
   theories and, 17–18
Guntrip, H. J. S., 7, 33, 99

Hamilton, N. G.
   on containing function and an-
      alyst's projective identifica-
      tion, 163–176

review of object relations
    theory, 1–20
on splitting/identification
    among healthier individu-
    als, 86–96
Hartmann, H., 10, 13, 66
Hartocollis, P., 18
Haugsgjerd, S., 7, 18
Healthier patients, splitting in,
    85–96
Heimann, P., 217
Holding environment, 7–8, 102,
    295. *See also* Container-
    contained concept
    fragile patients and, 65–68
Horner, A. J., 11, 12, 14
Horowitz, M. J., 13, 17, 76, 81
    on states of mind in psycho-
    therapy, 76–83

Idealization in narcissistic person-
    ality disorder, 210
Identification(s), 277
    normal, 277, 278
    psychotic, 277–279, 280
        mechanisms of, 278
        steps in, 277
Identity formation, 277
Insight therapy
    interpretation in, 68–72
    states of mind in, 79, 81
Internalization, 276
Interpretation(s)
    insight therapy and, 68–72
    interpretive moment and, 56–58
    interpretive setting and, 54–56
    modes of offering, 58–68
        expectation of patient re-
        sponse and, 59–61
        holding environment and,
        65–67
        patient's activity and, 62–65

timing and, 61–62
role of, 69–71
supportive therapy and, 68–72
Intersubjectivity
    negative therapeutic reactions
        and, 184–186
    psychopathology and, 186–187
        clinical example, 187–189
    therapeutic action of psycho-
        analysis and, 189–192
    transference/
        countertransference and,
        183–184
Introjection, 276–277
Introjective identification, 102
    by object, 116
    by self, 117
Isaacs, S., 3

Jacobson, E., 8, 30, 198, 276,
    278, 281
Jaffe, D. S., 106, 167

Katan, A., 70
Kernberg, O. F., 1, 4, 6, 7, 8, 9,
    11, 12, 13, 14, 15, 16, 17, 18,
    57, 86, 94, 107, 109, 152,
    157, 165, 166, 170, 185
    on ego psychology-object rela-
        tions approach to transfer-
        ence, 30–49
    on identification in psychosis,
        276–297
    Kohut and, contrasting
        approaches of, 196–211
Klein, M., 6, 7, 30, 34, 44, 87,
    95, 100, 102, 103, 105, 109,
    152, 164, 166, 185
    critique of, 6–7
    object relatedness and, 3, 4–5
    projective identification and, 6

Kohut, H., 1, 9–10, 11, 12, 13,
    15, 16, 18, 33, 35, 57, 141,
    153–154, 170, 182, 185, 187,
    190
  critique of, 10
  Kernberg and, contrasting ap-
    proaches of, 196–211

Lacan, J., 230, 231
Lachmann, F. M., 185, 191
Langs, R., 86, 95, 218
Lemaire, A., 232
Lester, E. P., 9
Lewis, H. B., 81
Lichtenberg, J., 16
Lipton, S. B., 16
Lipton, S. D., 174
Loewald, H. W., 55, 68, 167, 190
Loneliness, psychosis and,
    293–294
Loewenstein, R. M., 174

Mahler, M. S., 4, 5, 10, 11, 12,
    30, 276
  developmental phases, 8–9
Main, T. F., 18
Malin, A., 106, 108, 165, 217
Masterson, J. F., 4, 9, 12, 13, 14,
    15, 16, 86, 197
McDougall, J., 230, 232, 253
  on "dis-affected" patient,
    252–273
Meissner, W. W., 104, 106–107,
    166
Meltzer, D., 235
Menninger, K. A., 10, 11
Minuchin, S., 17
Misrecognition of affect, 230–249
  analytic setting and, 237–239
  anxiety and, 234
  clinical examples, 239–240,
    241–243, 245–248

developmental perspective,
    234–235
  eating disorders and, 243–245
  structuralization of, 236–241
  theoretical background,
    231–234
  See also Affect pathology
Mitchell, S. A., 11
Modell, A. H., 15, 174, 197
Money-Kyrle, R. E., 167
Morrison, A. P., 152, 153, 154
Motivation, Kernberg on, 30–31
Myerson, P. G., 150

Nacht, S., 175
Narcissistic personality disorder
  aggression in, 204–205
  borderline disorders/psychosis
    and, 205
  countertransference responses
    to, 209–211
    boredom, 209
    devaluation of therapist and,
      210
    idealization of therapist and,
      210
  descriptive features of, 197–198
  humiliation and, 205–206
  interpretation of transference
    and, 206
  psychoanalysis vs.
    psychotherapy for,
    202–203
  theories of, 198–202
    Kernberg, 198–200
    Kohut, 200–202
    psychotherapist and, 206–209
    relevance to psychotherapy
      of, 204–206
Negative therapeutic reactions,
    intersubjectivity and,
    184–186

Nemiah, J. C., 230
Neuroses/neurotic characters
    self-reflectiveness in, 296
    structural organization of, 31
"Normopaths," 253, 254, 256
Noy, P., 167

Object induction, in marriage, 116
Object relations theory
    cognitive/perceptual factors
        and, 13
    diagnosis and, 11–12
    etiology and, 12–13
    Freud's, 3
    historical overview, 1–11,
        100–104
    implications for future, 19–20
    imprecise terminology and, 11
    psychoanalytic drive theory
        and, 1–3
    splitting and, 3–4, 8, 9
    treatment and, 14–19
        family therapy, 17
        group therapy/psychiatric
            administration, 17–19
        individual psychotherapy,
            14–16
Ogden, T. H., 6, 86, 87, 95, 152,
    153, 155, 165, 166, 175, 210,
    217, 218, 219, 223, 224
    on misrecognitions and fear of
        not knowing, 230–249
    on projective identification,
        107–110, 171–172
Ornstein, P. H., 204, 205
Overmodulated states of mind, 77

Piaget, J., 9, 10, 183
Pick, I. B., 167
Pine, F., 55, 56
    on interpretive moment, 54–72

Potential space, 230, 233
Primary maturational failure,
    219
Projection, 279
    in marriage, 116
Projective identification
    clinical example, 6
    concordant/complementary
        identification and, 114
    containment of, 152–153,
        163–176
    countertransference and, 16,
        209–210
    couple therapy and, 99–134
    as curative factor, 157–160
    defined, 87, 279
    disengaging from patient's,
        220–227
    extractive introjection and,
        114–115
    family therapy theory and,
        110–113
    in healthier patients, 85–96
        clinical examples, 87–91
        therapeutic utility of inter-
            preting, 93–96
    Klein's concept of, 105–106
    mutual, 118
    projection vs., 279
    psychosis and, 278–280
    reinternalization of, 153
    review of literature on,
        106–110, 152–153, 164–166
    selfobject function of, 140–160
        clinical example, 141–152,
            155–157
    selfobjects and, 153–154
    and self psychology, integration
        of, 153–155
        therapy implications,
            155–157
    sex therapy theory and, 113

sources of confusion about,
    104
steps of, in marriage, 116–118
therapist's containment of,
    152–153, 163–176, 217–218
and transitional phenomena,
    157–158
valency and, 113–114
Pruyser, P. W., 4
Psychiatric administration, object
    relations theories and, 18–19
Psychoanalysis, therapeutic action
    of, 189–192
Psychopathology, intersubjec-
    tivity and, 186–189
clinical example, 187–189
Psychosis, vicissitudes of identifi-
    cation in, 275–297
capacity for self-reflectiveness
    and, 292, 293
clinical example, 281–291
loneliness and, 293–294
normal identification and,
    277–278
projective identification and,
    278–280
psychotic introjections and, 278
Psychotherapy
object relations theories and,
    14–16
states of mind in, 76–83
Psychotic introjections, 278

Racker, H., 40, 45, 114, 117, 172
Rangell, L., 217
Rapoport, D., 63
Reed, G. S., 35
Refractory borderline patient,
    215–227
clinical example, 220–227
theoretical/technical consider-
    ations, 217–220

Rhine, M. W., 166
on selfobject function of pro-
    jective identification,
    140–160
Rice, A. K., 17, 18
Rinsley, D. B., 4, 9, 12, 13, 14,
    15, 86, 197
Riviere, J., 185
Rosenblatt, B., 30, 57
Rosenfeld, H., 165
Roth, B. E., 17

Sadavoy, J., 18
Sandler, A., 30
Sandler, J., 6, 30, 57, 87, 110,
    165, 166
Schafer, R., 16, 174
Scharff, D., 113, 114, 115
on projective identification and
    couple therapy, 99–134
Scharff, J. S., 17, 106, 110, 114,
    115, 116
on projective identification and
    couple therapy, 93–144
Schwaber, E., 182
Schwartz, M., 18
Seale, A., 235
Searles, H. F., 86, 95, 218, 223,
    227, 238, 294
Secondary maturational failure,
    219, 225
Segal, H., 3, 102, 104, 105–106
Self, dual nature of, 291–296
self-reflectiveness, 292
self-representations, 292
Selfobject
defined, 153
function, projective identifica-
    tion as, 140–160
self-esteem regulation and,
    153–154
transference, 185, 191

Self psychology, 10
Self-reflectiveness, 292
  in borderline disorders, 293
  neurotic personality organiza-
    tion and, 296
  in psychosis, 292
Self-representations, in psychosis,
    292, 296
Semrad, E. V., 150
Separation-individuation phase
  practicing subphase of, 9
  rapprochement subphase of, 9
Shapiro, E. R., 17, 152, 153, 159
Shapiro, R. L., 100, 107,
    111–112, 152, 153
Silent patient. See Refractory
  borderline patient
Singer, M., 7, 18
Slipp, S., 17
Solomon, M. F., 17
Spillius, E. B., 6, 165, 166
Spitz, R. A., 9, 10
Splitting, 3–4, 8, 9, 32, 34
  clinical examples, 3–4, 14–15
  defined, 86
  in healthier patients, 85–96
    clinical examples, 91–93
    therapeutic utility of inter-
      preting, 93–96
  repression and, 87
Spruiell, V., 207
Stanton, A., 18
States of mind. See also Misrecognition of affect
  motivational organization of,
    79–81
  naming, 77–78
    clinical example, 78–79
  observation of, 76–77
    degree of modulation and, 77
  structure of, 81–83
  well-modulated, 77

Sterba, R., 296
Stern, D. N., 10, 11
Stolorow, R., 11, 182, 183, 185,
    186, 190, 191, 207
  on intersubjectivity in psycho-
    analytic treatment,
    182–192
Stone, L., 16, 66, 174
Stone, M. H., 281
Strachey, J., 55, 174, 190
Sullivan, H. S., 33
Supportive therapy
  insight therapy and, 68–72
  role of interpretation in, 69–71
Sutherland, D. J., 17
Sutherland, J. D., 101
Symbiotic phase, 8–9, 30, 276

Therapist. See also Countertransference; Projective identification
  containing function and,
    163–176
    clinical example, 167–171
  devaluation of, 210
  fear of not knowing and,
    237–238
  idealization of, 210
  as patient's selfobject, 140–160
  projective identification of,
    163–176
  reflective self-awareness of,
    183–184
Therapy. See also Projective identification
  ambiguity in, 158–160
  "doing nothing" in, 215–227
  misrecognition of affect in,
    237–239
    clinical examples, 241–243,
      245–248

object relations theory and,
14–19
family therapy, 17
group therapy/psychiatric
administration, 17–19
individual psychotherapy,
14–16
of refractory borderline patient, 216–227
with severely regressed psy-
chotics, 294–296
Tolpin, M., 8, 9
Transference
apparent absence of, 217
channels of communication of,
35–41
clinical examples, 35–36,
37–38, 39–41
intersubjectivity and, 183–184
mirror transference, 201–202
psychosis, clinical example,
187–189
selfobject dimension of, 191
unconscious present/
unconscious past and,
41–44
Transitional object, 8
Transitional phenomena, projective identification and,
157–158
Transmuting internalization, 1, 9

Treatment. *See* Psychotherapy
Tustin, F., 230, 235

Undermodulated states of mind,
77

Valence
in marriage, 117
Valency, 102–103, 113–114

Waelder, R., 16, 57, 174
Weiss, J., 226
Well-modulated states of mind,
77
Whole object relations/
relatedness, 4–5
clinical example, 5
Williams, A. H., 106
Winnicott, D. W., 15, 18, 30, 47,
65, 66, 100, 102, 157, 174,
182, 216, 219–220, 226–227,
230, 233, 234, 235, 295
holding environment, 7–8
transitional object, 8
Wolf, E. S., 154
Wong, N., 17
Wurmser, L., 81

Zinner, J., 152, 153
Zinner, L., 100, 107, 110–112